# MOTOR GUNBOAT 658

# MOTOR GUNBOAT 658

## THE SMALL BOAT WAR IN THE MEDITERRANEAN

## L.C. REYNOLDS

CASSELL

**Cassell Military Paperbacks**

Cassell
Wellington House, 125 Strand
London WC2R 0BB

Copyright © L. C. Reynolds 1955, 2002
First published by William Kimber 1955
This Cassell Military Paperbacks edition 2002
Reprinted 2003

L. C. Reynolds has asserted his right to be identified as the author of this work

British Library Cataloguing-in-Publication Data
A catalogue record is available for this book from the British Library

ISBN 0-304-36183-6

Printed and bound in Great Britain by
Cox & Wyman Ltd, Reading, Berks

To

Lt.-Cdr. Cornelius Burke,
DSC and two Bars, RCNVR

whose remarkable qualities of leadership,
tactical skill and seamanship
were chiefly responsible
for 658's spirit and success

# PREFACE

THIS is a young man's book—a book by a very junior officer. I have written it largely because I feel I have an unusual story to tell. When I was first commissioned, as an R.N.V.R. midshipman, I was appointed to a new motor gunboat building in a West Country yard. The boat and I stayed together for the rest of the war. I was in turn her navigating officer, her first lieutenant, and her commanding officer. When she finally paid off, two and a half years later, we had journeyed and fought together over the whole of the Central Mediterranean, and 658's proud record of operations was outstanding even among the hard-worked flotillas of the Coastal Forces, Mediterranean.

I was nineteen when I joined 658. When the war began I was still at school and, in common with the rest of my generation, I missed all the benefits of introduction to adult life in a world at peace. Most men who achieved responsibility in the war had a background of experience to fortify them: we had to gain our experience of life within the all-embracing experience of war.

Looking back over ten years it is difficult to place events in the perspective they held at the time. There was no question of enjoying the war, nor of considering it glamorous, nor of hating our opponents. It was all far simpler than that. The war had been entered: it had to be won. It was our duty to fight one part of it. Much of what we had to do was very unpleasant and frightening; being a destructive task, it was never truly satisfying But we were young, and the freshness of youth saw only a challenge to be accepted, and took away much of the bitterness of war.

We could be creative only in one respect. War has been said to breed but one virtue; a spirit of comradeship and community rarely seen in saner times. That spirit abounded in Motor Gunboat 658, and was, indeed, common in the small boats of Coastal Forces, both in the Mediterranean and in all the other theatres of war where they were used.

# ACKNOWLEDGEMENTS

The author acknowledges with grateful thanks the assistance he has received from Mr Dudley Pope, the author of *Flag 4*, which tells the whole story of Mediterranean Coastal Forces and therefore provides the broad setting within which *Motor Gunboat 658* can best be placed, for his most generous help in the provision and checking of factual material and his advice on many technical points; and from Lt.-Cdr. T. J. Bligh DSO OBE DSC★ RNVR; Lt. D. H. Brown RNVR; Lt.-Cdr. C. Burke DSC★★ RCNVR; Mr R. J. Collins; Lt. T. E. Ladner DSC★ RCNVR; Mr W. J. E. Last DSM; and Lt. A. T. Robinson DSC RNVR, all of whom provided photographs, material and advice; and Mr W. R. Lewis, who drew the plans of the layout of 658.

★★★

Forty-seven years have passed since this book was first published. In that time, research in German records has provided several instances in which more light is cast on matters that had puzzled me. These, and reflections on some of those who feature in this book, can be found in a new postscript at the end of this edition, in the hope that the reader may find them of interest.

L.C.R.

# CONTENTS

# CONTENTS

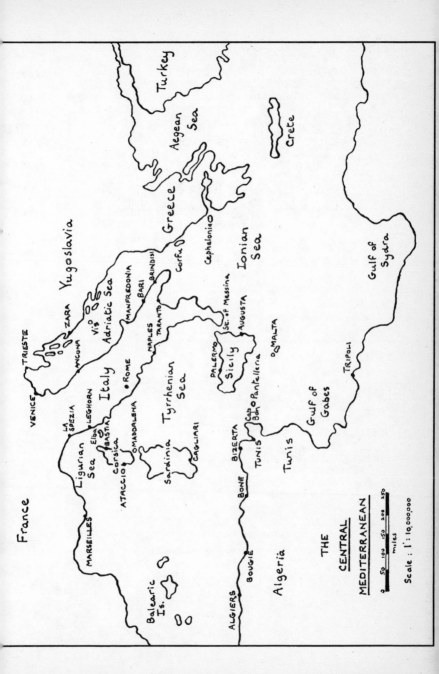

THE
CENTRAL
MEDITERRANEAN

Scale: 1" : 10,000,000

miles

0    50   100   150   200   250

II

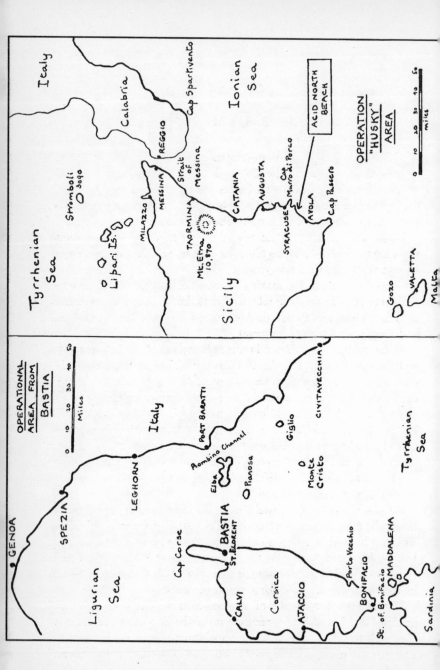

**OPERATIONAL AREA FROM BASTIA**

0 10 20 30 40 50
Miles

Ligurian Sea

GENOA

SPEZIA

LEGHORN

Italy

PORT BARATTI

Piombino Channel

Elba

Pianosa

Giglio

Monte Cristo

CIVITAVECCHIA

Tyrrhenian Sea

Cap Corse

BASTIA
St. Florent

CALVI

Corsica

AJACCIO

Porto Vecchio

St. of Bonifacio

BONIFACIO

MADDALENA

Sardinia

**OPERATION "HUSKY" AREA**

0 10 20 30 40 50
miles

Italy

Calabria

REGGIO

Cap Spartivento

Ionian Sea

Tyrrhenian Sea

Stromboli Soga

Lipari Is.

MILAZZO

MESSINA

Strait of Messina

TAORMINA

Mt. Etna 10,870

CATANIA

AUGUSTA

Cap Murro di Porco

SYRACUSE

AVOLA

ACID NORTH BEACH

Cap Passero

Sicily

Gozo

VALETTA

Malta

12

# CHAPTER I

## "YOU HAVE BEEN APPOINTED . . ."

I JOINED the group of midshipmen who were making forced conversation outside the C.O.'s door. We had been in H.MS. *St. Christopher*, the Coastal Forces training base at Fort William, for five weeks, and had finished both our classroom and sea training the previous day. Now we were waiting to hear our first appointments.

To some extent they would depend on our exam results and on our showing in the ship-handling tests; but even more, of course, we would be sent where the need was greatest.

One sub-lieutenant was making a book on our prospects. There were few takers; he was too well informed to make his odds very attractive.

"I'm offering ten to one on MLs, chaps. Short boats are at evens and Dog-boats six to four against."

So far we had only trained in motor launches (MLs), but we might well be called to the fast short MTBs and MGBs or to the new "D" class boats. In fact, the news we now awaited so anxiously might well decide the whole future pattern of life—and even its length.

Two weeks before, a midshipman had gone to an East Coast MGB Flotilla and had been killed on his first operational trip. This sort of thought made light-hearted conversation difficult, and we were glad to see the door open and the captain's secretary come to beckon us in.

The C.O., Commander Welman, stood behind his desk.

"Good morning, gentlemen."

He was a veteran of Coastal Forces, having served in coastal motor boats, the First War equivalent of MTBs. And he looked it. His face was deeply-lined and distinguished, and the "admiral's fluff" of grey hair on his cheeks gave him the look of a real sea-dog. The medal-ribbons on his left breast—among them the D.S.O. and D.S.C.—had been won in two wars and for a variety of escapades.

"I will read out the list of appointments straight away," he said gruffly, "and I need hardly remind you of the importance of security. You will travel to take up these appointments tomorrow morning. I wish you all good luck and good hunting when you get to your boats."

He began to read inexorably (and alphabetically) down the list. Except for noticing the type of boats which were coming up, I did not really take in any of the details until he came to mine. When at last he reached the "R"'s, the C.O.'s voice seemed to become louder, and I felt as if we were alone in the room.

"Midshipman L. C. Reynolds: Motor Gunboat 658, building at Brixham. Report to Captain (MLs), Brixham. . . ."

My heart leapt. I had got a Dog-boat, regarded by many as the plum job. I knew there had been at least one earlier in the list—had it been in the same flotilla?

The babble as we left the office was in sharp contrast to the tense silence of our entry. I sought out Derrick Brown and Gordon Surtees, two shipmates of long standing, and we hastily compared the chits handed to us by the captain's secretary as we left. A miracle had happened. Their Lordships could not possibly have known that we wanted to stick together, and yet our three chits read: MGBs 658, 662, and 663. Surely these three must be in the same flotilla? And they were the only three Dog-boat appointments in the whole list. The interview we had dreaded so long was over, and it had brought news we had not dared to expect.

At 1000 next morning we began the long weary rail trip south to Glasgow and London. After breakfast together at Euston, we parted and set off to our respective ports: Derrick to Littlehampton, Gordon to Brightlingsea, and myself to Brixham.

I settled into the unaccustomed luxury of my first-class compartment, and took out the notebook containing details of the various types of craft to look up a few facts about D-boats. I knew they were generally known as "Dog-boats", but I had never seen one, and had no idea of their appearance or performance. In fact, I had never seen even a photograph of one. The notes I had scribbled in my book during a lecture had been of mere academic interest; now they became vital statistics.

"Length 115 feet; beam 21 feet 6 inches; no funnel—side exhausts; hard chine design; one 40-mm. pom-pom; two twin .05-inch turrets; two twin .303-inch on the bridge; one twin Oerlikon (20-mm.); and one 6-pounder. Four 1,500 h.p. Packard supercharged engines; fuel capacity 5,000 gallons 100-octane petrol. Maximum speed about 30 knots at 2,400 revs. . . ."

I looked out of the carriage window at the wintry landscape rolling by, and tried to get a picture of what all this meant. 658 would be a pretty powerful boat, then—much bigger and more heavily armed than the short MGBs which had held the field so far, but much slower too.

I arrived at Brixham in the late afternoon, and got a taxi to the office of Captain (MLs), Brixham. Stacking my baggage outside the door I knocked at an office marked "Enquiries". Inside, a pleasant Wren second officer asked "What can I do for you?" and feeling very brand new and green, I replied "I've been appointed to MGB 658. I was told to report here to Captain MLs."

"Oh, I see!" exclaimed the second officer. "Come in and warm yourself up. We haven't had any signal about your appointment here, and I'm afraid your C.O. and first lieutenant have gone off to the training base at Weymouth." She looked keenly at my midshipman's tabs. "I say—how old are you? You look about the youngest we've had here yet—they *are* cradle-snatching now, aren't they!"

I flushed and ignored the question. "What do I do now, then? Do I wait till they get back, or join them at Weymouth?"

"Oh, I think you'd better join them," she said; "they only went three days ago, and 658 won't be ready for another two or three weeks at least. There she is, down there." She pointed through the window. Moving across the room, I saw for the first time that the office overlooked the harbour.

There, where she indicated, and surrounded by a miscellany of every type of fishing boat, lay a dark grey shapeless hull, of so little beauty that I hastily scanned the bay for a more elegant craft in the hope that I was mistaken.

"Not very beautiful, is she?" remarked the second officer, watching me closely. "She'll look a bit better with a mast and a coat of paint, though. We've turned out several Dogs from here—the boat-yard's over there. J. W. & A. Upham—and a damned good yard it is too. They'll build you a good ship all right."

"May I row over to her and have a closer look?" I asked.

"Certainly—you'll find a dinghy tied up at the foot of the steps down there."

I found the dinghy, and rowed over clumsily; the Navy hadn't given me much practice yet in boat-handling! As I climbed the side ladder, and swung over the gunwale, I gave a self-conscious salute. "658 may not be in commission yet, but after all," I thought, "she deserves a little respect on my first visit: it may pay dividends later."

There was no one on board, and I had soon had a quick look round all the compartments. The carpenters and painters were obviously putting the finishing touches below, and I was pleasantly surprised at the neatness and economy of the accommodation. What was obviously the wardroom was very minute, but was so well arranged that two officers would not be really cramped. The C.O. had a cabin to himself, only the size of a large larder, of course, but with space for a bed, a desk, chest-of-drawers, and a wardrobe. Luxury indeed! The engine-room was a confusion of pipes and wires, and I rapidly left it, wondering if I should ever be able to master the intricacies of such complex machinery.

Rowing back to the quayside in the fading light, I paused and rested on the oars, gazing at the bleak hull. My mind was full of doubts, of hopes, of pride—a strange mixture. What did the future hold? The cold North Sea? The warm Mediterranean? The Pacific? A brief spell of glory—or some colossal blunder on my part which would bring disgrace?

Question marks all of them—and only time could provide the answers.

## Chapter II

## NO TIME TO WASTE

SITTING in the train going to Weymouth next day, I found my-self thinking about a remark that sophisticated young Wren officer had made as she handed me my travel warrant.

"Oh, by the way," she said, "your C.O.'s name is Burke—Cornelius Burke—and the Number One is Pickard. Both of them are lieutenants, and they're both from Canada. Burke's a tough egg from the wild and woolly west—I hope he doesn't eat you! Cheerio!"

And it was difficult, after this, to avoid picturing these two as crude backwoodsmen who would make my life a misery. I had a shrewd suspicion that she probably had a routine line in leg-pulling for young officers joining their first boats; but I had always been rather easy meat for that sort of thing, especially if I regarded the subject seriously.

When I got to Weymouth, I booked in at an hotel, and after dumping my kit in my room, I set off to the base in search of Lieutenants Burke and Pickard. It took me some time to track them down, but finally I found them, gazing at a stripped-down pom-pom in the Gunnery Shed, their hands oily and the gun manual open beside them. There was no mistaking the skipper from the Wren's description, I thought. He certainly looked a tough egg—*and* rather wild and woolly. I saluted self-consciously and introduced myself. The C.O. returned the salute jauntily, beamed a wide grin and held out a hard, hairy (and oily) hand to grip mine firmly.

"We-ell, we're pleased to have you here, Pilot. This is Herb Pickard, the Number One—he's from Winnipeg. I'm Burke, from Vancouver."

Pickard smiled and shook hands and I knew immediately that I was on firm ground. There was strength, sincerity and friendliness apparent even in those few seconds' greeting. The skipper wiped his hands on a grubby piece of cotton waste and suggested that a drink was indicated. "I guess we've got that pom-pom drill weighed off, Pick—let's move along to the pub and put the Pilot wise on the routine here, shall we? By the way, what'll we call you? Everyone knows me as Corny, so save the 'sir' for formal occasions."

In the pub, we settled in a corner and I had my first embarrassing moment. "What's yours, Len?" I was, at nineteen, still T.T. merely because I had not found beer to my taste. Should I ask for a pint of bitter? I actually replied "A cider, please." To my relief no comment was made, and I relaxed.

The next hour was fascinating. Corny outlined the future prospects, and gave me an idea of the duties which would be my special responsibility aboard 658. I was to be navigating officer, signals officer, confidential books officer, and captain's secretary, all for the price of a midshipman; Pick's duties as Number One involved gunnery, victualling, general supervision of the ship's company and maintenance of the boat, all for the considerably higher price of a (Canadian) lieutenant.

But all this was routine beside the revelation that 658 was bound for the Mediterranean, and that Corny intended that we should break all records in commissioning and getting out there to begin operating.

"You see, Len, I reckon the big squeeze is bound to start in Tunisia in the next few weeks, and things will warm up at sea if Rommel's mob are going to be kicked out of Africa. When that happens, I want 658 to be there!"

It was 2nd March, 1943, and Montgomery's Eighth Army, and the First Army which had landed in North Africa the previous November, had been temporarily halted, the Germans being strongly entrenched in the Mareth Line south of the Gulf of Gabes in Tunisia. The strategic position made it clear that sooner or later the combined weight of the two great allied armies, with Eisenhower as Supreme Commander and Alexander in command of the whole front, must eventually be victorious.

I was overjoyed at the news that we were bound for the Mediterranean. In my spell at sea as an ordinary seaman, I had been bitterly disappointed to get no further from the coasts of Britain than making brief excursions into the Atlantic north of Ireland, to relieve the monotony of a regular Belfast to Barry Docks convoy run! Now, I visualised the Mediterranean sun and calm azure seas, and thought gloatingly that life would be far easier for me as Pilot without the additional complications of fog and tides, both of which we could expect to miss in the Mediterranean. We learned better later.

During the general conversation, I soon realised that this was no ordinary partnership I had joined. Corny and Pick, who had only met a week or two earlier, had already, with their common outlook and accent, established a firm and genuine understanding and friendship. They had been working really hard, quite apart from the training programme at H.M.S. *Bee*, on details of the captain's standing orders, the proposed routine, and on other details of organisation. Neither had been in D-boats before—Corny had been in command of a short MGB at Lowestoft, and Pick had been Number One of a short MTB; but with characteristic thoroughness they had already discovered a great deal of the snags and problems in converting a newly-built hull into a competent fighting unit.

There was only one Dog in Weymouth at this time—665—with an old Canadian pal of Corny's, Peter Thompson, in command. She too was bound for the Mediterranean and it was natural that we should spend a lot of our time aboard her. H.M.S. *Bee* was a working-up base to polish newly commissioned crews or refitted boats into operational order, and the routine was indeed tough. A very complicated time-table was arranged so that lectures (for both officers and men) occupied the days, and frequent tactical exercises occupied the nights. The programme for each boat gradually worked up in a crescendo, so that by the time she was due to leave, she had an efficient crew, accustomed to snatching odd hours of sleep and hasty meals between fuelling and sea-time, and therefore prepared for operations immediately she arrived at her operational base.

It did not take me long to realise that Corny and Pick were determined that 658 should have every chance of becoming an efficient and happy ship, and their preparations for this were so thorough that they allowed themselves very little time for relaxation.

Most evenings they spent in their hotel rooms, working at details of organisation, and although I was roped in to help in minor ways on occasions, I was comparatively free. I spent a good deal of time with Pick during the day, in the gunnery rooms, where we practised the various gun-drills with a gunnery instructor to ourselves, and thus learnt far more than previous training in large groups had accomplished. I also met radar for the first time, and spent hours learning routines for warming up and operating the sets. The lectures on operational tactics fascinated me most, however, especially as the lecturer and many of the group had first-hand experience of their subjects. My mouth must frequently have fallen open in my ignorance and wonder.

I went out on a night exercise in SGB 6 (a steam gun boat), which was later to become one of Peter Scott's *Grey Goose* flotilla. I rapidly became very confused (inevitable when I had no real grasp on the details of the exercise). Lights flashed all around and dark shapes loomed out of the night, disappearing again rapidly. Suddenly, at about 0200, came the unexpected signal: "Exercise abandoned, return to harbour". Immediately everyone started speculating about what had happened. The next morning the story unfolded. Three Vospers had gone aground at something like twenty-two knots, the helmsman having been given the course as *North* 30° East instead of *South* 30° East. It was a lesson I noted carefully for future reference!

After a week of intensive training, I was sent off to H.M.S. *Dryad*, the navigation school near Fareham, for a short course on celestial navigation. Corny knew that we should be running out to the Mediterranean under our own power, and had insisted that I should be given the chance to practise taking sun sights and star sights, which had naturally received little attention in our general training courses owing to pressure of time.

Imagine my pleasure to find on arrival in H.M.S. *Dryad*, that Derrick Brown had just turned up, and that his boat (663) was not only in the same flotilla as ours, but that his skipper, Tommy Ladner, was also a Canadian, and a life-long friend of Corny's from Vancouver.

There seemed no doubt that we should be pally ships as long as we could keep together in the future. 663 was working up on the Hamble River, and was nearer commissioning than 658. On the second day of our course, while we were peacefully following a lecture on tides, the door burst open, and in rolled Gordon Surtees, red of face and cheerful as ever, his arms clutching the large pile of navigational tomes which were apparently essential, and issued to all officers taking the course.

Nothing could have been more pleasant than a reunion with these two, my closest friends as yet in the Navy, so soon after parting, but now with so much more to discuss, involving the boundless future rather than the limited past of our acquaintance.

Gordon had been appointed to the Senior Officer's boat, MGB 662, and thus knew rather more about the general situation than did Derrick and I. Our S.O. was Lt.-Cdr. Norman Hughes, who had been in "C" Class Gunboats at Yarmouth, and our flotilla was the 20th MGB flotilla. 662 was a good deal further from completion than 658 and 663 (work had begun later on her), and it was obvious that she would not be commissioned in time to sail to Gibraltar in the convoy we hoped to join.

In view of this, Gordon had been able to take a short leave period, which left Derrick and me green with envy. We were fairly certain by now that our boats would be commissioned so rapidly, and our C.O.s would be so keen to get out to the Mediterranean, that we stood very little chance of more than a few days' leave before sailing.

After a week of intensive practice with the sextant, in which we used the sharply marked summit of Portsdown Hill as an artificial horizon, we felt confident to take the necessary sights and work out positions when we finally had to pit our wits against the Atlantic and its lack of signposts.

Arriving back at Weymouth, I found that our crew was due to arrive next day. Corny had arranged for them to be drafted to Weymouth for a training spell before taking them down to Brixham, so that we could prepare for our Mediterranean voyage as soon as trials were completed and the boat commissioned.

Corny, Pick and I speculated a great deal about the quality and temperament of the individuals with whom we should have to live. The two motor mechanics had already been appointed, and were at Brixham standing by the boat. They were two pleasant men but neither had any sea experience whatsoever. The "Chief" had the rating of chief petty officer but that elevated position was due to mechanical experience in Civvy Street, not in marine engine installations in small craft!

On the 17th March 1943, the ship's company of MGB 658 marched up to the gate of H.M.S. *Bee*, with the coxswain, Petty Officer Roberts, in charge. Roberts was a well-built solid Welshman, and a Regular Navy man. I liked him from the first, but found his faintly patronizing air towards "Hostilities Only" officers and ratings rather difficult to overcome. He was always extremely loyal to both officers and men, and would never hesitate to bring anything to our notice if he felt the happiness of the boat or the men was affected.

Next was the leading hand ("Killick") Maguire, who was a great asset immediately. He was a cheerful and efficient little Lancastrian, very tiddly in his best uniform, and he had been an A/B in a Vosper MTB at Dover, where he had seen a good deal of action, including the ill-fated attack on the *Scharnhorst* and *Gneisenau* during their dash through the Straits of Dover.

Apart from these two key ratings, there were two other "Active Service" men (i.e. on regular engagements), the electrician Smith, and the leading stoker, Welsh, who both looked knowledgeable and sound men. But the rest were an amazing assortment. Not one of them had done more than a week's sea-time, put in aboard the MLs whilst training in *St. Christopher*. This meant that only four of a crew of thirty had ever been to sea before: the others were so raw that the coxswain had almost to teach them the difference between port and starboard. We had been given a labour squad, not a crew!

Some of them had AA3 badges on their arms, having completed a light-craft gunnery course at Whale Island. Two or three were older men, over thirty, who looked solid and dependable. A few were bright-eyed, intelligent youngsters, obviously good material, and the rest were the good-hearted, mixed bunch you would expect in such a widely-gathered selection. We had cockneys, Hampshire yeomen, North Country tykes, and Lancastrians, noted for sharp wits. It was now our job to knit this miscellany into a harmonious unity. It seemed a mountainous task.

The six days the crew were in *Bee* were busy ones for everyone. Corny's immediate concern was to discover who would make the best gunners, and he got down to this straight away. First he took them to the .22 range, contending that a "good eye" would show itself just as well there as in a pom-pom turret. He ignored the existence of the AA3 badges, and promised that the guns would be given to the best shots, and not necessarily to those who had had the advantage of studying the gunnery manuals previously! The results of the .22 shoots were borne out by further tests on the .303 range at H.M.S. *Attack*, and it was soon clear that two of the eighteen-year-old seamen, Preston and Day, and two of the older men, Watt and Howe, were to be key men when it came to allocating the turrets.

Friday 23rd March saw the whole crew and officers aboard a train bound for Brixham. This time, when we arrived, MGB 658 looked more like one of His Majesty's ships, as her mast was stepped, she had a coat of paint, and she looked very smart, lying placidly at her buoy in the harbour. As soon as possible we were aboard, and while Corny and Pick were noting all the improvements and progress made I was making a quick survey of all the various gadgets and apparatus which would be in my charge.

The next three days were hectic. The boat was brought alongside on the grid so that the shafts could be inspected and worked on when the boat dried out at low water; the ammunition, naval stores, food and comforts, were received and checked, and acceptance trials were held in Torbay.

In these three days I saw a good deal of the work of the Upham's

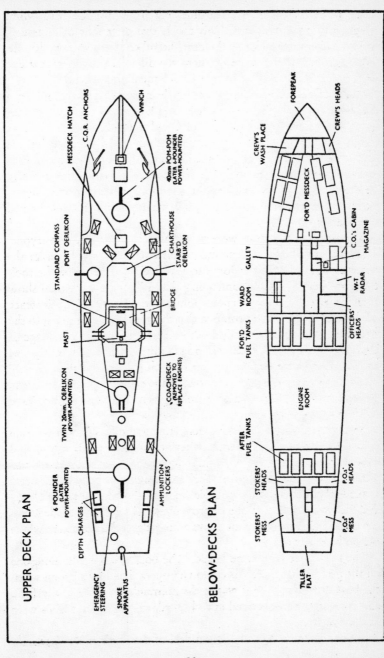

## UPPER DECK PLAN

MESSDECK HATCH

C.Q.R. ANCHORS

WINCH

40mm POM-POM
(LATER 6-POUNDER
POWER-MOUNTED)

STANDARD COMPASS

PORT OERLIKON

CHARTHOUSE

STARB'D OERLIKON

BRIDGE

MAST

COACHDECK
(REMOVED TO
REPLACE ENGINES)

TWIN 20mm. OERLIKON
(POWER-MOUNTED)

6 POUNDER
(LATER
POWER-MOUNTED)

DEPTH CHARGES

EMERGENCY
STEERING

SMOKE
APPARATUS

AMMUNITION
LOCKERS

## BELOW-DECKS PLAN

FOREPEAK

CREW'S HEADS

CREW'S
WASH PLACE

FOR'D MESSDECK

C.O.'s CABIN

MAGAZINE

GALLEY

W-T

RADAR

WARD
ROOM

OFFICERS'
HEADS

FOR'D
FUEL TANKS

ENGINE
ROOM

AFTER
FUEL TANKS

STOKERS'
HEADS

P.O.'s
HEADS

STOKERS'
MESS

P.O.'s
MESS

TILLER
FLAT

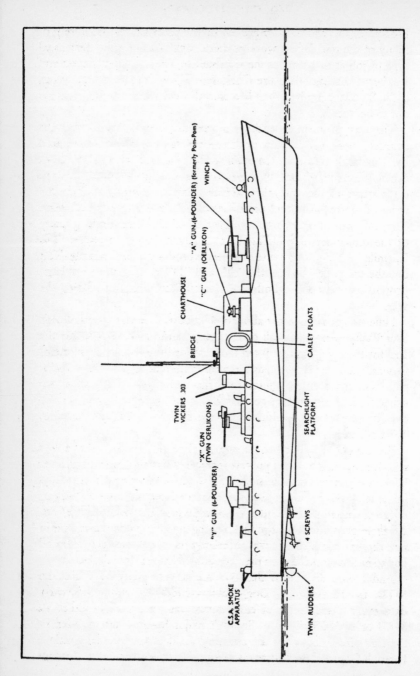

WINCH

"A" GUN.(6-POUNDER) (formerly Pom-Pom)

CHARTHOUSE

"C" GUN (OERLIKON)

BRIDGE

CARLEY FLOATS

TWIN VICKERS 303

SEARCHLIGHT PLATFORM

"X" GUN (TWIN OERLIKONS)

"Y" GUN (6-POUNDER)

4 SCREWS

C.S.A. SMOKE APPARATUS

TWIN RUDDERS

24

boat-yard, and was most impressed by the pride and craftsmanship of many of the old, skilled workers there. 658 was not quite their usual type of job at that time as she was built to a precise specification and was largely made of parts pre-fabricated all over the country; however, the hull was the result of their labour, and a well-found craft she turned out to be, too.

The way these small yards, in ports and river towns all over the country, were used to turn out the hundreds of small craft required by Coastal Forces and Combined Operations, was a triumph of organization and vision. In order to speed up the construction in the early stages of the war, the Fairmile Marine Company designed a series of motor boats, and prefabricated all the fittings for each class. Thus many firms built parts which yards assembled, eliminating many of the difficulties of building in so many dispersed localities. The Fairmile "A" did not go into large-scale production, nor did the "C"; but the two other classes, the "B" and "D", provided a very large proportion of the total number of Coastal Force craft built during the war.

I knew a good deal more about 658 by now. She was powered with four Packard engines, each of 1,500 h.p., and supercharged; and the fuel for these was carried in ten tanks divided into two compartments forward and abaft the engine-room, amounting to about 5,000 gallons of 100-octane (i.e. high performance) petrol. There were two other small engines (the "gennies") also in the engine-room, to run the dynamo which provided the electricity for cooking, lighting, W/T and radar.

For a small boat, 658 had an impressive array of guns. She carried a 40-mm. pom-pom in a power-operated turret on the fo'c'sle; twin Vickers 0.5 turrets on each side of the chart-house; twin Vickers .303s in the wings of the bridge; a power-mounted twin Oerlikon (20-mm.) over the engine-room, and a 6-pounder (nearly 3-inch calibre) aft. All these guns meant a large ship's company to provide crews, and in fact the full complement was three officers and thirty men, who all had to be accommodated in the very limited space below decks.

And I soon discovered that 658 might very easily have been an MTB. In basic design, all Dog-boats were identical, and in these early days every alternate set of eight boats was completed as either an MTB or an MGB Flotilla. So 658's major function was decided in the first place simply by the arbitrary accident of number position. Later all Dogs in home waters were given torpedo tubes, but this fate never overtook 658 in the different conditions of Mediterranean operations, where even the Dog torpedo boats functioned mainly as gunboats.

There was little enough ceremony to mark the occasion when, on 26th March 1943, His Majesty's Motor Gunboat 658 was received into the Royal Navy and flew her commissioning pennant proudly for the first time. There was a party at noon, at which a toast was made to "658 and all who serve in her", and our guests included the builders, Admiralty engineers, Captain MLs and his staff, and Alan Lennox-Boyd, the M.P., who was C.O. of another Dog lying at Brixham at the time.

For me, the occasion was most memorable in that Corny thrust a gin and lime into my hand and said "Drink that, Midshipman Reynolds, and that's an order!" I meekly obeyed, and afterwards found myself less shy and much more sociable when we entertained guests aboard.

The B.B.C.'s one o'clock news, which someone had turned on, opened with a report that the Mareth Line had cracked in Tunisia, and that the Germans were retreating. Corny tilted his glass a little, and murmured reflectively: "We'll have to get a move on, or we'll be too late, y'know!"

As many of the men had not had any leave after their training period, some just had to be granted in spite of the hurry, and four days was allocated to each watch. I took my leave with the second party, and the four days after commissioning were full of incident.

The runs over the measured mile between Brixham and Berry Head ascertained our speeds at various revs, the compasses were swung, and gunnery trials held. To make the process more exciting, on one occasion an unpleasant gale blew up whilst we were out, and on our return to the harbour, we found that the high wind made it very difficult to pick up the small ring on the mooring buoy. Corny manoeuvred magnificently as we continually slipped past that wretched buoy, but even so was dangerously near to going aground once or twice. He afterwards confessed that he had had horrible visions of mangled props and bent shafts, two days after commissioning. We were therefore highly gratified to receive a signal from Captain MLs, whose office overlooked the harbour: "Congratulations on the seamanlike way in which 658 came to the buoy in this afternoon's gale."

As soon as the second watch returned from leave, arrangements were made for our departure to Milford Haven, the port from which we were to sail for the "Med". We left Brixham proudly, with our pennants fluttering from the yard, and gravely acknowledging the farewell waves of the workers from Upham's yard and Captain ML's staff, who all turned out to see us off.

Our first sea voyage, and my first real navigational responsibility, was the short trip round to Dartmouth, where we fuelled and spent the night before setting out for Milford Haven at 0730 next morning.

I was on my mettle to make a success of the navigation, and took great pains in laying off courses and checking our position very frequently. It was an interesting and enjoyable day—except for a little engine trouble through petrol pressure failure all went well—and I was happy to find that the swept-channel buoys and bearings on landmarks ashore all came up just as I forecast and plotted. In a way, it was a new and exciting game of skill, and I could see that Corny and Pick, who at first kept an unobtrusive eye on the navigation, were soon content to leave it to me.

We sailed past the Eddystone Light and the Lizard, rounded Lands End and struck across the Bristol Channel to Milford. It was 2245, and several hours after sunset, when we slipped through the boom and anchored under Great Castle Head. There are few more agreeable sensations than to sit snug in a wardroom discussing a successfully completed voyage, however short, and I was a very contented young midshipman when I turned in at about midnight. It was especially pleasing to reflect that the last time I had entered Milford Haven (nine months earlier) I had been a bewildered ordinary seaman getting in the way of the fo'c'sle party as one of His Majesty's cruisers had come to anchor! It seemed a very long time ago.

Next morning we took a pilot aboard and moved up the river to Pembroke Dock, which was to serve as the assembly point for our convoy. Here, as we berthed alongside the old hulk of the *Warrior*, we had our first view of the boats which were to be our companions on the voyage to Gibraltar; and there was Derrick Brown waving us in alongside, and two lieutenants standing on the bridge of 663 to whom Corny shouted a boisterous greeting. They immediately came aboard, and were whisked down to the wardroom, where I was introduced to Lieutenants Doug Maitland and Tommy Ladner, C.O.s of 657 and 663 respectively.

Corny had talked a great deal of these two, and I had gathered that the three of them had been great friends from their schooldays in

Vancouver. They made a trio of fascinating contrasts, and yet they were in many respects complementary one to another. Maitland, the senior, was outwardly hard-bitten and crisp of speech; Corny was rugged, forceful and decisive in all his actions; and Ladner possessed a penetrating brain, a serious nature and a far more sensitive personality. They all had enormous zest for life and a refreshing ability to throw off the weight of responsibility and to relax light-heartedly off duty, when their sense of humour was rarely dormant.

At the beginning of the war they had enrolled in the R.C.N.V.R. as early as possible, and had soon managed to get moved across to England. After a difficult period in 1940 when it seemed that there was little for them to do (Corny spent some time demolishing the docks at Le Havre and got out of France just in time), they were all appointed to Coastal Forces, and served in short boats on the East Coast till 1942.

Corny was very proud that he had been a first lieutenant in the 6th MGB Flotilla at Falmouth, when all the C.O.s were R.N. officers until they were joined by one Lieutenant Robert Hichens R.N.V.R., who later became a legendary figure in Coastal Forces. Tommy had also served in Hichens' famous flotilla in 1942, and Doug had been a "half leader" (i.e. senior C.O.) in another MGB flotilla.

After two years of operations the three of them had gone together to the Admiralty, applied for the foreign service leave which was due to them, and arranged that on return from two months in Canada they would be appointed to three of the new Dog-boats. So the coincidence of this union of three C.O.s of such long-standing friendship was due rather to careful planning than to any quirk of fate!

We used this waiting time to work-up, with frequent gun drills, actions stations, emergency routines and the like, and we found it a good opportunity, too, for getting to know the officers of the other boats as they arrived from their building ports all over the country. Every day, one boat would be unofficially appointed "duty drinking barge", and a mob of officers would descend to the wardroom to discuss matters over a glass of gin.

At one of these parties someone switched on the radio. The war in Africa was holding our attention closely, and there was a pause in the conversation as the news began. The hubbub rose again as interest fell away, until Tommy Ladner suddenly snarled "Quiet!" The voice of the announcer seemed to be personally addressing us rather than a vast unseen audience, and there was that sort of breathless, tensed silence in the wardroom which was rare—and the more memorable for being so.

"... *The following communique was issued by the Admiralty today:*

"*On each of the last two nights, light coastal forces have had short, sharp engagements with enemy patrol craft close to the Dutch coast.*

"*As a result of these engagements considerable damage has been caused to the enemy craft and many casualties must have been inflicted on their personnel.*

"*During the course of last night's engagement it is regretted that Lt.-Cdr. Robert Peverell Hichens, D.S.O., D.S.C., R.N.V.R., was killed. The other casualties sustained during these two nights were two officers and two ratings wounded. The next of kin have been informed.*

"*All our ships returned safely to harbour.*"

Tommy sat looking into his glass, his mind back to the summer of 1942 when he had followed Hichens night after night as a C.O. in the famous 8th MGB Flotilla. I myself had never met him, but I knew well his amazing story of leadership and determination which had done more to give Coastal Forces their reputation as the Navy's most constant striking force at this time than any other single factor.

Just before we sailed, Peter Scott, son of Scott of the Antarctic and himself a distinguished Coastal Force commanding officer, made an inspiring broadcast in a B.B.C. Postscript on St. George's Day. Derrick and I heard it in the lounge of a hotel in Milford Haven after a leisurely meal. It seemed to me that Peter Scott, knowing we were on the threshold of life in Coastal Forces, was giving us a personal message of inspiration derived from the acknowledged leader of our proud little ships.

"*In this sort of fighting, as I suppose in any kind of specialized fighting, there are men who combine those particular qualities of cool leadership and complete knowledge of the technical side of their job so perfectly that their battles are successful where others fail. Such a one was Lt.-Cdr. Robert Hichens R.N.V.R. whose loss two weeks ago was a most tragic blow to Coastal Forces and indeed to England—he was known throughout Coastal Forces as 'Hitch', and most of the tactical theory of Motor Gunboats was first developed and practised by him. But the chief thing about him was the way he could lead and the confidence he installed into the officers and men of his flotilla—and it wasn't limited to his flotilla, this inspiration. It spread around and developed the spirit which puts our Coastal Forces on top whenever they meet the enemy, by virtue not of their guns but of their determination.*

*"The officers and men who fight these battles will not forget Robert Hichens. He left a rich legacy—the fruits of his energy in the development of the boats, and the fruits of his experience in the way they should be handled and fought—and then that other thing—that example of courage that makes people think, as they go into action: 'This would have been a mere nothing to Hitch.' "*

After nine days at Pembroke Dock, the convoy moved downriver to the inner basin at Milford Haven, all ready now to start when the powers-that-be gave the word, and the weather was suitable.

There began ten weary days of waiting, with everyone keyed up to a high pitch of tension. We were "on top line" and this anti-climax was hard to bear, especially when we remembered the shortness of our foreign-service leave.

But at 1600 hours on 30th April 1943, the order to leave was finally confirmed, and we sailed with our untried boats and untried crews to do battle first of all with the turbulent Atlantic.

## CHAPTER III

## BISCUITS IN THE BAY

ONE by one, the seventeen ships of the convoy passed through the lock and into the outer harbour beyond. We were the fourth to leave, and as we moved slowly through the narrow channel, Corny suddenly sniffed and swung round to Pick. "Petrol! Can you smell it, Pick? Quick—where?" He clanged the telegraphs urgently back and forth, and the roar of the exhausts reverberating against the lock walls was chopped off abruptly. We flung lines ashore, and warped alongside, with Pick rushing round the upper deck. Within a few seconds, he found a thin stream of green liquid flowing over the side from the air vent of one of the petrol tanks.

With a line of boats astern impatiently shouting and pressing klaxon horns, just as bad-tempered as cars in a London traffic jam, the motor mechanic hastily switched his petrol feeds and put the trouble right. The engines roared again, and at last we were off.

By the time we emerged into the outer harbour the two escort trawlers and 657 were already through the boom. We looked back and watched the line of Dogs and MLs moving out behind us, each with a stream of pennants billowing out to give the scene the colour and gaiety of Milford Regatta rather than the solemnity of a final parting. I suddenly had a picture of row upon row of fluttering handkerchiefs waving in a symbolic farewell. When would we next see England? If war took its normal course, some of us would not come back. . . .

I noted the time as we passed the boom, and watched the two escorts, black smoke pouring from their ancient funnels, streaming out to their station ahead while the convoy formed up. Fancy giving us trawlers! Why, we should have to protect *them* if anything happened! One Dog-boat's broadside was nearly as powerful as their combined fire-power.

But from the briefing we had had, I knew their real function was to act as navigational guides and anti-submarine screen. We were going to make the whole voyage with only one of our four engines running at a time, in order to save petrol; so ten knots would not strain even this escort's resources.

In a very few minutes, the convoy was formed up like orderly chessmen at the beginning of a game, and set course to the westward. We were in four columns, with two lines of MLs sandwiched between the four Dog gunboats to port and four torpedo boats to starboard. Each line was a cable (200 yards) apart, and each boat half a cable astern of the next ahead. At least it *should* have been: life for the next seven days was largely governed by these two simple distances!

A Sunderland flying-boat from the Coastal Command base at Pembroke Dock floated gracefully over as we got under way. To her pilot we must have resembled a string of thoroughbred hunters and racehorses being carefully exercised under the benevolent eyes of two elderly and out-of-breath carthorses.

We were second in line in the port column, and as we plunged westward towards southern Ireland that first evening, a heavy rolling Atlantic played immediate havoc with our ship's company. Within half an hour, the running of the boat was in the hands of four or five experienced men, and the remainder—including myself—were rushing periodically to lean, with agonised spasms, over the guard rails. The human stomach is quite remarkably adaptable, and I found myself after one unpleasantly gruelling bout returning to a more normal view of my duties.

I climbed to the bridge and found Corny, Pick and Roberts, the coxwain, all serenely occupied, as though oblivious of the dismal plight of so many of their shipmates. The coxswain murmured a request to Corny, and called to Maguire (the leading hand) who was keeping look-out watch in the wing of the bridge.

"Take over the wheel, Mac," he said. "I want to make sure none of these blasted ODs are spewing all over the messdecks. Some of 'em are so green they'd be sick in their pockets if we didn't tell 'em it was the wrong place!"

Corny chuckled. The coxswain rarely bothered to conceal his irritation with the hurriedly-trained human material at his disposal; yet he managed to keep the crew happy and could often be seen patiently explaining a point of seamanship to one of the young hands. We decided we were lucky in our senior rating.

He was back a few minutes later, his face a picture of amazement and contempt. "I've never seen anything like it," he growled; "there's only four men on their flat feet apart from us here on the bridge—and two of them are being supported!" He turned to Pick. "We're going to find it a bit dodgy in the engine-room, sir. Both the motor mechanics are flaked right out, *and* two of the stokers; there's only Leading Stoker Welsh and one youngster down there at the moment—and y'know Welsh is a new hand at petrol engines. He's always been in the big stuff and he won't be able to cope with anything tricky if we get a breakdown."

By now I felt well enough to take a prowl round the upper deck to see for myself how things were shaping. Even with the recent rendings of my own stomach fresh in my mind, I was not prepared for what I saw. At each gun were one or two men, their gun-telephones with close-fitting earpieces giving them the air of bewildered rugby forwards, slouched miserably in the turret seats. I felt that even if we passed a juicy unarmed German merchant ship with engine trouble and no escort we should still have a job to hit it at more than a hundred yards.

In other corners, small groups of pale, heavily-clad seamen sheltered silently from the wind and spray. Few stirred as I passed by. It was as though they had all signed a separate peace and were now resigned to a cruel fate.

But at last my faith in the imperishable spirit of the British matelot was restored.

In the lee of the charthouse, braced with their feet against the upper deck petrol tanks, A/B Smith and Stoker Arthur Francis were deep in conversation. Smith was very popular with his mates, and with several years at sea behind him he was busy pulling the young stoker's leg. Francis, a cockney lad of eighteen, was easily impressed, and as I came by he looked up.

"Is it true our orders have been changed, sir? Smithy says we're going to South Africa instead of the Med because we're too late for the North Africa do!"

I grinned and passed on.

"You see," said Smithy confidentially. "The skipper hasn't told the midshipman yet—he probably hasn't had a chance to. But I had the buzz straight from Sparks, who got it from 'is pal in the signals office back in Milford, who 'eard the Chief Yeoman telling the coder to keep 'is mouth shut."

"Cor!" breathed Francis reflectively. "South Africa! That's a long way, ain't it?"

Before nightfall, we worked out the watch routine. As I had never yet stood a night watch, Pick and Corny would obviously have to share them, and Corny decided to take the "middle" (from midnight to 4 a.m.). I was to stand watch with him, and also to help Pick out as much as possible in the daylight parts of the first and morning watches.

That first night we all stayed on the bridge till about ten, when Corny and I turned in leaving Pick to strain his eyes alone to pick out the minute speck of blue and the patch of slightly less dense blackness which were all we could see of 657, half a cable ahead. As this was a dark moon period, each boat showed a shaded blue stern light to help the boat astern keep station, and already the high seas meant that the boat ahead was only visible when she lifted out of the troughs of waves.

I seemed to have been asleep for only five minutes when at midnight a hand roughly shook my shoulder. "First lieutenant's compliments, sir. It's your watch. I've shaken the captain."

I was still fully dressed except for my boots, and as I drew myself up on the bunk, I had a terrible urge to go on sleeping. My whole body craved sleep, and my head began to sink back to the pillow. Corny's head appeared in the doorway.

"Come on, Pilot, get out of it. This is where life really begins for you!"

That first middle watch was a nightmare. Corny had served in fast "short" MGBs, where close station keeping was a matter of honour as well as operational necessity: to find himself now in an ungainly craft in mountainous seas, wallowing along at a steady ten knots and a hundred yards apart, all in pitch blackness, was an unpleasant reminder that he had much to learn about his new boat.

The helmsman could not see the boat ahead—he merely steered a compass course, his eyes glued on the faint red glow of the binnacle, and his arms moving constantly to correct every twist and sliding turn of the bows by rapid movements of the wheel.

The officer of the watch's main task was to concentrate on keeping that minute patch of blue and grey within the double orbit of the binocular lenses—and quite apart from eye strain it was extremely exhausting.

By the end of the middle watch, when Pick, heavy-eyed and less lively than usual, relieved us, I was very nearly asleep on my feet. My eyes stung with salt spray, and even the skin on my cheeks felt weary with the impact of the lashing wind. I stumbled below, pulled off my oilskins, and climbed fully clothed on to my bunk. Sleep came quickly, but so did the awakening. At seven the ruthless hand of the bridge messenger clapped mercilessly on my shoulder.

"First lieutenant's compliments, sir, and he told me to say that it's horrible up top, but not so horrible as it was three hours ago."

This time I made sure of a hasty wash, and felt the better for it. On deck, the light of day instilled a confidence and lack of crisis which contrasted sharply with the uncertainties and doubts of the past night. 657 ahead and ML 240 to starboard, the king-pins of our existence, were clearly visible, and it would obviously be comparatively simple to keep them that way.

I gravely noted the course and engine revolutions, the recognition signals and the state of the weather, and took over my first spell as solitary officer of the watch.

It was remarkable more for the things that did not happen than for any excitement. Ten minutes of it were taken up with receiving and passing on a semaphore message relayed down each line from the trawler ahead, giving our position at 0600. We carried no signalman, and although Corny and Pick were both quite proficient with lamp and flags, I was always summoned rapidly to the bridge if I was available.

I had Corny shaken at nine o'clock, and he climbed up to the bridge for a look round before taking his breakfast. His keen eyes swept around the heaving sea, taking in the situation in a few seconds. As he did so, the motor mechanic appeared at the back of the bridge. His face was a sickly yellow, and beads of perspiration stood on his forehead in spite of the biting wind. "Excuse me, sir. I'm afraid I've had to stop the generator—both of them are running hot and we're working on them. We'll try to get one going as soon as we can, but . . . well, we don't seem to be able to stay below for very long at a time, sir."

Corny looked at him, and could see he was in no condition to be harried. "Right. Do your best, Chief. I suppose we've got no electricity at all till you get one going?"

He turned to me, "Hell! and that means we shan't get any cooked breakfast or a hot drink unless we can keep a Primus stove steady." He disappeared below scowling.

The Primus could *not* be kept steady. One experiment which nearly set the galley on fire was enough to prove that. There was no hot drink, and no cooked breakfast. Or dinner. Or supper. In fact, not until the seventh day of the voyage did we have our next cup of tea, let alone a hot meal.

Even this hardship was borne philosophically. In place of hot meals, we fed on a variety of ready-prepared foods, and some of the combinations were grotesque, considered in retrospect. Cold meats (mainly corned beef) with pickles and crushed ship's biscuits; herrings from the familiar oval tins, with shredded wheat; tinned cheese and jam; tinned milk in every possible form; and—as a luxury—tinned pears or peaches; these formed the main diet. It was monotonous in the extreme, but nutritious enough to keep us going with sufficient energy. But I was amazed to hear very little nattering from the men on this score—they must have sympathised with the engine-room crew!

We could not even be generous with the issue of fresh water. The tanks contained 125 gallons, which meant about half a gallon a man each day for all purposes, and this was little enough. A careful check was made regularly, but so conscientiously did the crew follow the restrictions that fifty gallons remained when we reached Gibraltar. I suspect that half the crew didn't bother to wash—they looked like it!

We settled into a regular routine on this second day which set the stamp on the whole memorable voyage. For most of the daylight hours all the crew could be seen on deck, the non-duty watch squatting in groups in the few sheltered spots to leeward of the bridge and the engine-room hatch. All three officers would be on the bridge, and I soon discovered that both Corny and Pick loved to play with the sextant whenever I got it out to take a sun sight. They were both very competent navigators, and insisted on helping in this way; but I noticed that they never volunteered to work through the succession of logarithms and haversines to achieve the numerical result!

In these circumstances taking a sight at all was itself an adventure, as the crazy roll of the boat made the whole process one of accurate timing rather than skill in adjustment. Whoever was taking the sight would wedge himself firmly between the mast and the bridge chart table or in the wing of the bridge with a seaman holding him firmly in place to enable him to use both hands. The sun, which in any case shone very fitfully, had to be hunted in the sextant mirror as it swung up and down, until experience decided the right moment to shout "Now!" so that the deck-watch time could be noted.

Fortunately, the plotting of our position from our own sights was not strictly necessary as the leading trawler was acting as our pilot and was passing back the estimated position every morning and evening. Our efforts were intended for emergencies only.

But such an emergency very nearly arose on the evening of the second day, when, with a horrible cough, the engine on which we were running suddenly stopped. We heard the duty motor mechanic trying each of the others in turn, but none responded. By this time the two boats astern of us had passed by; 663 had been rude enough to line her decks and shout abuse, while Tommy Ladner, with a malicious grin on his gnome-like face, had offered Corny a tow.

As the convoy dwindled into the distance, the enormity of the situation began to sink in. Here we were, "Harry Four"[1] in the middle of the Atlantic! The "Chief" reported that it was only petrol pressure trouble, and sure enough, after switching the feeds about a bit, two engines roared into life and we moved off after the convoy.

We were carrying 3,000 gallons of petrol in specially-built tanks on the upper deck besides the 5,000 gallons below decks, and we found this extra load an embarrassment in more ways than one.

We were always conscious of petrol. In normal circumstances a cigarette lit in the wardroom meant a naked flame only a foot or two from a compartment holding 2,500 gallons of extremely explosive fuel; with these upper deck tanks literally encasing us in petrol, it was always necessary to have it in mind.

On the third day out the wind freshened and the sea grew rougher, the swell shortening and becoming far more uncomfortable. The convoy reached 13 degrees west, calculated to be far enough into the Atlantic to avoid serious aircraft attack and the U-boat concentration in the Bay of Biscay, and therefore we altered course to due south. We now had this beastly short, high sea tumbling us along from the starboard quarter, and making the boat's motion far more erratic and violent than before. We could not even use the wing engines for a time, as the corkscrew rolling took the wing propellers right out of the water.

But suddenly our attention was distracted from the sea to the air. A series of staccato "A"s sounded on the gun buzzer, and Preston in the pom-pom turret was pointing up on the port bow.

"Four-engined aircraft, sir!"

"Action stations! Hoist Flag 'A', Pilot!" Corny and Pick studied the plane. "It's a Focke-Wulf Condor all right. It's not likely to attack us —it's only shadowing."

Sure enough the aircraft circled round and round the convoy, about a mile away, as unpleasant as a vulture waiting for its prospective prey to die. The gunners got very impatient, and were all for having a go at it, but the range was obviously too long, and they had to be disappointed.

We became so used to its presence that at one time we quite forgot it was there. There seemed no point in staying at action stations, but

[1] "Harry 4": a flag hoist meaning "4 engines out of action".

Corny kept the number ones of the guns at their stations in case of any attack. At noon it disappeared, and the trawler ahead immediately ordered rapid changes in course and speed to attempt to throw him off; but in the late afternoon "George", as we had dubbed him, resumed his stooge patrol! Another message was passed down the line, and a flurry of excitement swept with it. "Prepare to open fire when ordered."

Only the pom-pom could possibly approach that range, and so young Preston had the privilege of firing 658's first shots in anger. Although the barrage was completely ineffective, we all felt a little elated at having opened our account with the enemy. At dusk, our unwelcome visitor left us, and we began to wonder how good his contact was with his U-boat pack, and whether they were in an advantageous position to intercept us.

The middle watch began quietly enough, with every nerve strained to hold the shaded stern light ahead. Corny and I didn't talk much, but concentrated on the empty blackness enveloping us on all sides.

At 0100, the peacefulness of the night was suddenly shattered. A disembodied stream of tracer came floating in from the port bow, well for'd of us but flicking towards 657 ahead. I had never seen tracer coming in my direction before. It was quite remarkable, the way it floated lazily nearer and then flicked past and seemed to curl away—as it was missing us. My eyes and mouth opened wide, and my bemused brain awoke to hear Corny rap "Action Stations! Port wheel, Cox'n!"

While I—still bewildered—fumbled for the second buzzer from the left and rang a series of urgent "D"s on the alarm, Corny had steadied up on the bearing from which the firing had come, and had rung down for all engines and more speed. Everything happened at once. Figures stumbled on the bridge—Pick, wild-eyed, startled out of a deep sleep, followed by the two Vickers gunners. At each turret the number ones climbed in and waited for information. In our present state, encumbered with deck petrol tanks which not only made us more vulnerable but also restricted the arcs of fire of the guns, we did not relish surface action. I stared out ahead, but by now the tracer had ceased. The only evidence of the attack was the flickering light of a fire aboard 657. She had been hit, then! I thought with horror of the connecting pipes between all the petrol tanks, and prayed that they would be able to control the fire quickly enough to stop it spreading. Otherwise, with 8,000 gallons aboard. . . .

We could only assume that the attack had come from a surfaced submarine and as we charged along the bearing towards its position every hand and eye was tensed ready to strike. But there was nothing to find. In the pitch blackness, the enemy had disappeared—dived presumably—and Corny made a wide circle and struck our original course again, although we could no longer see any ship of the convoy.

So "George", our shadower, had done his job well! We could only admire the navigation involved in such an accurate interception on a very dark night, but were grateful that the attack had been so lightly pressed. 657's rapid return fire (she had managed several bursts from the 0.5 turret almost immediately) may have discouraged the U-boat, which probably expected to achieve complete surprise.

About an hour later, as we followed astern of the convoy, queer things began to happen a mile or two on the starboard beam. Several small searchlights swept around, but there was no tracer, so it could hardly be another attack, and we therefore held our course to regain our station. We passed 663 and 648 (the two astern of us in the line) and were overjoyed to see 657 ahead ploughing along apparently unaffected by her damage.

When dawn came the convoy was all present and correct, sailing serenely on if a little ragged in station, and we semaphored to 657 to see how they were. Doug Maitland, not given to heroics, merely replied, "All now well, slight casualties only, one petrol tank burned out and considerable experience gained in fire fighting!"

For me, the night left only a sensation of immense confidence in Corny's leadership. He had not hesitated, but had reacted immediately in taking aggressive action. His coolness and efficiency had been felt all over the boat, and spirits were lifted high. The weather was still unpleasantly bad, and the day wore on with little excitement and the usual discomforts. A cup of tea or of ship's cocoa (always called "ky") would have been like nectar, but there were few grumbles.

When I set off round the upper deck on a leg-stretching social tour I found the usual groups squatting in the most sheltered places huddled in oilskins and overcoats, very much on form and now convinced that they were true seamen, having weathered four days of the Atlantic in a small boat! They certainly looked far more at home than they had on the first evening out.

Towards the evening of 5th May came a rapid, but nevertheless almost unnoticed, change in atmosphere and weather. The sky cleared and showed its blue for the first time, the wind dropped and the sea calmed. Conversation began to be directed forward to Gibraltar and the Mediterranean rather than back to Brixham and Milford and "home". This mood was enlivened even more by a signal which told us that at 0100 we should be altering course to east-south-east on the last leg of our voyage, instead of ploughing interminably southward as we had been for the past three days.

Next morning we sighted the first ships we had seen since we left England. A battleship with three escorting destroyers steamed past at 25 knots, on the opposite course to ours, and I made the entry in the log: "1130—sighted battleship with destroyer escort." When I next opened the log I found beneath my entry, in Corny's unmistakable hand, "1150—decided friendly!" H.M.S. *Duke of York* looked very majestic and powerful as she passed, and was light-hearted enough to flash "Hope you get there" to our senior officer.

For the rest of the day, we restored the boat to order in readiness for our arrival at Gibraltar next morning. We could now gauge the water supply accurately, the whole crew shaved, scrubbed out, and wallowed in cleanliness for a change. To complete the renaissance, the chief M.M. rushed up to report that at last he had managed to get one of the generators going, and we could have that long-awaited cup of tea. We dined ravenously that night on hot soup, stew, and a solid currant duff!

The biggest surprise came at dusk. A signal was passed back from the *Coverley* (the leading trawler):

"*Estimated time of arrival Gibraltar* 0730/07. *Rig for entering harbour, ratings half blues, officers blues. Prisoners will be met by escorts.*"

The word "prisoners" shook everyone. We flashed up Doug, but he knew nothing, so we tried ML 240 to starboard. He pleaded ignorance, but tried the ML in the next column. Eventually, and at fifth hand, we discovered that Charles Jerram in 667 and Tom Fuller in 654 (the two Dogs at the end of the starboard column) had picked up survivors from a German U-boat on the night of 657's clash. So *that* had been the commotion we had seen! The searchlights had been the Aldis lamps of the Dogs sweeping the sea for survivors. But how had the U-boat been sunk?

We heard next day that the whole thing was rather a mystery! The trawler *Coverley* had picked up a submarine by Asdic, and had turned sharply to port to attack. She may have rammed the submarine. On the other hand, survivors from *two* U-boats were picked up, and stated that they had been in collision with each other. Apparently this was the price of hunting in packs!

Admiralty records, however, attribute one sinking to the trawler by ramming and the other to aircraft attack, which in the circumstances of that dark night hardly seems likely.

In any case, the two Germans aboard 667 soon became very useful, as one of them was found to be an expert cook, and could even bake delicious bread! By the end of the voyage, they were on excellent terms with the British crew.

During the night the first land we had seen for seven days showed up as a dark smudge on the port bow. Soon the lights of neutral Tangier appeared, like fairyland after the British blackout. At dawn most of the crew were on deck to catch their first glimpse of the Mediterranean. The sun came up dead ahead, due east, and we seemed to peer up a dazzling rippling roadway of light which led not only into the eye of the sun, but also beckoned us on into the ancient sea beyond. There was the Rock on the port bow, already large and menacing.

As we approached, a small fleet of HDMLs came out towards us, and one came alongside to put aboard a young officer to act as pilot. As we shook hands, we immediately sensed a new atmosphere. The subbie was wearing a white cap cover, and this seemed to crystallise our thoughts. We had arrived! Here, there was a different Navy, and a different job, and we could leave all the past behind us and concentrate on the future.

"Good morning, sir." He saluted Corny. "Welcome to the Mediterranean. What sort of a trip have you had?"

"Bloody awful," growled Corny. "But what's more important— what's our routine? We haven't been able to listen in to B.B.C. wavelengths. What's been happening out here?"

The subbie pulled out a newspaper from his inner pocket.

"I thought you would want to know that, so I brought out today's paper."

Corny stared at the headlines.

*"Big Retreat Begins. Afrika Korps Prepares To Evacuate Tunisia."*

We looked at each other. Were we too late?

## Chapter IV

## DOG AND BONE

ON our way into the harbour we gathered a great deal of information. The Dogs which had arrived a month before (mainly of the 19th and 32nd Flotillas) had been hard at work, and had already made a name for themselves. But it had been hard won. The Senior Officer, Lieutenant P. F. S. Gould D.S.C., R.N. had been killed and 639 sunk by an attack after a thrilling series of successes. Stewart Gould had been renowned as the great MGB leader at Dover, and his loss was a sad and telling blow to Coastal Forces generally and to us in particular. Everywhere men spoke highly of his courage and leadership.

The subbie had brought with him a list which showed the order in which we were to visit various parts of the dockyard. The plan was to rush us through Gibraltar to Algiers in thirty-six hours, and this involved continuous work for the whole crew. The idea really took our breath away. We had been at sea for seven days with little sleep, very cramped conditions and in unpleasant weather. What we all wanted more than anything else was to bath, change into pyjamas, and sleep for twenty-four hours. And instead, here we were faced with thirty-six hours unremitting toil! It was a lot to ask.

On the other hand, for two months we had been rushing events, restricting leave and leisure and even skimping training, for the one purpose of getting out to Tunisia before the war finished there. Were we to throw away our sacrifices lightly? For the time being, at least, we were given no choice. Within four hours, we had been invaded by shipwrights who wrenched off the bolts securing the deck tanks, and by ordnance artificers who readjusted the firing arcs of the gun turrets. A crane plucked off the tanks, and at once we had a feeling of freedom: we could now walk our decks without taking climbing exercise.

Next we were rushed to the victualling yard to take on fresh provisions, and to the fuelling berth to take on a complete load of petrol. It was a relief to remember that it would at least all be below decks.

All the time, we looked longingly at the inviting prospect of Gibraltar. The sun shone from a cloudless blue sky, and we could see a fruit-vendor with heaped baskets of oranges and bananas at the dock-yard gate. The soldiers working around the docks wore khaki shorts, and looked more alert and fitter than the men we had left behind in April's gloomy Britain.

At last we were guided to our berth in the Coastal Force Base, and there was a chance to relax. Leave was piped, and the duty watch, granted a "make and mend", were soon all fast asleep except for a solitary quartermaster.

At tea time, Corny returned from a conference of C.O.s in the operations room at the Base. "Panic's over," he said. "It looks as though we're too late. They reckon North Africa will be clear of Germans within three days, and they've got enough boats to mop up any attempted evacuation by sea. I guess we'll have to wait till the next big push—wherever that will be—for our chance to help the war along."

Each day that followed brought news which bore out Intelligence's predictions. On 8th May, the day after our arrival, Admiral Cunning-ham made his famous signal to his ships patrolling off the Cap Bon peninsula: "Sink, burn and destroy. Let nothing pass." For the follow-ing forty-eight hours destroyers and Coastal Force craft reaped a rich harvest of prisoners escaping from Tunisia in every conceivable small craft—even in rubber dinghies! This blockade was officially named "Operation Retribution", but those taking part dubbed it the "Kelibia Regatta", which summed up their high spirits at the Army's great victory.

The end had still not come when we left for Algiers on the 11th May, although obviously it must be soon. As we set off on this voyage of nearly 450 miles, we found it encouraging to reflect that six months earlier it would have been considered a major operation; even now no convoy reached Malta without stiff air opposition from the Sicilian-based Luftwaffe. We found it vastly more enjoyable than anything we had experienced before. At last 658 was a fighting craft, able to fire her guns on every bearing; her crew had been knitted into a team by their common experience of a 1,600 mile voyage, and now knew the strengths and weaknesses of all its members.

And above all we had perfect weather. A cloudless sky and mill-pond sea, which made 24 knots a sheer delight, gave a tremendous feeling of power as the whine and throb of the engines thrust the boat forward, leaving a frothing chasm tumbling in its wake. Here too was the chance for close station keeping; not as close as we normally kept later, but still thrillingly daring to an easily-impressed midshipman.

When we passed the boom at Algiers at 1500 a signal was rushed to us that we were required to fuel and leave again at 0600 next morning! We had begun to realize that there was a sense of urgency in the Mediterranean. There was still no news of the final surrender in Africa, so perhaps we were going to be in time, after all.

It took us the rest of the afternoon to fuel, but we sent one watch ashore to sample the atmosphere of North Africa, and we each slipped ashore to have a rapid look round this strange French-Arab city. But the fun really started after nightfall, when an air raid began with no warning whatsoever. It was quite unlike any air raid I had experienced before in London, Portsmouth, or on the South Coast, as in this case a fantastic barrage of light anti-aircraft guns opened up, so intense that it seemed to form an umbrella of criss-crossing tracer over the harbour. The crash of bombs into the basin only a hundred yards away left me breathless, but soon all sight and sense was blotted out by an evil-smelling sulphurous smoke-screen which descended—too late—to protect the harbour. After the all clear I slept uneasily. The noise and violence of both the attack and its repulse had brought us suddenly into the Mediterranean War, and now I began to wonder how I would stand up to the personal tests of courage which were bound to come. I had always hated air raids at home; I thought it would make all the difference if I had something to do and think about during an attack. But it seemed that there would be little point in opening fire with our pea-shooters when the target would not normally be visible, so I would have to put on a bold face even if I did not feel very confident.

Early next morning we sailed for Bone. It took us two days to reach our destination in the end, as 657 had engine trouble and we had to spend a night in the little port of Bougie en route. Bone was full of shipping, and we now joined up with the Dog-boats which had passed through their first spell of operations. They had many experiences to relate. Tunisia had finally fallen the previous day, and there was an air of jubilation abroad.

We quickly settled into the routine, and began our first serious working-up programme, both within the boat and as a unit of the 20th MGB Flotilla.

Up to this time, we had been so busy just *getting to* the Med that our efficiency had not measured up to real operational requirements. Now Corny set about this situation with his usual determination.

His outlook was typical of a Canadian who had been educated in a very "English" school on Vancouver Island. Although his ideas and energy were characteristic of the New World, he had a tremendous respect for British institutions, even though he was not above making cracks at them to provoke an argument.

It was his tremendous zest for life that made him an outstanding leader. If he had an unusual idea, he would follow it hard till it was either successfully carried through or proved impracticable. He could turn on his immense charm at will; but if he detected insincerity or shallowness in others, he could become rigidly hard and unfriendly.

To his own shipmates, the officers and men of 658, he was always the undisputed boss. Occasionally, he was severe in judgment and exacting in his demands. When this happened, it was accepted that we had not measured up to his standards, and such was his hold on the men that, instead of grumbling, they would shake their heads and say: "Blimey, what a skipper!" and then get on and put the matter right.

But in normal circumstances a twinkle was never far from his eyes, and his fiercest grimaces were well known to us as forlorn attempts to hide an effervescent sense of humour. His rugged aggressive exterior left no doubt about the strength of the man beneath.

Every night, almost without exception, there was an air raid, and I found the inevitability of the attacks hard to stomach. As 2100 approached I would begin to glance at the clock in the wardroom and to listen intently for the alarm. I could never settle to anything after the evening meal and I envied the others their apparent lack of imagination. Later I was to learn that the only difference in fact was in the degree of concealment of their emotions, but I was not to know this at the time.

Bone was an important supply port, and the German airfields in Sicily, Sardinia and Pantelleria were able to send out strong bomber strikes to attack it. The raids led to one benefit for us, however. We formed a very pleasant liaison with a famous trio of destroyers, *Loyal*, *Lookout*, and *Laforey*, and when they were in harbour, we would normally lie alongside them to receive power from their dynamos in order to rest our own overworked "genny". The crew were given the use of the destroyers' showers and canteens, and we were invited to use their bathrooms. All this hospitality was greatly appreciated, and the R.N. destroyer officers would often spend an evening in our ward-room in a quiet poker session.

On one such evening, the alarm sounded, our guests fled, our engines burst into life, and we were just moving off when *Laforey* opened fire with her 4.7s! 658 shook and rattled with the con-cussion, and we shouted at each other deafly. As soon as we moved out into the harbour, with 663 close by, the dense, acrid fumes of the port's smoke-screens enveloped us, and we were blind as well as deaf. Our searchlight could not penetrate the fog, so we blundered slowly across the harbour, sounding the klaxon, until there appeared, a few feet off the bows, the hulk of a cargo ship sunk by bombing a few weeks earlier. We managed to avoid collision, and tied up to her. Corny then began bellowing into the night with a megaphone to help Tommy Ladner get alongside. 663 was nearby (we could tell that from the noise of her engines) but we could see no sign of her. Suddenly her stem appeared a few yards away heading straight for our engine-room. But catastrophe was averted, and we waited together for the all clear to sound.

Towards the end of May a heavy air assault began on the small island of Pantelleria, the key to the Sicilian Channel. We watched the formations of bombers heading out to sea, and heard of the results in the B.B.C. bulletins. It seemed probable that this was to be the next objective, and we began to wonder if we should be used in an assault.

On the 31st, however, we knew our next move. We were ordered to sail to Malta next day with 663. For me, this meant my first opportunity to take full navigational responsibility for a long voyage, and I prepared the courses carefully and checked them with Derrick, who would be following astern.

We rounded Cap Bon by night, and all next day we steamed east-ward. In mid-afternoon I gave Corny a time and bearing for sighting Malta. The time came, and passed, and Corny called down the voice pipe to the charthouse.

"Say, Pilot, just check your bearing and time, will you? There's nothing in sight in any direction, and visibility's pretty good."

I checked rapidly, but found my dead-reckoning position to be accurate, and scrambled up to the bridge puzzled and anxious. The sky above was absolutely clear and blue and, apart from heat haze obscuring the horizon, visibility could not have been better. "We should have been able to see the island at at least ten miles, and that was nearly fifteen minutes ago!"

I began to blush and get really hot under the collar.

"Hold it," said Pick. "Here comes your salvation. Look—through the mist." Quite suddenly, the golden line of Malta spread before us, and the hitherto invisible wall of mist which must have obscured it melted away.

I breathed again.

So at 1550 on the 2nd June, 1943, we arrived at Malta for the first time, sailing into Marxamaxett harbour and tying up at Sa Maison. The yellow bastions, glaring in the strong sunlight, towered impressively above us. The fo'c'sle party, in immaculate white rig, paraded smartly, our pennants Sugar-Six-Five-Eight fluttered proudly from the yard, and we piped the still as we passed the famous Submarine Base at Manoel Island.

We felt that at last, after our long voyage, we had arrived. We were ready for work.

## CHAPTER V

## DOWN TO BUSINESS

OUR first visitor was not Captain Coastal Forces, nor even an officer from the Base. He was a little Maltese Jew in a trilby hat, known to everyone as "Mr. Greenberg" as he was the representative of that prominent tailor in Valletta. He very rapidly secured orders from most of the crew for uniforms of varying descriptions. No self-respecting matelot would ever wear a "pusser's suit" for number ones ashore; they all had suits made to flatter, with a specially cut front and extra wide bell-bottoms! We were to be visited by Mr. Greenberg very frequently throughout our commission, and although we were a little doubtful about him at first, he eventually became a welcome and comforting sign of the unchanging routine when we returned to Malta after long absences.

He was not the only "local" to make an immediate contact, either. Coastal Force Base Malta was named H.M.S. *Gregale*, after the strong north-easterly wind which seasonally blew straight into the harbours of Valletta, and raised a swell which made the berths alongside very uncomfortable for small craft.

It was housed in a row of hotels and villas on the other side of Marxamxett harbour, and any journey across to the Base at this time meant a long dinghy row. However, on the second day we found that we had been adopted by "Joe", the owner of a spotless dghaisa, who in return for very minor "perks", would transport any of us for a much-reduced fare, and could also be relied upon as efficient dhobeyman.[1] The dghaisas are a feature of Malta which cannot fail to attract newcomers. They are long boats, after the style of Venetian gondolas, but are sculled with two oars from a standing position.

It took only a few days for us to decide that June was obviously going to be a quiet month, but that it also heralded preparations for some big operation. Inevitably, the questions "Where?" and "When?" rapidly became the major topics of conversation. Sicily seemed the obvious target for an invasion although the South of France, Sardinia,

---

[1] Dhobey: laundry.

Crete and Greece were all eagerly put forward by some of our amateur strategists. Pantelleria was captured soon after our passage to Malta, and the islands of Lampedusa and Linosa fell to token forces shortly after.

More and more Dogs arrived from Bone, until a strong force was working-up together. There was little news of the two convoys which had still to arrive from England (including 662, with our S.O. and my friend Gordon Surtees) except a vague idea that they were due at the end of June.

On the 6th June, Corny returned from a visit to the Operations Room.

"Well, fellers, I guess we're on the job tonight." He handed me the sailing orders. "See you've got all the minefields and swept channels marked, Pilot. And Pick—you'd better do an extra careful check of guns today. This is our first real test, and I want everything to go with a bang."

I studied the orders. "Being in all respects ready for sea . . . MTB 633 and MGBs 658 and 663 will proceed to patrol the Sicilian Coast from Cape Passero northward to Cape Murro di Porco."

Ten minutes later Derrick and I were sitting in Joe's dghaisa on our way to the Base to visit S.O.O. (Staff Officer, Operations). We had already made his acquaintance, and knew we could expect every help in the way of chart corrections, weather reports, and intelligence on the Sicilian ports. S.O.O. was a young R.N.V.R. lieutenant named Tim Bligh[1] who sported a wonderful beard and a forceful manner. He had only been ashore a few weeks, after losing his boat. He had been in command of a Vosper until she had gone aground whilst patrolling a shallow and badly charted enemy-held bay and Tim had destroyed her by firing a two-star cartridge into bilges filled with petrol. This episode (or perhaps the explosion which followed) had earned Tim the title in a colourful Press report, of "The man who laughed at death"! He took a long time to live that one down. What we did not know then was that Tim was destined to become, by the end of the war, the most well known of all Coastal Forces officers in the Med.

At 2000 that night, the three boats slipped out through the boom and headed north-east towards Sicily. We saw the S.O. in 633 ahead wave his arm in a circular movement above his head, and Corny turned to give Tommy the same signal. "Increase 200 revs," he

[1] Later Lt.-Cdr. T. J. Bligh D.S.O., O.B.E., D.S.C., R.N.V.R.

ordered, and I moved the handle which passed this instruction to the engine-room.

W/T silence was always kept as long as possible, and all signals were kept to a minimum. By day, simple hand signals indicated increases, decreases, and orders to stop, while at night, a small blue signal lamp was flashed astern down the line, the letter "I" meaning increase 200 revs, "R" reduce by 200 revs, and "O" meaning stop. No visual signal would normally be made forward up the line, as it might possibly be seen by enemy craft ahead, so it was a case of keeping eyes skinned for signals which were not repeated and had to be acted upon without the sender knowing whether they had been received.

Almost at once, a flag hoist appeared on the S.O.s halliards. "Preparative Flag Five, sir," I called. Corny motioned to Pick, waiting with loud-hailer mike in his hand. "Stand by to test guns, Pick."

Gunnery control was Pick's job, and there were three ways of transmitting orders to the gunners in their turrets. The "sound-power" telephones worked effectively when newly adjusted, but were easily put out of action by salt water and careless handling; the gun buzzers were excellent for definite orders such as open and cease fire, but were useless for giving any detailed information; and so the loud hailer—a simple loud-speaker system directed both forward and aft—which could be heard above the roar of the engines and even the guns when at full blast, was most frequently used.

When the flag fluttered up to the yardarm ("close up" in naval terms), Pick immediately ordered each gun in turn to fire a short burst in a safe direction.

I looked round the ship and saw the gunners eagerly talking to the loading numbers at each turret. They were obviously confident and pleased all had gone smoothly. For a small boat, we could certainly boast a tremendous fire-power, and the power-operated turrets, which could twirl round at a touch of the gunner's fingers on his joystick control, looked very efficient.

Quite quickly, darkness fell and a careful check was made of "darken ship". The height of indignity would be to receive a signal from the next astern, saying: "You have a light showing on the starboard quarter". With Tommy and Derrick astern this would have been especially hard to live down, and we took great precautions to see that it never happened.

As we approached the Sicilian Coast, we were amazed to see the lighthouse on Cape Passero (the south-eastern corner of Sicily) shining as brightly as it would have been in peace-time. Surely it wasn't normally lit? Did this mean that a convoy was expected? We kept our fingers crossed.

We patrolled about three miles from the coast, scanning the sea inshore with radar. Our radar set was really designed to detect aircraft, and was not very effective with surface ships. But it was all we had, so each boat in turn kept watch on radar for a set period. The screen was in the W/T office below decks, and in fact the "sparker" and the radar operator were the only two ratings allowed below decks (apart from the engine-room crew) during a patrol. We were very lucky in having an experienced and very conscientious operator who had already qualified for his leading seaman rating. In fact, Gunning did not profess to be much of a seaman, but he was quite remarkable on his radar set.

The aerials above the mast were directional, and were worked by hand from the office below, the direction in which they were pointing being recorded on the scale beside the set. Across the screen were two lines at right angles, the horizontal one looking as though it was growing grass, with minute fingers of green light flickering out from it. Should a target appear, and the aerials be accurately pointed at it, a definite green "blip" would appear above the line, and its distance from the vertical would indicate the range.

Reports were always given in the form of a relative bearing—that is as an angle with our own line of advance, using Red for port and Green for starboard.[1] But to detect a firm target, especially a small one, from among the perpetual "grass", and from the 360 degrees of sweep, was an expert's job, and we were confident that Gunning was an expert. He was a Welshman, and we could normally gauge his excitement from the intensity of his accent as he called his reports up the voice-pipe to the bridge.

On this, our first patrol, he was very disappointed when he reported after two hours that he was closing down as arranged. "Not even a gremlin to get me worked up tonight, sir! I can usually manage at least one or two false alarms, but I haven't had a smell of an echo on this watch."

All round the deck there was a stir of activity. Every two hours the watches changed. No one went below, but the new watch kept lookout from their gun turrets, and those just relieved settled down on the

[1] e.g.: "Red Three-O": 30 degrees on the port bow; "Green Nine-O": on the starboard beam.

hard deck near their guns and tried to snatch some sleep. All was very quiet.

Suddenly the situation changed. We saw a flickering searchlight swing to seaward and begin to sweep to the north of us. Was there anything in the wind? Had we been detected? Perhaps a convoy was about to leave Syracuse!

We stopped, cut engines, and lay quiet for a while, listening for sounds of motors. We were only a mile and a half off Syracuse, and if we were to catch any shipping, we were in the ideal position. Ships entering and leaving harbour were likely to be psychologically un-prepared for attack—they might well be occupied with the routine of preparing to anchor or to take up moorings, or conversely stowing the gear away, or busy with a hundred other duties and thoughts.

Then the searchlight passed right over us. I experienced for the first time the horrible sense of vulnerability the sudden glare of illumination brings. It was like undressing in the beam of a car's head-lights. I looked round apprehensively. Surely every shore battery in Sicily had now got us in its sights.

But no shells whined out towards us from Syracuse. Engines were started up and slowly we turned and ambled off down the coast again. We did this for the rest of the night, punctuated with another long spell of lying with engines cut.

At 0440 the welcome sight of 633 turning homeward told us our first patrol was virtually over. We knew, however, that dawn was a dangerous time for aircraft attack, and our orders clearly told us to be more than forty miles from Sicily by first light. The Luftwaffe had plenty of planes and airfields in Sicily, but the R.A.F. could only fly its fighters from Malta, which was too far away to maintain adequate protection over a long period. In fact, the Luftwaffe ruled above these waters and it was extremely discomforting to think of those venomous Me. 109s and Ju. 88s waiting to have a go at us.

As Corny and Pick had not taken any rest during the night, whereas I had managed to snatch two short spells while we were lying cut, I had the doubtful privilege of the watch for this return passage. Conscious of the danger from the sky, and especially from the eastern sky where any aircraft would hardly be seen approaching out of the eye of the sun, I strained my eyes and made sure the lookouts were on their toes. But the effort after a virtually sleepless night was almost im-possible. I found my eyes closing automatically and shook myself angrily, realizing the awful crime I was involuntarily committing.

Drastic measures were necessary. I talked to the helmsman and got him to talk to me. I bathed my eyes with eye lotion to tone up the muscles. Finally I had a brew of tea made and sent it round the upper deck. The three hours dragged slowly by, and I was never more pleased to see land than when the low yellow coast of Malta came in view.

As we entered harbour, I took my place with the fo'c'sle party and was horrified to find myself dozing off on my feet for a second or two. And all my ideas of an immediate long sleep were swept away when we tied up.

The boat had to be brought to readiness before we could relax. Pick gave his orders: "Both watches to breakfast, work ship and clean guns 0800, fuelling 1030, pipe down after dinner."

Very few of the crew went ashore that afternoon. If I had not been setting an example on a bunk in the wardroom, I should have found every man-jack of them sprawled on the deck or on the messdeck with their "heads down"—the Navy's phrase for sleeping.

During these few weeks, 658 and 663 were seldom apart. We normally lay alongside each other, and rarely went to sea independently. It was natural that the crews should become both great rivals and (paradoxically) great cronies, and they frequently went ashore together. We had already done so many trips in company that our lads had named 663 "The Shadow" as she was always astern of us, Corny being slightly senior to Tommy. In the wardroom, too, 663 were constant visitors and it was more usual than otherwise to find either Tommy, Derrick or Barry Syrett, the first lieutenant, sitting at our table at tea or over a drink in the evening. 657 had been delayed in Bone with engine trouble, and although later the three boats were very close, 657 never achieved the same place in our affections as "The Shadow".

Tommy Ladner was a remarkable man. Often very quiet, he would become very excited if his point of view demanded it, and his lawyer's mind and tongue were a formidable combination. He was thoughtful, too, and paid more attention to detail than Corny or Doug. Whereas Corny would demand a high standard, and leave its achievement to Pick or myself, only checking that all was well when next the matter was raised, Tommy would persist and remind his officers frequently and see personally that his wishes were being carried out. Both methods worked, but Tommy expended far more nervous energy his way!

It was at this time that I received the nickname which stuck to me for the rest of the war.

I had always been a very keen member of the Scout Movement, and early in Naval training I had joined the Navy's branch of that movement—the Deep Sea Rover Scouts. On my first visit to H.M.S. *St. Angelo*, the great accounting base for Malta, I noticed that the paymaster lieutenant-commander who was in charge of all our pay accounts was wearing a Scout wristlet badge. I introduced myself, and made a very valuable friend.

This impressed Corny and Pick no end—that their young Pilot could immediately strike an acquaintanceship with a senior accountant officer seemed remarkable to them. When I spent each Tuesday evening at the meetings of the Malta Deep Sea Rover Crew, and occasionally brought down a fellow member to have a look at 658, they could not resist dubbing me "Rover" Reynolds.

As the whole thing was very light-hearted, there seemed no reason for me to object, and very quickly the name stuck. Pick and Corny would salute me gravely with a Scout salute over one eye as I came aboard, and this practice even spread later to our good-humoured senior officer when he travelled with us on operations.

During this quiet period, Corny began to get restive about replacing our 0.5 turrets by single Oerlikon guns on each side of the bridge. He argued that that the 0.5s were primarily anti-personnel weapons, whereas the 20-mm. Oerlikon shells were particularly explosive and would do far more damage against craft and men, and in addition the gun was far simpler in operation and less liable to get stoppages. It had a greater effective range and fired nearly 500 rounds a minute.

Eventually he persuaded the Base gunnery officer to try out his pet scheme, and within a very short while we had the mountings and were going out for trials. The vibration was rather excessive but we had tremendous confidence in the new guns and felt that in every way they had improved our armament.

At the end of June, without any advance information, Lt.-Cdr. Norman Hughes arrived with the other five boats to complete our flotilla. One old friend was 665 with Peter Thompson in command, to whom we had said farewell three months before at Weymouth. But for Derrick and me the big event was the arrival of Gordon Surtees, and we soon put him in the picture on the routine at Malta. As the S.O.'s Pilot, his secretarial duties were heavy, but he had a super efficient Number One (Bill Darracott) who had everything very carefully organized.

The new Dog-boats were not the only recent arrivals in Malta. A trip to *St. Angelo* for pay took us across Grand Harbour and gave us a magnificent view of the fleet assembling there. I recognized the old battleships *Warspite*, *Malaya* and *Queen Elizabeth*, but the cruisers and destroyers were too numerous to identify. In our harbour, Marxamaxett, every beach and jetty was crowded with landing craft of every sort, and every day brought further newcomers.

On the 28th June, we were detailed for an anti-E-boat patrol off St. Paul's Bay (where St. Paul was ship-wrecked nineteen hundred years before on one of his voyages). To us, it was a very dull affair; we dubbed it a "zizz patrol", a term of contempt used for patrols where nothing was likely to happen, and where everyone not on watch could sleep peacefully without much fear of disturbance.

This patrol was as uneventful as we had expected, and was only memorable for me because midnight saw the arrival of my twentieth birthday. As I was on foreign service this meant my automatic promotion from midshipman to "temporary acting sub-lieutenant". Consequently, as we approached the boom that morning Corny held the megaphone to his lips, and addressing the forward party, roared: "Sub-Lieutenant Reynolds to the bridge, please."

Wondering what this was all about, I dodged up to the bridge and there, with a genial beam, Corny informed me that it was my privilege to take the boat alongside in celebration of my promotion. I began the job with some internal trepidation, but with as little fuss as possible.

Both Corny and Pick handled the boat well, and in my apprenticeship taught me that flamboyant handling at high speed was stupid, as it never left any margin for emergencies; and also that good handling involved completing any manoeuvre with the smallest number of telegraph orders possible. This was rubbed home firmly when Corny sent me down to the engine-room whilst manoeuvring, first to watch, and then to assist in handling the gear levers, which was no light job even without a flurry of orders.

We had planned a dinner party in our wardroom to celebrate my birthday and promotion, but this was soon squashed when we heard on getting in from our "zizz patrol" that we were due for another patrol off Sicily with 663 (as usual), 640 and 634.

It was similar to our first patrol, but had a more exciting climax which helped me to remember my birthday more vividly. Both 634 and 663 had to return to harbour with engine defects soon after we had sailed. I made a note to pull Derrick's leg about poor maintenance, and settled down to keep the watch on passage to the patrol area while Corny and Pick had a short sleep.

We searched carefully up the coast of Sicily as we had on our first patrol, and apart from the probing searchlights near Syracuse, there was little to raise emotions of either hope or fear. Twice the radar office buzzer heralded reports of possible targets, but each time Gunning reluctantly decided that the "echoes" he was watching were nothing more than "ghosts". His eyes and fingers were so sensitive that he could pick up the slightest reaction of his set; he sometimes had firm traces on his screen which were certainly not ships, but were very difficult to explain away without invoking the supernatural.

At 0300, the S.O. decided that as it did not seem likely that we would meet any enemy ships, we should spread a little alarm and despondency by carrying out a bombardment of the harbour at Avola Marina, about twenty miles south of Syracuse. This action seemed very justified from three points of view: to lower the enemy morale, to do some damage, and to give our gunners some night-shooting practice.

We stopped a mile off Avola and the S.O. shouted across from 640.

"Corny—now there are only two of us, we'll go in a bit closer than we decided and make two runs. Keep close to my tail. Remember that we can't afford to damage the boats—if things get hot we'll have to beat it—fast!"

Corny waved in reply. "Stand by, Pick," he said, "and tell the gunners this is their chance to show what they are really worth. I want continuous firing the whole time we're on target."

We turned into line and crept in towards the shore, our bows well up in 640's wake. I noticed that the Sicilian blackout wasn't very good; the air-raid wardens and police of Avola Marina were not as efficient as in my home town! Lights sparkled here and there, and gradually the dim outline of the harbour wall became firmer in my glasses.

Over the R/T came a crackling, unreal voice. "Preparative Flag Five."

Immediately Pick passed on the warning to the gunners. "Stand by to open fire at Red Three-O. We shall be turning to starboard."

At 200 yards range, 640 swung round to starboard and increased speed.

"Flag Five!" ordered the R/T.

Pick pressed the gun buzzers, and simultaneously the two boats opened fire.

In an instant, 658 changed character. From a silently marauding domestic cat she became a vicious, spitting tigress snarling defiance at an unseen enemy.

The noise astonished and deafened me. The crack and stutter of our guns rolled back from the ancient walls of Avola and stunned my mind with its intensity. At this range nothing could miss so extensive a target, so long as the gunners aimed low.

We watched the 6-pounder shells striking against walls, each raising a cloud of smoke and dust and a spurt of yellow flame. The pom-pom and the Oerlikons hammered continuously, their tracers searing a brilliant path through the darkness and thudding home in rhythmic bursts of sparks.

The first run was over in two minutes, and we turned sharply to starboard to come round to the opposite course. By this time, the garrison had awakened and several spouts of machine-gun fire floated out towards us. The S.O., very conscious of the order to keep the boats out of trouble, opened the range a little and then passed the word to open fire again. The Oerlikons now had a definite point of aim at the sources of the machine-gun fire, and soon all but one were silenced. The run had almost finished when the first heavy shell from the shore fizzed overhead and raised a water spout two hundred yards to seaward.

At once "I"s blinked from the S.O., the engines roared, and we followed 640 out at twenty-four knots, weaving left and right to throw off the attentions of the battery.

Three minutes later, we stopped and looked back at Avola. A cluster of fires glowing redly were all the visible results of our bombardment. But we had baptised all the guns *and* the gunners, and with the future stretching ahead this was more important to us than the doubtful amount of damage we had inflicted on a Sicilian sea-side resort.


Some days later, at about 1230, I saw Corny returning from the Base in Joe's dghaisa. I moved to the gangway and saluted him as he came aboard.

"Find Pick and bring him down to my cabin, Rover—and bring in a bottle and three glasses while you're about it, too!"

There was just room for the three of us in the C.O.'s cabin. Pick and I sat on the settee and Corny had the seat by his bureau. When we each had a full glass in our hands, Corny said quietly:

"It's going to be Sicily, fellers—in a few days from now. And it's going to be the biggest invasion fleet in history."

## CHAPTER VI

## COILING THE SPRING

I LOOKED into my glass and then raised my eyes to meet Corny's. My thoughts were confused. I had no yardstick to help visualize the magnitude of such an invasion. I naturally thought mostly about my personal part in it all. Would I be up to the job? How would I feel in action? It was bound to come now. But however bad it was, it would be something to be able to say in years ahead: "I was at Sicily."

Pick asked: "What's our job going to be?"

"Our flotilla will be acting as an anti-E-boat screen during the landings, and patrolling in the Straits of Messina at nights. But here's the pay-off—the real sixty-four dollar question: How long can we operate without any reliance on a Base? They want us to stay at the beach all day and patrol all night until they capture a port from which we can operate. Bobby Allan's ready to move his Mobile Base in as soon as possible, and we'll fuel from tankers off the beach."

Pick pursed his lips and looked thoughtful. The machinery of a Dog-boat was fantastically complex for its size. Four main engines with all their cooling and fuelling mechanism; two auxiliaries, working constantly; two intricate electrical circuits and the radar and W/T; gun turrets worked by hydraulic pumps off the main engines; all these were subject to a multitude of faults and without any one of them the boat was severely handicapped. To keep them all running efficiently would mean an immense effort and a great deal of skill and intelligent improvization on the part of our engine-room crew. In fact, this was a great challenge, and amidst our doubts we had one great consolation.

Our chief motor mechanic on the outward voyage had suffered so chronically from sea sickness that we had reluctantly to put him ashore at Bone. In his place we had been lucky enough to receive Petty Officer Motor Mechanic William Last.

Bill Last was a veteran in Coastal Forces, and could already look back on two years of MGB operations. For more than a year he had been a motor mechanic in short MGBs off the East Coast, and as far back as November 1941 (just before I joined the Navy) he had been mentioned in dispatches after a bitter fight with E-boats in which he was wounded. He had commissioned 640 with Stewart Gould and had brought her out to the Mediterranean in the convoy before ours, and it had been our good fortune that he had been available just at the time we needed a new "Chief".

He was a tall, dark, Oxfordshire man with a flashing smile and considerable charm, and he proved to be a prince among motor mechanics, especially in action. He had tremendous courage and physique, and a real aptitude for dealing with emergencies. We all felt that if engines could be kept going, Last would be the man to do it. His leading motor mechanic, Bert Burrows, was a young and efficient little cockney who had been a Post Office telegraphist before joining the Navy, but had lapped up technical knowledge in training so that he was probably as sound as Last in his grasp of theory. This made them a very solid combination.

But even with our confidence in the crew, there was still the awful problem of spares. We had already found that the supply of spare parts for all the complex machinery of our boats was criminally poor. It had been difficult enough to keep 658 in state A (ready for operations) so far; would it be possible to operate night after night without needing repairs and replacements? and if we did, would they be available?

Our meeting broke up, and that afternoon each of us in turn read through the fifty closely-typed pages of foolscap which contained the details of organization and operations for the naval side of the invasion. These were kept in a large envelope heavily marked "Operation Husky —Most Secret" and as Corny handed it over to me he said: "Put this in the safe, Confidential Book Officer, and for heaven's sake remember that if you lose it we'll probably both be court-martialled and shot."

He need not have reminded me. The thought of the red-hot document in our small safe kept me awake at nights until the invasion began.

When I settled down to read it, the vastness of the organization began to sink in. At H-hour on D-day, nearly two thousand ships would converge on Sicily from every direction. I had no idea what two thousand ships would look like, and tried to picture them as dots on a page. Two thousand! That meant twenty lines with a hundred dots in each line. And many of the ships were coming direct from America and Britain and Egypt, through waters which less than a year before had been the most dangerous in the world, and where the Luftwaffe and the U-boat were still highly effective enemies.

The broad plan of "Husky" was to land huge forces simultaneously at 0200 on the 10th July in two main areas: American troops on the south-west coast, and British and Canadian troops on the south-east coast.

Our flotilla, operating together for the first time, was concerned mainly with the landing by Canadians and the Lovat Scouts at a beach (named "Acid North") just south of Syracuse and Cape Murro di Porco, which we already knew quite well.

The days between this early briefing and D-Day itself are among my sharpest memories of the war. The whole population of Malta was discussing the operation and many of the ideas of time and place were very wild; I found the knowledge and the great weight of secrecy was a heavy burden. We all knew the importance of security, and yet it seemed impossible that the Germans could be unaware of our objectives and timing when so many knew the facts.

The tension among the officers of our boats mounted daily. The tremendous challenge to our efficiency both in maintenance and in fighting strength seemed overwhelming. After all, our boats were still completely untried; they had not really faced the enemy yet.

The commanding officers of the boats were virtually alone in their experience of action; they alone had seen and heard and smelt the fury of close surface battles; they alone could visualize the possibilities of failure and therefore understood clearly the magnitude of the task before us.

Corny, Doug and Tom felt all this very keenly. For them, the last two days became an agony of suspense. Nothing could have been more natural, then, that on the evening before we were due to sail, a wild party should result in Monico's, the most popular bar ashore. When the Canadians arrived, they found the upper bar crowded with officers of the famous 51st Highland Division. They had just arrived from North Africa, and had an extremely cocky confidence which soon had them dominating the whole bar. They began to perform various highland dances both on the floor and on the tables, and the evening rapidly became more hilarious. Up to this point, the Army had undoubtedly held the focus of attention, and Doug Maitland suddenly felt he couldn't let them get away with this any longer.

After one particularly spectacular act, he took advantage of a brief interval of silence and approached one of the more prominent dancers.

"Say, Captain, have you ever enjoyed the occupation of having a drink and then eating your glass?"

A roar of derision greeted this question. Maitland turned to the barman and ordered a sherry in a long-stemmed glass. He downed the sherry and solemnly proceeded to eat the bowl of the glass. When he had finished—watched intently by a great circle of spectators—he put down the stem and pushed it towards the young Highland Division officer.

"Now, sir, I've left the greatest delicacy for you—how about it? Any takers?"

No one stepped forward. The Navy had won the day! From that point the party never looked back. Its climax was a game of rugger between the Army and Navy which, by its violence, attracted the Military Police. At its height, Corny inadvertently dropped a chair out of the window which landed most unfortunately on the head of the Provost Marshal, arriving to investigate. This gentleman, an irate Colonel of Marines, did not appreciate the act at all, but found on enquiring a complete ignorance of the dastardly deed. Burke, of course, looked more innocent than anyone else.


On the morning of 9th July (D-1), all the commanding officers, with their navigators, reported to the Base for final orders.

Luckily for us, our own orders were far less complicated than the mammoth bundle we had already studied, and were contained on half a sheet of signal paper.

"The 20th MGB Flotilla will patrol off Syracuse and Augusta from 2330, returning to 'Acid North' beach at first light. . . ."

There followed details of the other Coastal Force movements for the night, and limits were laid down beyond which we should not venture "unless in pursuit of the enemy".

Lastly, S.O.O. handed round to each Pilot a copy of a message to the whole invasion fleet from C.-in-C. Mediterranean. This was to be read to the crews just before leaving harbour.

We returned to 658 in Joe's dghaisa and, as we climbed the ladder, Pick greeted us with raised eyebrows, and Corny motioned him to follow us below. We worked out the day's routine, and Pick sent for the coxswain to give him the details as they affected the crew. When Roberts knocked at the wardroom door, his face was as expressionless as ever; but his eyes flickered and his eyebrows rose when Pick said; "No shore leave today, Cox'n. We shall be going out at 1600. Harbour stations at 1530—and tell the crew to be prepared for dirty weather— the forecast's bad."

"Aye aye, sir." The coxswain asked no questions, but we all knew that such an early start would set the tongues wagging on board and send "buzzes" from one end of the boat to the other. No one could be sure if it was the real thing or just a routine patrol—but the time of harbour stations was a pointer which would not be ignored.

All day a troublesome swell bumped us uncomfortably against the boat alongside, and every few minutes that afternoon one or the other of us knelt up on the wardroom settee to get a glimpse of the weather through the ports. Finally Corny could stand it no longer.

"I'm going to try to get my head down for an hour in my cabin. See everything's ready, Pick."

Pick and I clambered up to the bridge and stood looking around the harbour. Already many of the landing craft had gone, but the swell and the taut, flapping ensigns told us, even in the shelter of Marxamaxett, of a strong, blustering north-west wind. Through the entrance we could see a tumbling, heaped sea dappled with flecks of spume. We had seldom met worse conditions, and never operated in them, let alone invaded a continent.

It was still blowing hard and looking more grey and miserable than ever when Corny came to join us on the bridge. Naturally he had not slept at all.

"I'll talk to the crew on the messdeck now, Pick."

"Aye aye, sir."

Pick walked aft and spoke to the coxswain.

The shrill call of the bosun's pipe sounded, and the quartermaster on duty roared down each hatchway: "Clear lower deck. Muster on the forward messdeck."

Within two minutes, a knock came at the wardroom door.

"Ship's company all present, sir," reported the coxswain.

Corny led the way along the twelve feet of passage which separated the officers from the men in our crowded boats.

As he ducked through the watertight door into the messdeck, he motioned the men to sit.

"In half an hour, we shall be sailing to play our small part in the invasion of Sicily—Operation 'Husky'. We may be away for weeks. I'm going to tell you a few details now so that you have some idea of what's going on. I will try to keep you informed throughout the operation."

A ripple of movement passed through the crowded messdeck. Eyes met and exchanged messages, but in all of them I read only keen anticipation. This was what they had all been waiting and working for. Most of them looked really interested as I held up a chart for Corny.

He pointed out the main landing beaches and our patrol area. He showed them the gathering points of the huge convoys approaching from all directions. There were gasps when he told them of the American divisions sailing direct to the beaches from the United States, and of Canadians coming straight from Britain.

Then Corny read the C.-in-C.'s message.

*"We are about to embark on the most momentous enterprise of the war—striking for the first time at the enemy in his own land.*

*"Success means the opening of the 'Second Front' with all that implies, and the first move towards the rapid and decisive defeat of our enemies.*

*"Our object is clear and our primary duty is to place this vast expedition ashore in a minimum of time, and subsequently to maintain our military and air forces as they drive relentlessly forward into the enemy territory.*

*"In the light of this duty, great risks must be and are to be accepted. The safety of our own ships and all distracting considerations are to be relegated to second place, or disregarded as the accomplishment of our primary duty may require.*

*"On every commanding officer, officer and rating rests the individual and personal duty of ensuring that no flinching in determination or failure of effort on his part will hamper this great enterprise.*

*"I rest confident in the resolution, skill and endurance of you all to whom this momentous enterprise is entrusted."*

When he finished reading, he looked long and hard at the crew. "Well—that's it, fellers. Are there any questions before we go to harbour stations?"

There was a stir on one side of the messdeck. Stoker Arthur Francis was on his feet.

"Excuse me, sir. Will there be any shore leave in Sicily?"

The great gust of laughter which followed blew away the signs of tension, and the men began to pull on their sea-going gear.

Obviously we need not worry very much about our crew.

## CHAPTER VII

## HUSKY DOG

N O SOONER had we shown our noses out of the harbour than we realised just how bad the weather was. I made a note in my notebook, "North-westerly gale blowing", and later found written beneath it in Corny's unmistakable writing: "Sea— Harry Roughers". We found it difficult to maintain the appointed speed of eighteen knots and the rough beam sea played havoc with our station keeping, but the long line snaked its way painfully towards Sicily.

Seas broke over the fo'c'sle and trickled into the chart-house, and my charts began to get wet—an infallible indication that the weather was really bad. Then sea water caused a short circuit in the W/T cabin, and I rushed below to help extinguish an electrical fire. To cap it all, the "short" put the radar out of action for a while. Even Pick on deck was having extra worries, with a tricky stoppage on one of the guns during the brief testing shoot.

As night closed down on us, we had a grandstand view of the softening-up air raids on Avola, Syracuse, Augusta and Catania. But we were already wet and miserable and our thoughts hung in advance of time, probing the unknown mysteries which lay ahead. I thought, too, of the small landing craft bucking towards Sicily, and of their wretched cargoes of fighting men who were highly trained for war but ill-equipped to battle with the sea.

It seemed too much to hope that the whole complex plan could go through in these conditions without some major hold-up. Would these boats be able to beach? Would the weather ruin the whole thing? There could only be one answer. The weather must not be allowed to ruin it. The spirit of the men and the ships must overcome the problems and risk all rather than fail.

We patrolled slowly backward and forward about a mile off Augusta and Syracuse, getting wetter and colder and more miserable for nearly two hours. And then, as if to strengthen our suspicions that this whole operation was ill-fated, Pick reported that we had lost contact with the boat ahead! On this night of all nights, when confusion must on all account be avoided, the flotilla was split into two units, out of touch with each other. We could not risk breaking wireless silence, but kept on patrolling in the correct area until, with a sigh of relief, we picked up the other unit about half an hour later.

At about 0200, the crucial moment when the landing craft were due to touch down, the wind suddenly dropped, and the sea calmed surprisingly quickly, leaving only an uneasy swell to remind us of its earlier malevolence. It was as though a Divine Providence extended a hand to calm both the sea and the thousands of men about to be thrown into battle.

Nothing stirred out of Syracuse and Augusta. It seemed incredible that the Luftwaffe could have missed sighting our convoys that afternoon and evening, steaming steadily towards the beaches. Surely they must have wind of the plan by now? But there were no attacks, and we began to lose the tension of the night. Suddenly it was back. In the first dim light of dawn, Pick sighted flecks of white on the horizon. Through the binoculars, we picked out six boats moving south at high speed. E-boats!

The alarm bells shrilled, the crew ran to action stations, and the S.O.'s boat leapt forward, increasing rapidly to full speed. Each boat swung in behind and bows lifted as the flotilla surged ahead. It was fascinating to watch the small specks, shrouded in spray, growing larger every moment.

A daylight clash between D-boats and E-boats! Six of each, too. This was going to be a classic party. Wish we'd had a bit of time to work-up together. Still, we knew Doug and Tommy were all right.

"Range 1,200 yards, sir."

"Stand by, Pick."

Corny looked hard through his glasses.

"Hell! They're Vospers. What an anti-climax."

We ploughed quietly southward towards Murro di Porco, wondering what we would see when we reached "Acid North". However great our expectations, they did not compare with the incredible sight which opened up as we rounded the point.

I had seen the Coronation Review of the Fleet in 1937 off Spithead, and the hundreds of ships I saw before me now, in neat lines, immediately brought that picture into my mind. All was so peaceful! No ships were bombarding, no aircraft dive-bombing: it was far more like a review than an invasion. But the variety of ships had any review knocked cold. Stretching into the distance down the coast, further than the eye could see, were rows and rows of warships, merchantmen, and landing craft, at first glance all motionless and inactive.

But one got the key by peering through the binoculars: the landing ships lay with their davits hanging empty, their complement of assault craft already disgorged. As I swept round towards the beach, I could pick out the tiny boats moving between the shore and their parent ships. Tank-landing craft were lying hard up on the sandy beach, and blue-grey wood smoke drifted upward from the burning shell of a peasant's cottage.

I turned my gaze inland, to the higher land rising behind the coastal plain. There, smoke was thicker and occasional flashes which lit the low clouds of early morning spoke of a grim artillery battle in progress behind the peaceful hills.

The coxswain was our expert in ship recognition. He picked out the cruisers and other warships and could usually identify them by name if they had some small characteristic different from the rest of the class. He was on his mettle this morning. "That's the *Erebus* out there, sir—15-inch monitor. And that's a Colony cruiser over there; yes, I think it's the *Mauritius*."

"Wreckage in the water on the port bow, sir!" reported the look-out from the wing of the bridge.

"Thank you, Maguire." Corny and Pick levelled their glasses.

"Good God! It's a glider—with American markings."

We moved up closer and looked, aghast, at the pitiful sight. Maroon berets floated near the wreckage, bearing silent testimony of a human tragedy that had gone unnoticed among the night's momentous events. As we moved southward, we sighted two more partly submerged gliders. Gloomily we wondered just how great the effect of the storm had been on this and many other similar individual parts of the operation.

Suddenly we were distracted from our thoughts by the "sswwsh" and "crack" of a heavy shell landing nearby. A spout of turbid water rose about a hundred yards astern. This was good shooting. Who was responsible? We looked round suspiciously at *Erebus*, lying a mile to seaward. She looked quite innocent. Then someone spotted a flash from a battery on Murro di Porco, five miles away. They had certainly got the range quickly. Shells began to fall around us, all uncomfortably close and the nearest only fifty yards astern.

The S.O. altered course away violently, and we saw him signalling to

*Erebus.* Almost immediately, we saw that mighty gun platform belch fire and smoke. We trained our glasses on the battery ashore and acted as interested but unofficial "spotters". In one minute the battery had ceased fire (for good) and we politely thanked *Erebus* for her assistance.

Our orders were now to find a suitable point in the anchorage, cut engines, and allow one watch to pipe down in order to get some sleep while the going was good. This wording proved literal.

It was 1010 when the first dive-bombers arrived. We knew that until some airfields were captured (they were the most urgent objectives) the Luftwaffe would have supremacy over the beaches. Our fighters from Malta could not remain long enough to give effective cover owing to their range, and we had been expecting to see the German planes earlier.

The first we knew of the attack was the thump-thump of a pom-pom opening up, and a row of black dots in the sky. Corny was below having a late breakfast, and came rushing up to the bridge as I pressed the alarm buzzers. No aircraft came near us, but we had front-row seats as we watched the dive-bombers hurtle down towards the anchorage about two miles away. Soon the sky was peppered with the black puffs of exploding anti-aircraft shells and tracer, almost invisible in the bright light, soared into the sky. We heard two explosions, and soon smoke began to pour from a stricken ship much further south. But not all the aircraft got away scot-free. We saw one plunge into the sea and another with one engine on fire bucketing awkwardly away to the west. We felt impotent—the range was too great to open fire, so we had been forced to stand by and watch.

We stayed at action stations all day, and the raids continued spasmodically. The aircraft seemed to have one policy only—to swoop on the anchorage from the west and hope their arrival was so sudden and unexpected that they would receive no attention, and then to roar away to the east and return inshore by a roundabout route. Twice we opened fire with the pom-pom and the Oerlikons, but as the attacks were never directed at our flotilla, the range was always rather extreme and we had no success.

In the afternoon, the S.O. was told by signal to bring the flotilla alongside H.M.S. *Bulolo*, the headquarters ship flying the flag of Rear-Admiral T. H. Troubridge. There we received our detailed instructions for the night's patrol and, after a short stay, moved away to seek a quiet anchorage in which to rest until the evening.

An ominous roar of engines from over the land gave us a few seconds warning of the next attack. This was it! This time we were well and truly in the target area. The flotilla scattered and Pick ordered independent firing by all guns. I leapt to the starboard Vickers .303 mounting. I had no navigation to do, so I might as well have a bash at them.

The guns kicked madly in my hands and the bullets sprayed out ahead of the oncoming aircraft. The sky seemed full of them and all round was the roar and stutter of anti-aircraft fire. I heard the whistle of bombs and remembered I hadn't put my tin hat on. I crouched down behind the ply-wood bridge; then realizing how stupid that was, I grabbed my tin hat from its stowage and jumped back to the gun. In a flash the two pans were empty. I worked feverishly to change them and looked round for something else to fire at. All the time I knew that these pop-guns would only be effective if a great deal of luck was on my side—but it made such a difference to be *doing* something aggressive instead of merely encouraging the crew to greater efforts.

A stick of bombs from a high-flying aircraft screamed down and straddled right across our line. We saw 657's stern lift and she suddenly disappeared in a great spout of water which seemed to rise from beneath her. Breathlessly we watched the water cascade down again, and there, to our relief, was 657 still moving along. Corny closed her. "Are you O.K., Doug?" he shouted. Maitland leaned over the side of his bridge. "Four men injured down aft, and we're making water a bit. Too close to be healthy, wasn't it!"

Again the gun buzzer rang, and this time Day, in X gun, pointed high in the sky, shading his eyes with one hand. "Spitfires arrived, sir!" he called.

Enthralled, we watched the dog-fights until suddenly one of the Spitfires went into an uncontrollable spin, and plunged dizzily down towards us. It was a terrifying moment. There was no point in moving, although I personally felt like jumping into the sea, it seemed so certain to hit us. No one could tell where the stricken plane would crash. My mouth was dry, and I didn't want to watch, but I couldn't drag my eyes away.

Down it came, lurching crazily and accelerating as it screeched through the air. With a sickening crash it roared into the sea only fifty yards from us. When the great spout of water descended, nothing but ripples were left on the surface. It was useless to look for the pilot.

The attacks continued intermittently throughout the afternoon, all by Ju. 88s and Do. 217s. It was a most uncomfortable period. The air cover seemed very ineffective, and by now two merchant ships were blazing and sending up huge columns of black smoke as a token of the severity of the raids. The S.O. sent 657 off to the hospital ship *Talamba* to transfer her wounded men. They would have been better aboard 657 as the *Talamba* was bombed next day and one of them was killed.

At 1930, the flotilla re-grouped and we set off (rather thankfully, as it seemed certain that Acid North would be a hot spot that night) for a further patrol off Catania.

This relief was accentuated later when we saw in the distance signs of a severe air raid raging on the bearing of Acid North. Muffled explosions and the complex interlacings of red tracer told their tale, while over Augusta and Syracuse palls of black smoke indicated heavy raids by the R.A.F. Our own turn came at first light after an uneventful night, just after we had turned southward to return to Acid North.

A Ju. 88 appeared from right ahead, and swooping down the line dropped a stick of eight bombs down the starboard side, all missing wide. Two further attacks were made by single aircraft, flying very low, and every boat of the flotilla got in a good burst at each. In 658 we saw no results, but 660 (the last boat in the line) claimed to have shot one down.

Back at the beach once more, we were told to patrol off the anchorage and to keep a good look out for U-boats, which were suspected to be in the area. Our engines had been running continuously for thirty-six hours, and we were beginning to run short of fuel, so at 1100 we were ordered alongside the tanker *Empire Lass* to take in the 3,000 gallons of petrol we required.

Fuelling was the most monotonous and unpleasant task at the best of times, and accidents had been sufficiently numerous in coastal force boats for everyone to be very conscious of the strict rules necessary whilst engaged in it; all electrical circuits were broken and the boat left lifeless while the green highly explosive liquid slowly gurgled aboard. And it *did* arrive slowly, too, much to the annoyance of the tanker officer.

It was a standing order that every drop of petrol which came aboard must be filtered through chamois leathers to see that no water could enter our tanks and cause a breakdown at a difficult moment. The tanker naturally wanted to get rid of us as quickly as possible, and could have given us 3,000 gallons at high pressure in no time at all, but instead the interminable but safe routine of slow filling and constant filtering took us two and a half hours. Not that we were keen to stay as long as this; air raids punctuated the process every half an hour and we felt decidedly unsafe all the time we were there. Blast from a near miss could easily have ignited the petrol and blown the *Empire Lass* (and ourselves) to Kingdom Come.

There followed a peaceful three hours when the non-duty watch were able to get to sleep without interruption, for a change. All too soon it was time to rendezvous with the flotilla, and to start once more past Murro di Porco for our patrol.

This time, however, it started with a bang. We had only just formed up and were testing guns when six small black aircraft streaked towards us from the land, coming in from astern.

"They're F.W.190s aren't they, Pick?" yelled Corny.

At once we knew that this time the attack was being aimed directly at us. This was going to be personal combat between us and the enemy. It was a heaven-sent chance, too! The gunners were closed up and had just tested guns. They had learned a lot in the last two days.

Pick checked the loud hailer, still in his hand, and then gave his orders.

"All guns select targets independently. Open fire!"

By opening fire before the first Focke-Wulf had really begun its swoop down, Pick prevented a direct approach. The pilot banked slightly to port instead of flying straight over us. His machine-guns blazed but his alteration of course sent the bullets scudding into the sea a few yards to port. But as he banked, A/B Day in the twin Oerlikon turret had him exactly in his sights and gave him a long searing burst which ripped down his fuselage. Splinters flew and the tail of the aircraft seemed to hang drunkenly down. As we cheered wildly, the plane plummeted into the sea. The others in the line, seeing both the fate of the leader and the frightening spread of flak pumped out by five Dog-boats, pulled away without pressing home the attack. The third in line left it too late, however. One of the boats further up the line riddled him with Oerlikon shells and, with smoke pouring from the engine, he dived straight into the nearby hillside and blew up. The attack was over, and 658 had made her first kill. Young Day was surrounded by grinning matelots all promising him their tots next day!

Our patrol on this occasion was the first on which we penetrated deeper into the Straits of Messina. Everyone was expecting E-boats to begin to arrive from Naples through the Straits, or from Bari and Brindisi and Taranto round the "heel" of Italy, and traffic was also anticipated across the Straits, bringing reinforcements from Italy across to the battle area. The whole of the Straits were therefore divided up into patrol areas so that several flotillas could operate simultaneously without fear of accidentally attacking each other in the darkness.

Normally the smaller areas well into the Straits were the province of the short MTBs (the Vospers and Elcos), which were faster and much smaller targets for the shore batteries to hit. Area C, to which we were detailed on this night, was a central area dominating the exit from the Straits and also the likely approach from the east. Radar watch was always kept by each boat in turn, which increased our area of search and likelihood of interception considerably. But once again there was no sign of any surface movement, and our third successive night was a blank.

Back at Acid North, we went straight to the tanker *Empire Lass*, and were attacked even before we had started to connect up hoses. It was much more satisfactory to fuel early, however, as it meant that dinner could be cooked in peace, and the routine was not disturbed. We were lucky enough to get our water tanks refilled from a friendly Liberty Ship, and then managed to get bread and provisions from the H.Q. Ship *Bulolo*. After three days we had run right out of fresh food, and our diet was becoming very dull and unvaried. The whole crew, too, was very tired and beginning to show signs of strain, but after our successes against the aircraft and our luck in escaping any damage so far, spirits were high and morale very sound indeed.

It seemed that the powers-that-be had also noticed the constancy of the flotilla's operations, as a signal was received from *Bulolo* ordering us to anchor close inshore and rest till 2000, which meant a more or less firm guarantee that we should not be disturbed. Indeed, apart from two or three minor false alarms, we had a fairly peaceful day and all felt better for it.

At 2000 (it was now 12th July, D+2), we heard the news we had been expecting and awaiting anxiously since the landing. Reconnaissance had reported that twenty or thirty E-boats had been sighted at noon proceeding south through the Straits of Messina. It sounded as though we could expect a bit of excitement fairly soon.

Keyed up at this news, it was even more of an anti-climax than usual that yet another patrol brought no contact with the enemy; but events the next morning brought some compensation. On our way to patrol, 659 and 662 had been detached for special duty, to proceed to Augusta with the landing ship *Ulster Monarch* to cover a landing of raiding troops right inside the vast harbour. We naturally knew nothing of their adventures, but it transpired later that the landing was strongly opposed, and 659 (Lieutenant Bob Davidson) was sent for more ammunition, while 662 (Lieutenant Tim Bligh) was despatched to Syracuse at midnight. She was singled out for ten dive-bombing attacks whilst en route. Gordon's description of this afterwards was very graphic and colourful and we gathered it was not a pleasant experience. Meanwhile, 659 had succeeded in sticking herself well and truly aground in one corner of Augusta harbour, and was unable to get herself off despite the frantic efforts of her C.O. One can hardly imagine anything more disconcerting for a commanding officer than to have his ship stuck hard on the "putty"—helpless—only a few hundred yards from an enemy blockhouse! Fortunately, it was a dark night and, anyway, the garrison of Augusta was too busy repelling land attacks to worry overmuch about a small boat in the harbour.

Next morning, then, as we passed off Augusta harbour at first light, we were greeted by flashing from H. M. cruiser *Newfoundland*. Her message told us that most of Augusta was still in enemy hands, but that we were to enter and render 659 all the assistance we could! We could hear light-arms fire occasionally and see artillery still active in the town, but otherwise the scene appeared quite peaceful.

Augusta had a huge harbour and its docks and jetties were very modern, so it was obvious that it would be a very important capture for the Allies.

We crept quietly and slowly forward to the gap in the huge sea wall, and found the boom open and no defences manned. By 0800 we had all passed gingerly through the entrance, and the S.O. (now in 660) ordered us to wait while he approached 659, which was visible near the blockhouse over to starboard.

As we waited, we moved alongside a large lighter (one of several in the harbour) bristling with anti-aircraft guns. This had obviously been left hurriedly in the night, and very little attempt had been made to destroy valuable or secret equipment. The guns (mainly Bredas) were complete with tool-kits, spares and ammunition: confidential books of signals were still in the cabin below decks. We removed three Bredas which were welcomed by the Base next day, and then at 1100 saw a large merchant ship, flying the White Ensign, moving into the harbour.

She was the *Antwerp* and she had on board Party "Glutton", a complete naval party trained specially to take over Augusta harbour when captured.

She contained a complete Base under a naval-officer-in-charge (N.O.I.C.) and staff of officers. Our flotilla was immediately placed at his disposal, and began to tow lighters of equipment, and to ferry men, from *Antwerp* to the Base, without delay. This kept us really busy all the rest of the day until 1700, when we were detailed to do some ferrying of senior officers.

After efforts by a variety of ships to tow 659 off the putty a destroyer was eventually successful and she was able to rejoin the flotilla after minor repairs. Thereafter the shoal where she had grounded was always known as "Bob's Patch", after Bob Davidson her C.O.

All through the day F.W.190s had been making attacks, but none of them had been pressed home very hard. Now, however, they began to become more attentive, and two of them singled us out for special attention. We had just secured to a buoy in a "quiet" corner of the harbour, and were entertaining a group captain and major to tea in the wardroom. As the screech of bombs sounded, I jumped to my feet and Pick scampered up the hatch to control the fire. I was most impressed by the R.A.F. type who continued to raise his cup to his lips and did not even pause in his conversation.

Pick and I reached the bridge and, hearing the roar of low-flying aircraft becoming louder every moment, we saw the two F.W.190s circling round to come in for a second run, this time at ground level and obviously intent on a machine-gun attack. The twin Oerlikon gunner—"Happy" Day again—was already in his turret and was calmly waiting for the aircraft to come within range. As they roared nearer, he opened fire and sent stream after stream of tracer swinging towards them.

The first black, stub-winged fighter banked sharply away down the starboard side, but the second came straight in from astern. However, before the pilot could press his firing button, black spots suddenly appeared in the nose and wing, wreckage showered, and a sheet of flame sprang around the fuselage as if by magic. The plane roared close over us and, like a furious blue-bottle drawn involuntarily to a candle flame, careered madly on until it ploughed into the harbour about half a mile away. Once again Day had done the trick, and this time completely on his own.

Two hours later there was another severe attack and bombs fell all round us—but we still bore a charmed life and suffered no damage.

At 1930, we were ordered to go alongside in the inner harbour, and Corny reported to the N.O.I.C. When he came back and told us the news, we didn't know quite how to take it! Apparently the Germans were counter-attacking, and there was a slight possibility that they might re-enter the port during the night, and recapture it. Rather than risk all his port party, N.O.I.C. was withdrawing for the night and all shipping was evacuating the harbour *except* (and, we thought, rather an important omission) MGB 658. We were to remain alongside all night, and bring off the last few troops from any rearguard action.

The rest of the 20th Flotilla left harbour during the evening, 663 having 125 extra men aboard, and 660 a mere sixty. 663, with this incredible number of passengers aboard, had great difficulty in making Syracuse successfully, but with Tommy's skilful seamanship, managed it after a nightmarish trip. The deck was so tightly packed that only number ones of guns could be in their turrets, while the rest of 663's seamen were wedged at harbour stations! Every slight turn sent her heeling over alarmingly, and to get alongside at Syracuse Tommy had to go full astern for some time to take the way off her! 660 remained at sea all night rather than risk the tricky entrance.

Meanwhile, we were given orders not to open fire to reveal our presence during any air raid, so we revised our watches to give maximum rest to the crew, and everyone got more sleep than they had had for days. We went to action stations at dawn, and found this a wise precaution, as the "hit and run" attacks with both bombs and machine-guns restarted at 0600. However it seemed that the town was now safe from recapture (we heard that "Monty" had turned on one of his famous artillery barrages), and ships of all shapes and sizes began to flood back into the huge harbour.

The speed with which supplies poured in amazed us. Fleets of the great ungainly tank-landing ships (LSTs) began to arrive with their aggressive high bows which gaped open when near enough to the beach. One of our tasks was to deliver signals to them indicating the fact that air cover was so weak they would have to keep A.A. guard continuously. This was emphasised at noon, when a formation of twenty-four Ju. 88s made a determined attack, damaging several ships. It was 2015 before we got out to our favourite mooring buoy, and after only two hours there, we were ordered to bring in yet another convoy of LSTs.

It was a pitch black night, and in the already congested area of the harbour (nearer the Base) this was a tricky job. However, we picked up the convoy just outside the boom and brought them in on our tail, leading them to the point at which they were to beach. This seemed to be the signal for the heavens to open, for bombs to crash down, and for every ship in the harbour to add to the noise and the inferno by firing wildly upward.

By the time we had settled in the new arrivals, it was midnight, and we reported to N.O.I.C. for further orders. We were told to patrol outside the harbour until first light, and breathed a sigh of relief. It would be far more peaceful outside than in. We passed out through the boom once more and took up our patrol.

Next day, the Mobile Coastal Force Base which was to become so familiar to us in many different ports in the future, began to take shape. Commander Robert Allan R.N.V.R.[1] whom we had first met at Bone, was in command, and set up his Base in an excellent part of the harbour, with a long, comfortable stretch of jetty.

He had gathered together a very versatile Base staff, and they seemed to be able to tackle most problems. At this stage, however, the maintenance and repair shops had not got fully into their swing, and in any case we were having very few troubles in spite of the almost continuous running the engines had been doing. We therefore rather treated C.F.B. as a convenient berthing place when we needed to be alongside to collect ammunition stores, or signals, but otherwise whenever possible we went out to secure to our buoy in a remote part of the harbour, quite close to the pleasant green vineyards.

After seven days of almost continuous running, several boats with defects had had to return to Malta, and operations had settled down to a regular pattern. It was obvious that no boat could continue to operate every night for an indefinite period; it was therefore decided that normally every other night would be left free for rest.

This soon proved a rather unpopular idea, as our first two "rest" nights (the 18th and 20th July) were both largely occupied by very unpleasant air raids during which, although we were at buoys well-dispersed about the harbour, we certainly got no rest. It was so hot at this time that we preferred to try to sleep on deck; but with shrapnel from the port's A.A. guns falling around like rain, it was not healthy to carry on sleeping. The second night was particularly bad. Two sticks of bombs fell very close, and when the smoke cleared it revealed two large

[1] Now Commander R. A. Allan D.S.O., O.B.E., M.P.

merchant ships blazing furiously. One of them was an ammunition ship to judge by the pyrotechnics.

Our patrols were never uneventful, although we did not once succeed in making contact with the enemy on the surface. Time and time again we would intercept or receive signals indicating that E-boats and destroyers were about in other parts of the Straits, but never in our area. However, we had several more brushes with aircraft, although the daytime air cover was improving vastly as the R.A.F. got use of airfields in Sicily and thus reduced the range of their operations. We soon applied to miss our stay in harbour, which was no rest to us, and welcomed the very sensible decision of "Operations" to use us as an anti-E-boat striking force anchored in the bay outside Augusta. Here we were reasonably clear of the raids and very handy to repel any attack by surface craft.

On the 22nd July, we were honoured by a visit from C.-in-C. Mediterranean (Admiral Sir Andrew Cunningham), who inspected the Base and boats accompanied by the newly appointed Captain Coastal Forces, Captain J. F. Stevens R.N.[1] It seemed that our existence and the constancy of our operations were being officially recognised.

Shore batteries and searchlights along the shores of the Straits of Messina began to be increasingly unpleasant, and we soon had the majority of them plotted on our charts and knew where we could patrol close into the coast. Already one of the Elco MTBs had been hit by a 4-inch shell and had been towed into harbour stern first with bows completely missing, and several boats had received slight damage from splinters.

The most exciting of our patrols took place on the night before we returned to Malta for engine overhaul and routine maintenance. We received orders to bombard the railway station and sidings at Taormina, right by the sea, and set out at 1930 with Norman Hughes (the S.O.) aboard us, and Doug (657) and Bob Davidson (659) astern. It was soon obvious that the R.A.F. had been there first, as there was a big fire blazing at Taormina already. However, we crept in to 500 yards, and then straightened up parallel with the coast. On the signal "Flag 5" everyone opened up with all guns, and shells simply pumped into the target. "Y" gun (the 6-pounder) was handled so enthusiastically that its barrel was hot very quickly, and the captain of the gun had to cease fire for a moment to let it cool.

[1] Now Vice-Admiral Sir John Stevens K.B.E., C.B.

I was so intently watching the target that my attention was distracted from the course we were steering, until a quiet word from the coxswain made me look round quickly to see a huge rock looming up ahead, rather similar to the stacks in Torbay. We had run right across the bay and were in danger of hitting the other side. Rapidly we ceased fire, swung round and continued firing again. Some answering fire was immediately received, but only from light arms and machine-guns, which we ignored. In the twelve minutes of the attack, our 6-pounder got off ninety rounds, each one laid and trained on the target, and considerable damage had been done; and, we thought, much fear and despondency had been aroused in the garrison of Taormina.

The next day (28th July) 658 sailed for Malta. In nineteen days, our engines had run for nearly 300 hours, and we were long overdue for both the 100-hour and 200-hour routines to which we normally adhered religiously. Several boats had already arrived back in Augusta from a spell in Malta, and as we were the *only* coastal force craft which had not been back since D-1, we were despatched without delay.

The boat which returned and its crew were in many respects vastly different from those which had set out nearly three weeks before. Instead of an inexperienced, loosely knit crew, not altogether sure of its capabilities, we had a seasoned band of veterans bursting with confidence and guns' crews to be proud of.

We therefore entered Marxamaxett Harbour proudly, and with some ceremony. We put our gramophone by the loud-hailer microphone, and "Hearts of Oak" played us in. We were given a rousing reception by the boats alongside, and berthed with 663. There was no thought in our minds of anything that evening but relaxation, and after Corny had reported to the Base and to C.C.F., a very enjoyable party followed. More than anything, however, it was sleep we all wanted. It was wonderful to be alongside and know there was little prospect of being disturbed.

The next morning, Corny routed me out of my bunk, and we went over to the Base for breakfast. This was untold luxury. After the dull and unvaried food we had been enduring, to sit at a polished mahogany table, to be waited on by suave Maltese stewards, to have a choice of three cereals and omelettes to follow, was all like a dream.

During the forenoon we were invaded by engineer officers and Base staff, and P.O.M.M. Last and his engine-room staff were complimented highly on the state of the engines after their very heavy running. The gunnery officer from C.C.F.'s staff inspected our guns and seemed very impressed with our ammunition expenditure; we had certainly baptized all the guns very adequately.

We were very proud when a special messenger brought us a "Memorandum" from the office of the Captain Coastal Forces. On one side, C.C.F. indicated that he intended to issue "Orders of the Day" to commend outstanding performances in maintenance and operations, and would grant special leave where possible. On the reverse was the following:

*Order of the Day No. 1.*

The C.O. of HM MGB 658 and his company are to be commended in that:

a. The senior officer of their flotilla reports that the boat has taken part in fourteen operations in nineteen days.
b. The senior officer also reports that the boat has been in State "A" since 1st July, due to consistent hard work on the part of the ship's company.
c. On arrival at Base the boat was found to have been so well maintained that she could have been got ready for sea again in four days.
d. A grant of special leave is being arranged.

This was a most pleasant and unexpected surprise. We were naturally delighted, and (again naturally) agreed with all Captain Stevens said; but we had hardly expected our achievements, which were painstaking rather than spectacular and therefore of the sort that usually escape official notice, to be recognized so promptly. However, this was our first real introduction to C.C.F. ("Charlie-Charlie" was our affectionate name for him) and we were to learn that he missed very little, and was always as ready to hand out congratulation as to indicate disapproval. The characteristic which particularly endeared him to us all in later days was his desire to know even his most junior officers personally.

He went out of his way to meet us informally and was always a welcome guest to any wardroom.

We sailed again for Augusta on 10th August, well set up by our spell in the luxurious and comparatively civilized surroundings of Malta. In the fortnight that followed we carried out operations every other night, mainly up the Straits of Messina or close to the toe of Italy. One of them was particularly interesting.

The Army was being held up in north-east Sicily near Catania, and a secondary landing was planned to turn the flank. In this, we were given an unusual job, and at first sight it was not particularly pleasant. Troops were to be landed in small assault craft from landing ships, and as these big parent ships could not move too near to the shore, it was necessary to give the LCAs a marking light to guide them in to their landing point, their navigational facilities being negligible. We were, in fact, to act as a lighted signpost.

On the night of the 15th August, the senior officer embarked with us, and we set off with 660 and 663. I was very anxious to have the navigation exactly right as we had to find the precise beach, station ourselves exactly one mile from it and direct the LCAs in. Imagine my chagrin when, on our way north, reports began to flood in over the W/T that some Vospers were in action against E-boats, and we were requested to intercept them.

We had two hours to spare before our landing job, and so we naturally hared off into an intercepting position, and began to make frequent alterations of course as we searched. Normally this would have been thrilling, but I was far too concerned with keeping the dead-reckoning navigation accurate to enjoy these diversions. The S.O. did everything he could to find the enemy, and to make the plot as difficult as possible for me. He was unsuccessful in the former: I now had to discover whether he had been successful in the latter. As soon as we returned coastwards, I began to take bearings on our old friend Mount Etna the volcano, which was, on a clear day or night, always visible for a great distance, and was invaluable for running fixes. Having confirmed my position, I consulted that very useful book the *Sicilian Pilot* to check the outline of the coast. I was by now pretty sure that my dead-reckoning position was correct, and reported so to the S.O.

We crept in to the one mile position and noticed that there seemed to be a lot of activity going on ashore at Cap d'Ali, where the landing was to take place. Lights were flashing, small explosions split the air, and altogether the prospect did not seem too bright for surprise to be achieved. At 0208, we began to flash "A"s to seaward, over an arc of about 60 degrees, twice every thirty seconds. It was a great sight, at 0235, to make out dimly two long columns of LCAs gliding in quite silently towards us. As they closed, their S.O. came alongside and asked for the course in to the beach. Realizing the responsibility I was taking after all the events of the night, I gave them "South 80° West" with a somewhat quaking heart.

They were followed by LCTs and LCFs, while lying off astern of us were three destroyers ready to give supporting fire. At about 0300, just when the LCAs should have reached the beach, there was a most colossal explosion exactly at their beaching point and our hearts jumped into our mouths. What had happened? I would have given a month's pay to know.

Next morning, my discomfort increased when the S.O.O. at Augusta told me that the landing had been successful, but had been carried out six miles north of the intended position. Immediately I was ribbed by all and sundry that I had put the pongos ashore in the wrong spot. I spent an uncomfortable day, but had the last laugh when the report came through that evening. The LCAs had arrived at exactly the right spot, but on seeing the explosion, which had been a German rearguard blowing up an ammunition dump, they had turned north to seek a more suitable beach. They had found one six miles further north, and all the troops had gone ashore successfully.

This landing hastened a process that was already beginning, the withdrawal of the German forces to the north-east corner of Sicily. The Americans had advanced rapidly once past the sticky stage in establishing themselves and, having captured Palermo on the north coast, were rapidly pushing the German line eastward.

In the Straits of Messina, Greene-Kelly in 655 met some E-boats and destroyed two, giving the Dogs their first surface action during "Husky". The short boats were penetrating nightly right up to Messina, but the searchlights and batteries commanded the narrow straits so completely that there was no time to wait about for targets and consequently few attacks could be made.

This hazardous dodging of the shore batteries was not accomplished without loss, however. One Elco and one Dog-boat (641) were destroyed fairly early, and several short boats damaged. Finally 665 (Peter Thompson's boat, which we had known since Weymouth) received a direct hit in the engine-room which set her on fire and disabled her until she sank. All her crew were missing, and also a great friend of the Canadians, Lt.-Cdr. (S) E. N. Bartlett R.C.N.V.R., a Press Relations Officer who was out with Pete that night. Tommy Ladner was particularly concerned, as "Bart" (as he was usually known) had, apart from anything else, borrowed his typewriter for the trip.

A year later, Tom had a letter from him, written from a prison camp in Germany, in which he described their capture and apologized handsomely about the typewriter. Apparently he and Pete had struggled hard to save it, but had in the end only just managed to save their lives.

The amusing sequel to this story is that, in 1948, Ladner received a cheque for $58.50 from the Canadian Government in payment for the loss of one typewriter on Active Service. Bartlett had carried on a voluminous correspondence with the Canadian naval authorities during and after his imprisonment, until they had finally agreed to pay Tom his due compensation!

The story of Peter Thompson's imprisonment revealed, after his release, the significant interest the Germans took in Dog-boats. Early in "Husky" Lieutenant Christopher Dreyer with his 24th Flotilla had torpedoed one U-boat in the Straits of Messina and narrowly missed another, which was lost later. The Germans evidently guessed that the Dogs were responsible, and suspected that they were carrying some new secret weapon by which they could detect and destroy U-boats either submerged or on the surface. Perhaps the mysterious disappearance of the two U-boats which had attacked our convoy in the Atlantic on our way out may also have misled them. In any case, Thompson was kept in solitary confinement for nearly three months, taken to Berlin and continually questioned about details of Dog-boats, and finally even confronted by a complete set of plans of a Dog-boat! Despite all this he resolutely denied all knowledge of the Dogs' weapons. The Germans eventually gave up interrogating him.

## Chapter VIII

### FRESH FIELDS—AND PROMOTION

Q UITE unexpectedly, a signal arrived next day ordering us to Malta for docking and strengthening of the deck beneath our new single Oerlikons. We received the news with mixed feelings. It was impossible not to feel pleased about a return to the comfort and comparative civilization of Malta, but we felt certain that events were boiling up to a big climax in the area, and that we were certain to "miss out on something", as Corny put it. The prospect of baking in Malta Dockyard's odorous September heat was not inviting, either.

In fact, 658 was in the dockyard for three weeks, and for us it was an irksome, unsatisfactory time, preoccupied as we were with reports from the front, which seemed to emphasize our inactivity.

On the 3rd September, a typical Montgomery artillery barrage from Messina across the Straits preceded an amazing ferry service of men and materials to Italy. The tiny LCAs were invaluable and made trip after trip between the legendary Scylla and Charybdis until the whole of the seasoned Eighth Army was across the Straits and the breakout into the mainland of Italy began. Our boats began immediately to patrol along the south and west coasts of Italy; and some were dispatched to North Africa ready to proceed against various islands in the Sicilian Channel, and also to be ready to take a select party to Sardinia when required.

On the 8th September, news came through which startled everyone and set all Malta talking about possible developments. Italy had capitulated and the Badoglio Government had ordered all Italian troops and ships to cease operations. Would this mean the fold-up of the Italian War? Would the Italian Navy be able to get away from its ports before the Germans could act? These questions were answered for us very shortly after being posed, as on the 9th September news came through that a large Allied Force had landed at Salerno, near Naples, and had met with considerable opposition.

And the Italian Navy did manage to get away from their bases at Leghorn, La Spezia, and Taranto. On the morning of the 10th September, we knew that the Italian Battle Fleet was heading for Malta to surrender. Among the force escorting them in were MTBs of the 7th and 24th Flotillas. Some days later, on gunnery trials, we were able to take a cruise around the Italian fleet, lying anchored off Grand Harbour, beneath the guns of the ancient forts.

We discovered later that whilst we were propping up the dockyard wall in Malta, our friends of the 20th Flotilla and others were having exciting and eventful times in various colourful places. First, 663 (Tommy) and 657 (Doug) sailed from Algiers with Bobby Allan aboard to accept the surrender of the Galita Islands, midway between Bone and Bizerta. Their operations then moved to Salerno, where they were based on the famous Isle of Capri and worked closely with the American Navy for the first time, Lt.-Cdr. Douglas Fairbanks Junior U.S.N.R. being one of their senior officers.

By the time our refit was finished and we were discharged from the dockyard the Army had broken out from Salerno, and it was obvious that we should in future have to be based much further north than we had expected. Indeed, when we arrived at Messina and joined up with the remainder of the flotilla, the main topic of conversation was about possible bases.

Those who had been at Capri hoped the famous island would be selected; but as news had just arrived from Sardinia that the ancient island kingdom had surrendered, and that Free French forces in Corsica were rapidly driving the German occupiers eastward, we all had a shrewd idea that these would be our destinations. A boat was dispatched to Maddalena (the island port north of Sardinia and an Italian Naval Base) to report on its suitability. This, we thought, was the most likely solution to our problem.

On 28th September, a strange-looking convoy sailed from Messina, bound for Sardinia—probably one of the strangest ever, composed as it was mainly of fast coastal force craft, all creeping along at about six knots in order to escort the LCTs containing Bobby Allan's complete Coastal Force Mobile Base.

The voyage seemed ill-fated from the start. We had hardly left the shelter of the Straits of Messina and turned westward (we were due to stop in at Palermo), when a rapid worsening of the weather began to whip up a very unpleasant head sea. 658 buried her nose and bucketed into it, spray drenching the bridge and the sea curling over the deserted fo'c'sle. Next moment she swung dizzily upward, the bows rearing up to the sky, to hesitate momentarily there before plunging steeply down with a jolt which shook her from stem to stern. This short sea was much more troublesome and dangerous than the massive Atlantic waves had been.

We endured this for fifteen minutes, and then saw with relief that the S.O. was heading for the shelter of Milazzo, a small port just "round the corner" from Messina. There was not room for us in the tiny harbour, so we passed an almost sleepless night outside at anchor in St. Antonio Bay and were roused early next morning to weigh anchor and move inside with 660.

For a long time now our food had been extremely monotonous, and the sight of a town like Milazzo apparently unspoiled by occupation stirred Corny to send me ashore to try to buy some eggs and fresh fruit. In Augusta we had done very well for fruit, both grapes and melons being especially abundant, but since September we had missed this welcome addition to our diet.

All the food in 658 (and in every Dog-boat) was cooked in a galley neatly situated between the wardroom and the for'd messdeck. Indeed, the cook (who was a volunteer, and usually not a willing volunteer, for a month at a time) was often the best informed rating aboard and a great purveyor of "buzzes", as wardroom conversation was frequently audible in the galley! We all—officers and men—had exactly the same food and menu from day to day. If the officers cared to supplement the food by outside purchases, then it was usually a simple matter to persuade the cook to add them to our menu! We also paid a volunteer rating to act as steward for the wardroom, and as this was quite a pleasant job with a little extra money and an easy number when the crew were "working ship", there was rarely any difficulty in finding a "flunkey" (as he was inevitably called by the rest of the crew).

It always seemed to us a very false economy on the Admiralty's part not to provide us with a qualified cook. We could get along without a signalman and even a sick-berth attendant (although both would have been invaluable on many occasions)—but the lack of a cook was often a major factor in the boat's morale, and was frequently a serious problem.

As I jumped down to the quayside I rummaged in my mind for odd words of Italian I had picked up in the past few months. I could only remember that the word for eggs sounded very much like the word for grapes.

Luck was with me. A ragged, bare-footed boy of about twelve came by, on his way to scavenge at the docks, I guessed. I stopped him and trotted out my carefully prepared phrases, making appropriate signs with my hands. He looked at me with a curious wondering expression tinged with either pity or alarm. I was getting nowhere. Suddenly I had a brainwave. "Cock-a-doodle-doo" I wavered. A sudden, delighted flicker of understanding crossed the boy's handsome bronzed face. "Si, si, senor"—and he beckoned for me to follow.

Crossing a small square, I was led through the doorway of a peasant's cottage and ushered into the presence of an old, old woman whose gnarled face showed no surprise at the sight of a strange man in a war-like uniform. The boy gabbled breathlessly, I produced my two tins of corned beef, and the old woman nodded and moved over to a large tin trunk in the corner. From its darkest recesses, beneath a very mixed assortment of garments, she produced, singly and with loving care, twelve eggs wrapped in newspaper.

I took a chance on their antiquity, handed over the tins, and received the booty with a great sense of achievement. Eleven subsequently turned into excellent fried eggs, which were eaten with appropriate exclamations of relish aboard 658. The twelfth was so old it went off like a saluting cannon.

The next day we sailed on to Palermo, the capital and premier port of Sicily.

After the gale we had met earlier, the summer seemed to be breaking up. That was an unpleasant thought with our first winter of operations lying ahead of us. In Palermo, as we lay alongside *Empire Damsel*, the faithful old tanker which still accompanied us, another sudden squall blew up and was extremely violent for a few minutes. Perhaps the sea was reminding us that we had other battles to fight besides those with the Germans; we had found it easy enough to forget in the Mediterranean summer.

When we continued our voyage next day through a choppy uneasy sea, I was suddenly laid out by repeated attacks of severe stomach pains. Some evil bug tore my inside to pieces, and my interest in life became centred on the relative positions of the wardroom and the officers' heads!

Between spasms, I lay limp and useless on my bunk, and with the prospect of forty-eight more hours before we were due to arrive at

Maddalena, Corny began to look thoughtful. If this was appendicitis or dysentery, the best thing was to get me to a doctor—and fast. There was a glint in Corny's eye, and he disappeared up to the bridge.

Soon a message flashed across to the S.O.

*"Sub-Lieutenant Reynolds sick and in pain. Request permission proceed maximum speed to obtain medical assistance Maddalena."*

Ten minutes later this action was approved and 658 immediately shot ahead, leaving the rest of the Dogs enviously behind to continue their six-knot crawl.

I knew nothing of the rest of the voyage until, after a fitful sleep, I awoke to hear the ring of the engine telegraphs and the movement of feet on the deck above. I raised myself to look through the ports, and with a queer detachment saw the colourful quayside of Maddalena moving steadily closer.

Almost immediately I was rushed off to the Italian Naval Hospital and found to my horror that none of the three doctors who examined me spoke any English at all. However, my ailment was easy to explain in sign language, and by this means and with a few words of French, I managed to convey my symptoms and agonies.

They appeared to find nothing very serious, and when they had finished pommelling my stomach I was sent back to the boat with a large bottle of medicine. Whatever the mysterious malady was, its main effect was to enable Corny and Pick to claim themselves the first Canadians to land in Sardinia; they based this mock triumph on the fact that only two minesweepers had got there before us anyway!

As soon as the rest of the convoy arrived Commander Allan very quickly established his Base, and operations began. From Maddalena we could now patrol off the west coast of Italy as far north as the Island of Elba, although distances were rather extreme for regular operations, and the long passages to and from the patrol area added to a night's searching meant at least twenty hours at sea. This, of course, was within our range, but meant that any boat suffering damage or casualties would have a long trek home.

A day or two later the Vospers of the 7th Flotilla led by Lieutenant Tony Blomfield R.N. made their usual impressive entrance. They had obviously had a rough passage but, more important, the buzz soon got round that they had brought a batch of subbies and midshipmen from Malta with a list of new appointments.

It did not even enter my head that these appointments could possibly affect 658, so it was a bombshell when Pick and I returned from a visit to the Base and were called to Corny's cabin. A dark young R.N.V.R. subbie stood in the doorway. The C.O. held a sheet of paper in his hand and he looked very sombre. "Fellers—meet Sub-Lieutenant Tony Brydon. He's been appointed as 658's new Pilot."

My face fell. Pilot? That meant I should be leaving 658. Hell! We shook hands, my face stony. I hated Brydon's guts even before I knew him. Why did he have to turn up just as we had settled down together? Why did C.C.F. have to be so stupid to break up a happy combination? The whole thing was idiotic.

I suddenly became aware of Corny talking again. His face had suddenly changed and he beamed his pleasure. "You don't look very happy, Rover! Perhaps it will help if I tell you that you are now first lieutenant of 658, and Pick is appointed spare C.O. to the flotilla. Well done, both of you!"

The news left me speechless. First lieutenant? Could I do it? A moment's reflection and I felt better. Of course I could. Pick would still be about, too, until he picked up his own command as soon as a vacancy arose.

My attitude to Tony Brydon immediately changed, and I began to wonder what sort of wardroom companion he would make. I need not have worried. It only took a day or two to establish that he was in every way a great asset, and a stauncher friend and more reliable shipmate never existed.

We were at sea within a few hours and the new occupant of the wardroom did not even have the chance to stow his gear properly. We agreed to continue in our old jobs for a week or two, until I had handed over fully to Tony. Meanwhile I understudied Pick's job, especially in gunnery control, and gave Tony as much practice with the navigation as possible.

It was just as well we made these arrangements, as Tony's first patrol was no ordinary affair. After six months of preparation and waiting, 658 at last met some enemy ships and fought her first battle.

## CHAPTER IX

# THE BATTLE OF THE PIOMBINO CHANNEL

WE had been told to stand by for a patrol off Elba. We felt that now after the rather special conditions of "Husky" and of the war in Sicily in general because of the narrowness of the Straits of Messina, we could settle down to a period of operating which had a clearer purpose than before.

Our task was obviously to place a stranglehold on enemy coastal traffic moving from north to south Italy by night. In this way we could be of immense value to the Army, as the cargo of one ship was the equivalent of many train loads of supplies to reinforce the enemy lines facing our troops in the south of the peninsula. The Air Force had the task of cutting off supplies by day, and Coastal Forces undertook to prevent the passage of vessels by night, from La Spezia in the north to the mouth of the Tiber 200 miles further south. From Maddalena, Elba was about the most northerly patrol area possible, but we knew that soon we should be able to operate from Bastia, and extend our influence to cover Spezia and Leghorn.

All the routine preparations were made and we sailed at 1500 on the 14th October with Lt.-Cdr. E. T. Greene-Kelly as S.O. in MTB 633 (Lieutenant A. B. Joy) and 636 (Lieutenant F. A. Warner). On the way, 633 developed engine trouble and, in view of the length of passage, the S.O. sent her back to Maddalena and transferred to 636.

It took nine hours to reach the patrol area, which was covering the small port of Baratti, on the mainland of Italy just north of the Piombino Channel which separates Elba from the mainland. We believed that Baratti was used by convoys passing southward.

We had only been lying there a few minutes when, quite suddenly, Corny rapped, "Have a look at Green Three-O, you two. I reckon we've got our first surface target."

Through my glasses I made out a dark shape and my whole body went cold. For a moment, I could not even hold the target in sight, my hands shook so much. Then things began to happen. Greene-Kelly had also seen the target, and Sparks called urgently up the voice pipe: "R/T from the S.O., sir—Nuts Starboard."[1]

My heart seemed to be thumping audibly. After all these months here it was at last! I felt only relief that I could do my accustomed job of keeping the plot and that Pick's presence meant I should not be pitchforked into this action as gunnery officer, completely lacking in experience. I lowered myself down to the charthouse and checked our exact position. Tony stood beside me. I thought how lucky he was to get an action on his first patrol. Or was he lucky? Not if he had his head shot off! My rambling thoughts were cut short by the need to scribble details in my notebook.

0116 *Sighted vessel at Green 30, range approx. 4,000 yards, course East. Our course S.E. Position 42° 56.6′ N 10° 27.4′ E. Speed 12 knots.*
0117 *"Nuts Starboard" from S.O.*

As I wrote, we followed 636 towards the enemy, swinging gradually round to enable her to make a bow torpedo attack. The approach seemed to take hours. I glanced at my watch. It was still only 0119. Corny's voice floated down the voice pipe. "636 has just fired one torpedo, Rover."

"Aye, aye, sir. Time is 0119."

I scrambled up to the bridge, and my eyes blinked into the darkness. "Thirty seconds gone," breathed Corny. My eyes half closed as I steeled myself for a blinding flash. No one moved.

"Sixty seconds."

"Can't be much longer, sir—range was only just over 2,000 yards."

No explosion came. By this time the outline of the target had become much larger and clearer, and it looked like a large trawler. A white light flashed at us, and all hope vanished. "Make a note, Rover—challenging with D's."

The bridge gun buzzer shrilled in my ear, startling in its unexpectedness. "Another ship at Green One-Three-Five, sir," reported Day from X gun.

Pick's binoculars swung round and everything happened at once. 636 fired her remaining torpedo, the trawler opened fire, and we disengaged sharply to starboard.

"Open fire!" snapped Corny.

But as we followed 636 round, only the 6-pounder could bear, and the range was opening fast. There was no indication that the other

---

[1] Code for "enemy in sight to starboard".

enemy ship was going to interfere, and we lost sight of her. When the firing ceased, we drew up to 636 and stopped.

There was a short shouted conference between G.-K. and Corny and then the boats parted company. At the conference before sailing, a diversionary attack had been suggested, and apparently we were now to carry it out.

636 moved off to the southward, and 658 set course both to place the enemy up moon and to gain bearing.

Almost immediately, the enemy fired a 5-star recognition cartridge, and this was followed without any pause by a hail of tracer of every colour and calibre.

"Hold it, Pick," muttered Corny. "I want to wait until we've got 'em where we want 'em." For two long minutes we held this course, with shot and shell curling round our ears and churning furrows in the sea about us.

At last Corny's quiet drawl broke the stillness. "Starb'd wheel, coxswain." I noted the time in the notebook and marvelled at the calmness in his voice. The coxswain repeated the order as if entering harbour, and we steadied up and moved right down the moon's track towards the enemy ship. I had the sensation of driving towards a country house clearly visible at the end of a stately drive.

"Rover, challenge them with 'D's'—it may confuse them; it seems to be their current challenge."

I seized the lamp and flashed the letter several times and, sure enough, the enemy obediently stopped firing.

Every second counted now. We had begun our run in at 1,500 yards and were closing the range very rapidly. At 700 yards the enemy opened fire again. Every man on the bridge was half watching Corny. Why doesn't he order Pick to open fire? I thought. We'll all be killed before we even fire a shot at this rate! No order came, and I gritted my teeth. At last he said: "Stand by, Pick—another 50 yards then we'll let 'em have it!"

Every gunner sat tensed, eyes glued to sights and fingers poised on the trigger. Still we ploughed on, apparently unscathed.

"Open fire!"

The noise and smoke of 658's opening broadside came as a shattering shock even to us, and we knew it was coming. The gunners could not possibly miss, with the target clearly visible and the range down to 250 yards. Every shot told, and the stricken enemy turned away, her fire weakening.

Relentlessly Corny followed her round, murmuring quiet orders to the coxswain. Within two minutes she was stopped and on fire, and only one gun (a 20-mm.) was still firing. Soon even this was silenced, and we ceased fire and crept further in to watch her end.

Fires blazed along her whole length, and she began to settle. She was about 130 feet long, and we could see a large gun forward of a high bridge, and a low deck-house aft. From the variety of the guns she had used against us (we had spotted a 3-inch or 12-pounder, a 40 mm. and several 20-mms. and light machine-guns) we thought she was probably a flakship of some sort.

As we studied her intently, the pom-pom gunner (A/B Preston) reported another ship in sight at Red Two-O. Was this the other target we had seen, or 636 returning to the fray?

"Make the challenge, Rover," ordered Corny.

I flashed the letter "S" continually for about a minute, while the range closed and the guns remained trained on the rapidly closing ship. She was in an unfavourable position for identification, and Corny and Pick could not make out her outline at all. A moment later our doubts were resolved. A stream of tracer shot across the surface towards us, and flicked past the bridge.

"Open fire!" snapped Corny. "It must be this one's pal coming back for revenge."

Almost immediately, the 6-pounder scored a vital hit, and the ship stopped with fire spouting midships. The other guns, with the target so clearly marked, were just beginning to concentrate their fire when Corny shouted, with agony in his voice: "Cease fire for God's sake— it's 636!" We all gazed, horrified, and, as the fire spread, the sickening realization of the tragic truth came home to us.

"Why in heaven's name didn't they reply to the challenge—and why did they open fire?" Pick's troubled face looked all round at us and no one had any answer.

"Come on, men, we'll have to snap out of it," Corny rapped. "There are quite a number of 636's crew in the water—stand by to get them inboard."

Around the stricken ship, in the ghostly half-light of her own funeral pyre, men were struggling, on rafts or individually, to stay afloat. In no time we were alongside the biggest Carley Float and began to help the survivors aboard. But even as we did so, there was a shout from aft, and Howe, the captain of Y gun (the 6-pounder), reported a ship approaching.

It was a terrible decision to take, but this enemy had to be beaten off before our rescue work could be finished, or we would be "caught with our trousers down". With the desperate shouts of another raft-load in our ears, we gathered speed and shot off into the darkness. I thought of those men and the blank despair that must be in their hearts.

They knew we were their only chance of safety, and now we were disappearing. Perhaps we would be sunk as well, and even if we weren't we may not find them again.

"Try him with the German challenge again, Rover—it may work!" Yes, by George, they couldn't know who had survived the two fights, and they must have seen them going on as they approached.

But this time the enemy were more jittery, and in spite of our challenge they opened fire almost at once. We were nicely situated down-moon, and once again ran in closing the range as fast as possible. The enemy fire was heavy and rather more accurate this time, and a thud and blue flash midships told us we had been hit. "Casualties at X gun, sir," reported Maguire from the back of the bridge.

"Look after them, Mac," ordered Corny. "Right, Pick—open fire!"

The all-important opening burst was once again devastating. As the enemy turned wildly away, Corny followed every twist until the ship stopped. We moved closer and closer, and finally, when all reply ceased, we were able to see that this was a similar craft to the first we had sunk. She was now burning fiercely and had taken a crazy list to starboard.

Back we went to the position where 636 was still burning, and immediately found the other raft we had seen before we were so rudely interrupted. But even this time we were not allowed to complete our task unhampered.

A searchlight on the Italian mainland flashed on and swung round to pick up each blazing wreck in turn. When it reached 636 we were revealed for all to see lying stopped nearby. Immediately several shore batteries opened up (the range was about three miles) and shells began to crack and whistle past most uncomfortably.

It was soon altogether too hot to remain still, so we tried to shake off these unpleasant attentions by sheering off to the northwest at high speed, making smoke and dropping calcium flares overboard to simulate fires. We then stopped suddenly and began to creep slowly and silently back. We were lucky. The searchlight lost us, the batteries ceased fire in turn, and we were able to return to 636. After an hour's careful and patient search, by which time we had picked up two officers and eighteen ratings, we were sure no one was left afloat, and set course to the westward away from the battle area.

The two flakships and 636 all continued to burn brightly astern of us, and I found myself looking back reluctantly. "There, but for the grace of God, go I," I thought.

As soon as the third engagement was over Corny told me to hand over the navigation to Tony and to get busy looking after the wounded and the survivors. We had picked up Freddie Warner, 636's C.O. (an old friend of Corny's from Lowestoft), and his Pilot; but "G.-K." and the first lieutenant and seven ratings were missing. It was a heavy toll.

I made the soaking and shocked survivors as comfortable as possible in borrowed clothes and blankets in both the wardroom and the mess-deck. Freddy and several of his crew had minor wounds, but his leading hand, Chiswell, had a shattered shoulder, and 658's only casualty was a nasty one. The loading number at X gun, Ordinary Seaman Balderson, had been wounded in the stomach and there was little I could do for him.

In both cases I gave a shot of morphine, and labelled them with details of the injection so that any doctor would have all the necessary information. This much was routine from the First Aid lectures I had attended. But the extent of their wounds was far beyond my range of training, and all I could do was to apply field dressings as effectively as possible and treat for shock.

636's motor mechanic was lying on a stretcher, alive but unconscious, and without any sign of injury at all, just as he had been brought aboard. None of our efforts revived him, and he eventually died at about 0400. We could only imagine that he had internal injuries or shock. One of his stokers said that a 6-pounder shell had burst near him in the engine-room, putting all the engines out of action at the very beginning of the attack.

Freddie Warner, despite his painful leg wounds and obviously suffering from shock, impressed us all by his efforts to help and care for his men. It appeared that 636 *had* in fact sighted our challenge, but not in time to make the reply before one of the gunners had opened fire without orders. This had resulted in our fierce reply, the first salvo of which had wrecked the engine-room.

I had the sombre task of stitching the body of the dead rating in canvas, and at dawn we buried him at sea.

Freddie Warner insisted on taking the funeral service, and the silent scene on the gently swaying deck in the pale light was unforgettable. There was no well-drilled guard, no rifle shots, only a group of bare-headed men in sea kit, but the solemnity and sincerity of that burial service was more moving and memorable than the full ceremony could ever have been.

> *"Forasmuch as it hath pleased Almighty God of His great mercy to take unto Himself the soul of our dear brother here departed, we therefore commit his body to the sea . . ."*

The weighted canvas bundle slid silently and swiftly into the sea. This man's duty was done. Ours was still before us.

CHAPTER X

## FALSE NOSE

OUR worries were not yet over. We had several severely wounded men aboard who needed medical attention rapidly, and our fuel was getting low. It would have been impossible to return to Maddalena, so Corny had decided as soon as we had broken off the action to make for Bastia in north-eastern Corsica. We knew Bastia had been liberated by the Free French only a week before, but we hoped it would be open for us and that there would be an adequate hospital there.

Early next morning, soon after our solemn burial service, the walls of the Porto Vecchia (the Old Port) of Bastia lay before us.

It was comforting, nevertheless, to see 662 (commanded by Tim Bligh and with Gordon Surtees navigating) just entering the harbour as we approached. Her signal lamp flickered and disclosed that 662 had been sent to arrange port facilities. Our unexpected appearance added some urgency to these arrangements.

We drew in alongside Tim, and the crew began to clean up the mess on the upper deck. The leading seaman rigged the hose and water began to sluice over the decks. I had heard the expression "scuppers running with blood" but until this grey October morning they had been mere words. Now I saw deep-red streaks staining the boards and the scarlet water coursing over the side, and the events of the past night took on a new reality. The crew of 662 watched silently, and Tim and Gordon came down to hear our adventures.

But my job was to seek out the hospital and arrange for our two badly wounded men to be operated on. With some difficulty I found it and discovered that the Germans had left it in a pitiful state. Nuns had taken it over, and one French surgeon was trying to cope with the wounded from the recent battle of liberation. Water was almost non-existent, there was a terrible shortage of nurses and of medical supplies, and the place was appallingly over-crowded.

As I walked along a corridor filthy with unswept refuse and glanced into one of the wards my heart sank. The scene reminded me of a picture I had seen of a Crimean War hospital before Florence Nightingale got to work. The patients were ill-clad and dirty, and there was nothing but shabby blankets on the beds. Everywhere were signs of death and hopelessness. Could we send our men here?

I saw the surgeon and in halting schoolboy French described the men's wounds. He arranged for an ambulance to fetch them, and I signed a form giving him permission to operate as necessary. There was nothing else we could do.

That evening, we visited them and were horrified to find them still unwashed apart from their wounds, and lying half-clothed in a crowded ward. Balderson seemed to know he was going to die. In spite of his obvious pain he smiled and whispered to Corny: "Good luck in 658, sir—I was proud to serve in her." He died during the night, and our ensign flew at half mast for a second day. Chiswell, whose arm was amputated, made good progress and was sent home a few weeks later; Freddie Warner's wounds were also treated in this hospital, where he stayed to keep an eye on Chiswell's condition.

Next day we lay alongside the wreck of a merchant ship out in Bastia Bay and set about getting the boat ship-shape once more. There was much to be done, especially in reloading ammunition pans and lockers and overhauling guns. But above all we wanted to be quiet, and at last we had time to reflect on the crowded events of the action.

The tragic destruction of 636 and the accidental loss of such fine men completely overshadowed the fact that we had fought a very fine single-handed action; but for that, we could have had the pride and pleasure of sinking two enemy ships and making the final Victory a little more certain.

But even though we all felt the tragedy, it weighed most heavily on Corny. It was not his fault. Our challenge was seen too late, their gunner was light on the trigger, the angle of approach and the visibility made identification difficult; and, to crown the series of coincidences, our gunfire had (unhappily on this occasion) been too accurate.

Although Corny was free from blame, it was not hard to imagine his thoughts. There was nothing we could do to ease them. He was the C.O., and the burden was his alone. But there was no doubt of the effect of the action on the crew. From now on, there was a confidence in their fellows, and a realization of the importance of the routine maintenance of guns and machinery. All imagined ideas of what went on in a tough action were now consolidated, and every member of the crew felt himself a valuable link in a strong chain.

We returned to Maddalena next day and were very much encouraged by the warm-hearted welcome by the boats there. Everywhere we found genuine respect for our achievements and an understanding of our feelings; the comradeship of our community helped to dispel the gloom and put the whole thing in its broader perspective.

Unlike most Naval ports we had used up to this time, Maddalena was not visited by any large warships. Occasionally a destroyer entered, but it was normally a Base for Coastal Forces, submarines and minesweepers only. The Base staff obtained a very pleasant villa ashore, and the Base buildings and jetties were in a good sheltered position.

Once Commander Allan had established the Maddalena Base, he travelled north to Bastia and began to set up an advanced Base there, with full facilities for boats to operate. A glance at the chart confirmed its suitability as a striking point, as it was only thirty miles from Elba, whose mountainous sky line was normally clearly visible. Rapidly Bastia became more and more important, and Maddalena settled down as a "rear" Base, to which operational boats went only for rest, refit and docking, and for major stocks of food, supplies and ammunition.

Almost immediately, the 15th MTB Flotilla of the United States Navy also arrived in Bastia, and although their Base was in the small Old Port, and ours in the far more spacious New Harbour, we saw a great deal of their officers socially and operationally, and were soon on very good terms with them. Their PT[1] boats were extremely fine, but it was their radar which turned us green with envy. Almost at once, Corny cadged a ride in a boat of their flotilla so that he could see the radar in action, and he came back full of excitement about its possibilities.

To start with, their radar aerial was not directional like ours, but revolved constantly within the dome-shaped cover which surmounted a low mast. The screen was circular, and a pointer of green light swept round and round from its centre, illuminating with a blob of light any target up to a range of about ten miles. Its value for difficult navigation was quite remarkable, as a glance at the screen showed the boat at the centre, and instantly revealed the relative position of all the land around.

It seemed a natural and happy development, therefore, that almost immediately we began to work in mixed groups, with one or two PT boats acting as the "eyes" for two or three Dogs. On the whole,

---

[1] PT: patrol torpedo boats.

the targets we could expect were mainly of shallow draught and more suitable for attack by gunfire than with torpedoes, so the PTs were able to do a worth-while job in this way by helping us. They had some very fine sailors and coastal force captains, and although we were sometimes very critical of their efficiency and effectiveness, we thoroughly enjoyed their co-operation. One of their C.O.s had been in the flotilla of PTs immortalized in the book *They Were Expendable* during the retreat from the Philippines after Pearl Harbour.

After a month of bad weather and a series of uncomfortable and uneventful patrols, we were given our first "false nose" assignment. We preferred this description to the more usual "cloak and dagger", and entered into the spirit of the operation with great enthusiasm. By now, Pick had got his command in 655, and Tony and I had settled down to our new jobs in 658.

We first knew we had been selected for this special job when a message arrived asking Corny to go to see Bobby Allan in the Base. There he was introduced to a French capitaine de corvette (lieutenant commander) who was to be in charge of a party of three French agents whom we were to land furtively on the coast of Elba.

Next morning, the capitaine de corvette brought his men aboard, together with a great load of equipment. I looked at the heap growing on the deck, and turned to Corny. "How do they expect to get all this lot ashore? They will need a pukka landing craft not a ten-foot dinghy!"

We carried the gear below into the wardroom and the agents took great delight in showing off their gadgets to us. They had a portable wireless set for both receiving and transmitting, a rubber dinghy, packs, and a considerable and varied armoury of guns and knives.

Together we bent over the chart and carefully fixed the point on the island where they were to be put ashore. The Germans had evenly-spaced batteries and observation posts all round the coast; but Intelligence reports showed that it should be possible to approach unobserved and land the party in a certain little sandy cove protected by a short headland named Pointe Zanca.

Tactfully I mentioned the question of their equipment and hinted that four men with packs, weapons and wireless would be a very heavy load for our small dinghy. Why not use two rubber dinghies, and conceal them ashore?

But the agents would not hear of it. Quite rightly, I suppose, they felt that discovery of the dinghies might easily reveal their arrival and either result in their capture, or a tightening of security measures on the island. And capture meant death to them.

We sailed with several other boats and began the evening by patrolling the coast north of Elba, but saw nothing. The PT, using its radar, then guided us to our landing point and gave us an excellent fix from which we could run in on dead-reckoning without fear of putting the Frenchmen ashore beside a German sentry.

The night was pitch black and the low clouds reduced visibility almost to nothing. These were excellent conditions so long as we could find the exact landing point.

When we were about two miles off the beach we stopped and I went down aft to attend to the launching of the dinghy. We secured it carefully, and towed it astern as we crept in very slowly towards the black mountainous coast. The engines were silenced but to us they seemed to roar louder than ever.

Tony circled round the standard compass, rapidly taking bearings to check the distance from the shore.

"Two hundred yards, sir."

We crept a little nearer, and then stopped. Even the telegraph levers seemed to clang louder than usual. We spoke in whispers. It was 2255, and time for the party to land.

We lowered the companion ladder, and Maguire brought the dinghy round to it. I looked at the four Frenchmen and their load of kit, and thought once more of our dinghy. We solemnly shook hands, and the capitaine de corvette, who was in charge of the party and would be bringing back the dinghy, gave them their last orders.

Laboriously they climbed down the ladder. Their understandable tension made them clumsy, and the second agent stumbled as he stepped over the thwart, throwing all his weight on one side of the dinghy and rocking it madly. A flood of rapidly-spoken French abuse betrayed the anxiety of the man already in the boat: he clutched wildly at the gunwale, dropping his precious pack. Fortunately it fell on to the bottom boards.

Before number two had really settled himself, number three began to arrive. Hissing a warning at the two in the boat, he stretched out his leg and stepped on to the central thwart. Gingerly he transferred his weight and then found to his horror that the boat began to slide away from the ladder. Soon his arched body was forming an unwilling bridge stretched almost horizontally. He clutched the ladder for dear life and emitted shrieks of fear. We tossed another line down and pulled the dinghy in tight while agent number three settled down in the stern. All now seemed well, so the Naval officer turned, saluted us, and dropped efficiently into place. We passed down the oars, they waved, and we watched them draw away.

But the dinghy had only travelled a few yards when we were some-what startled to see the two agents hitherto sitting peacefully at the stern try to stand up—a very unwise move in a dinghy. The poor Naval officer, knowing the meaning of centres of gravity, rested on his oars and pleaded with them to sit down. They continued to move and the dinghy rocked obediently. Still they did not sit down; and as we watched, the bigger of the two lost his balance and toppled shrieking into the water. This sudden removal of some twelve stone from one side gave the dinghy a sharp list to port and, with the extra weight of the equipment, the water began to pour in.

The situation was not yet hopeless, as long as the three survivors kept their heads. But no, the agent in the bow seat bent over to try to pull his extremely frightened compatriot into the dinghy. However, the Frenchmen had defied the laws of stability once too often, and the dinghy rolled right over. There was a second's silence and then the ocean seemed to be full of splashing, shouting men. We dutifully counted heads. Yes, there were still four, though from the noise one might have tripled the tally.

We dropped the scrambling-net over the side and Tony secured a lifebelt to a heaving-line and tossed it towards the furthest swimmer. Maguire scrambled down the ladder and, holding on with one hand, extended an arm to help the first arrival on board.

No one would have thought we were only one hundred yards from an enemy coast. The night rang with the cries of distraught Frenchmen and the hoarse encouragement (in doubtful French) of 658's crew. Rapidly, two of the agents were man-handled aboard; but the other two still seemed unable to help themselves and continued to shriek in top register. Any trigger-happy German nearby (at this time of night, with all the noise, any German could be forgiven for being trigger-happy), must certainly be sounding "action stations", convinced the Allies (since the voices were shouting in French and English) were about to land in force.

One of the Frenchmen, his white face pathetically uplifted towards us, seemed to be trying to convey that he had broken his arm, but suddenly his voice died with a gurgle as he drifted under the water pouring out of the exhaust pipes in the ship's side. At this, A/B Smith took pity and dived in to support him until he too was heaved aboard.

But by now there was no sign at all of the fourth member of the party (the capitaine de corvette). Admittedly we could hear him (who couldn't?) but we could not see him. It took a moment or two to realize that he had got himself wedged under the chine near the bows. As the boat lifted in the slight swell, each surge gave the poor fellow a tap on the head for full measure. Once again Smithy dived over. Corny was becoming a little anxious by now, as a northerly wind had sprung up and it was drifting us very gradually towards the point, on which there was possibly a German battery. A few moments later Smithy re-appeared, pushing the Frenchman along towards the ladder. As soon as he was aboard, Corny went ahead on the engines and slowly and quietly turned 658 away from the beach.

When we were a couple of miles offshore Corny handed over the watch to me and disappeared down to the wardroom to see how the agents were faring. They had been dried out and were now dressed in clothing borrowed from the officers and men of 658. To give them their due, they were all willing to land and carry on with the operation, but two were obviously suffering from shock and the effects of swallowing too much sea-water. After some discussion, the capitaine decided to send one agent only ashore, in spite of the loss of the radio equipment.

At midnight, 658 sidled in once more to the close position, and this time a rubber dinghy was used, the redoubtable A/B Smith volunteering to help the capitaine to paddle the agent ashore.

We anxiously strained our eyes to watch for the dinghy's return, but it was so small, and they paddled so silently, that it was almost alongside before we spotted it, even with binoculars. Corny sighed with relief.

## CHAPTER XI

# MALTA FOR CHRISTMAS

APART from this excursion into the realms of "cloak and dagger" the long autumn months of 1943 working from Maddalena and Bastia brought little more than hard slogging into unpleasantly rough seas. But Maddalena and Bastia each had its distinctive atmosphere and we soon shook down to a routine which seldom varied.

Our comparative isolation in Maddalena and Bastia in many ways added to our difficulties. We were so far off the beaten track of normal communications, and there were so few other British personnel in Corsica and Sardinia, that supplies of all sorts were difficult to obtain. Some of the shortages were very bad for morale, and others affected operations. By the end of November, the position was so bad that no mail had arrived for six weeks, and the poor food situation was beginning to wear down the spirit of even the most cheerful crews.

In 658, we were at least blessed at this time with a very able cook, self-taught in every way, but with such a flair for the job that even tins of "meat and vegetables" were transformed into tasty pies.

During the Sicilian campaign, when food had got very short, he had taken the familiar "herrings-in-tomato sauce", grilled them in bread crumbs and served them as "Sicilian lake trout". He was still producing this dish occasionally, but it had changed its name to "Sardinian lake trout" as the flotilla moved north.

But even A/B Jock Elliot could do little with dehydrated potatoes and the various dried foods which now came our way. We saw no fresh fruit, meat or vegetables for months, and the only butter was a very rare allocation of a tinned and rather strong variety which was difficult to stomach; it was even a luxury to get freshly baked bread, but an arrangement was made in both Maddalena and Bastia for local bakers to supply a small amount for the boats and Base each day.

Maddalena particularly had very little to offer in the way of shore-going attractions for the men. Its rocky, arid island landscape was as barren and featureless as the Navy's own Scapa Flow, and there were no facilities for games apart from swimming. The men seemed to spend most of their time aboard even when free to go ashore, and this was certainly true of the officers in all the boats.

Corny was always seeking ways to keep 658's morale high, and his particular method of doing this in the wardroom is worthy of mention. One afternoon, he disappeared ashore and returned two hours later, his arms laden with packages.

"Take a look at these, fellers," he said, grinning. "I heard that there was a warehouse in the old Italian Base full of their naval supplies, so I took a look over there, and managed to persuade the store keeper to part with a few choice items. We'd better keep this under our hats, though, or the whole thing will fold up."

We inspected the parcels. The first contained a complete set of table linen—two tablecloths and napkins to match. The second revealed serving dishes, and a third a heavy, beautifully finished chromium sugar bowl with the monogram "R.M." (Reggia Marina). Apart from this Corny had obtained two flexible table lamps and some additional cutlery. It had been a good haul.

At lunch next day we instituted a new formal ceremony which was observed throughout the rest of the commission, and was most impressive to a casual visitor. Our steward was, at this time, a big jovial able-seaman from Yorkshire named Christon. He was given instructions to set the table carefully, and to be smartly dressed in whites when he served the lunch. At the appointed time, Corny gave the first order.

"Ah, gentlemen, I think we should take lunch. Would you kindly ring for the steward, Mr. Brydon?"

Tony pressed the buzzer, which sounded three feet away in the galley. A knock came at the door, and Christon's red face appeared.

"Would you serve lunch, please, Christon?"

A few seconds later, the meal made its appearance. The meat dish and three hot plates were placed carefully before Corny at the head of the table, and the two vegetable dishes in front of Tony and me. As soon as Christon had shut the door behind him, Corny ordered, "Vegetable serving party—shun!" Tony and I sat bolt upright. "Off-lids!" A hand shot out from each side of the table and, synchronizing the movements exactly, we removed the two covers. This was the moment to simulate pleasure and surprise. A forced smile spread over Corny's face as he peered first into the starboard dish and then into the other. "Why! *de*hydrated potatoes—oh! and dried peas!"

The corned beef on the large dish before him was then carefully served in exactly equal portions on to the three plates, and the dishes were circulated for individual serving.

All this rigmarole served its purpose at the time, and we found that to take a meal aboard a boat where a loaded plate was carelessly slapped in front of each officer by a scruffy steward, was a real let-down after our own pleasant standards.

Very occasionally—if, for instance, Corny had received a large food parcel from Canada—we would throw a dinner party with all the trappings. On these occasions Christon was magnificent. He would dress in spotless whites and carry a starched napkin over his arm. He would serve the guests and the officers in exactly the correct order, *and* look as though he was enjoying it, too.

At the beginning of December the Base engineer officers held an informal meeting over a glass of gin in our wardroom. They decided that we should have to have all our four main engines replaced by new ones. This was normally routine practice after 500 hours' running time, but in our case Last had kept the engines at peak performance until the log-books revealed that three of them had already exceeded 950 hours!

To our delight it was found necessary that we should sail to Malta for this work to be done. We felt we had earned a short break, and though Malta was not exactly paradise, it had far more of the characteristics of that place than Maddalena or Bastia could boast! And it looked as though we should be there for Christmas.

We took a new route to Malta this time, sailing southward down the Sardinian coast and then heading east to pass along the south-western coast of Sicily, so that we had now circumnavigated the island.

Even in three months, Malta had changed tremendously since our last visit. The nearest German airfield was now high up the Italian boot, and the danger of air raids had receded almost out of sight. The social life of Valletta and Sliema had been reborn, and now the seamen could have every entertainment and amenity that they had lacked in Maddalena.

Very quickly Christmas was upon us—our first in 658 and, for me, my first aboard ship. I had been on leave for the last two. I spent a good deal of time in conference with NAAFI headquarters to make sure of special food supplies, and they did a very good job. We had a twenty-pound turkey, Christmas puddings, four bottles of beer apiece for the crew, and all the necessary fresh vegetables.

The day itself was crowded with eating, drinking, and singing; Captain's Rounds involved drinking a tot on the messdeck. When I downed mine (I was drinking neat rum for the first time in my life) my throat burned and I gasped for breath. The usual songs began, and Corny was urged to sing his party piece. In the end he allowed himself to be persuaded, and we were treated to his vigorous but tuneless version of "There came a desperado from the wild and woolly west".

Then came the Christmas dinner, magnificently prepared in the six-foot square box which was honoured with the name of galley. How Jock Elliott cooked such a complex meal for thirty-five on his small electric stove, *and* served it hot, will always be a mystery.

After dinner, the petty officers and leading hands were invited to the wardroom for a glass of port. On the messdeck the unaccustomed joy of drinking beer aboard seemed to stimulate the crew once more to song. By 1500, the whole ship's company was either ashore or asleep, and Tony and I surveyed the messdeck which looked as though it had recently weathered a tornado. Fortunately, we were unquestionably State "C" (unable to move, let alone operate!) and so had been able to grant the widest possible leave.

Our refit was complete ten days after Christmas, and our sailing was immediately arranged. On the morning of our departure a signal from C.C.F. was brought aboard by special messenger.

"*Under a general revision and reconstitution of flotillas, the following boats will form the new 56th MGB/MTB Flotilla, under the command of Lt.-Cdr. J. D. Maitland R.C.N.V.R.: MGBs 657, 658, 663; MTBs 633, 640 and 655.*

*Lt.-Cdr. T. J. Bligh R.N.V.R. is appointed in command of the 57th MTB/MGB Flotilla. . . .*"

Doug Maitland our S.O.! And every one of the boats in the new 56th Flotilla commanded by a Canadian! It looked as though things might hum when we got back to Bastia. They did.

## CHAPTER XII

# HAT-TRICK FOR THE 56TH

ON our way northwards we discussed the reasons for the re-shuffle. Naturally, Corny knew that the "Canadian" 56th Flotilla had been discussed, but he did not know it had got beyond the blueprint stage. The mixing of MTBs and MGBs was a very sensible move in view of the probable targets we should meet.

When we joined the others at Maddalena after a rough and very uncomfortable trip via Bizerta, there was a great deal of news to exchange. We had brought up a big batch of mail, and although it was already January 19th the sacks contained a good deal of long-overdue Christmas mail. The arrangements were so poor that mail was held at Malta and only sent up to Maddalena and Bastia when a Coastal Force boat was making passage there. There seemed to be a lack of understanding in higher circles on the enormous importance of a regular mail delivery to the boats, and it was some months before an air service to Sardinia improved the situation considerably.

We also found that our efforts to improve the social life of the flotilla by bringing up a crate of gin and of scotch for distribution, were very popular. They had not been easily gained, either—but at this time, overcoming the problem of the rationing of spirits was difficult but not impossible if one could spin a good enough yarn. Later in the war, NAAFI would only issue the strict ration of one bottle per officer per month on receipt of the boat's spirits log book, and this virtually put an end to the application of "one-upmanship" to NAAFI.

As far as the shooting war was concerned, the news was a little disturbing. While we had been away, German destroyers taken over from the Italians at the capitulation and both faster and more heavily armed than we had appeared in our area and our boats had had one or two narrow squeaks with them. Pick had fired both his torpedoes at one on his first patrol in 655, but had not managed to hit. It had become normal routine to patrol with an American PT boat as radar guide, and already this system was proving successful in ensuring an accurate plot of the enemy's movements.

There had been changes aboard 663, too. I was delighted to hear that Derrick was now Tommy Ladner's first lieutenant, a promotion that seemed to me to be long overdue. Their new navigating officer was a young and handsome subbie named Tony Marriott, who besides being excellent company proved to be an immense asset in Corsica as he was bi-lingual; in fact he spoke French with rather more facility than English. Although the social advantages of this were very rapidly appreciated, on operations Tommy and Derrick were horrified to hear Tony busily occupied with the navigation, mumbling away counting in French! At first they found this most disturbing, and wondered how far their lives could be trusted with an ignorant foreigner; but their fears were soon resolved when the results of the strange murmurings proved him to be an accurate and effective navigator. Indeed, his value was soon extended when it became common to use 663 as the boat most suited for operations with French Intelligence agents, especially for landings on small islands such as Monte Christo and Pianosa, both south of Elba.

Next day we moved up to Bastia and were immediately briefed for our part in a large-scale landing operation.

Far to the south, the Allied armies were bogged down between Naples and Rome, unable to make progress except by bitter fighting in appalling weather. In an attempt to cut off the German forces from their main supply lines from Rome, a landing was now planned at the port of Anzio, about thirty miles south of Rome. It was hoped that our forces would move quickly into Italy, link up with the Fifth Army and be ready to move on to Rome after isolating the strongpoint at Cassino. (In fact the Germans reacted unexpectedly and prevented any real penetration from Anzio, giving our armies a long arduous winter battle before the advance to Rome could begin.)

Our part of the Anzio landing, with the American PT boats, was to confuse the enemy into believing that simultaneous landings were being made, by creating a diversion at the port of Civita-vecchia, to the north of Rome. It was hoped that this dummy landing would at least cause a delay in the despatch of troops to the Anzio area. Our instructions finished with the invitation for us to "create as much alarm and despondency as possible in the neighbourhood".

The main method was to play records of invasion noises over large loudspeakers: anchor cables running out, and instructions being shouted to landing craft, and that sort of thing. We all carried fireworks to simulate the flashes of big guns, and the PTs had the loudspeakers on board and looked a little embarrassed by the whole idea. To make as much noise as possible would be a refreshing change from our normal stealthy approach.

We sailed at 1700 and set course direct for Civita-vecchia. It was good to be a real team at last. Doug was leading in 657, 658 followed, and then came Tommy in 663, Peter Barlow (in 659 on loan from the 57th Flotilla) and Pick in 655, the only torpedo-boat. Just before midnight we kept a rendezvous with the PTs four miles south of Giglio Island and moved in at 14 knots towards the beach.

It was at this point that our programme was interrupted. Suddenly the R/T loudspeaker crackled and every face turned towards it. The orders said no one was to break wireless silence unless it was urgent. What was up?

"Hallo, Wimpey, this is Stan." We looked at each other. Stan Barnes was S.O. of the PTs. They must have seen something.

"I have a target at Red 40, range 2,800 yards. Shall I leave it to you and carry on with the main job?"

Immediately we heard Doug reply.

"How many are there, Stan? Sure we'll take them on."

"Looks like one big and two small. They're all yours, Wimpey. Good luck."

We watched the line of PTs swing away to starboard. A lamp flicked twice from 657, and we increased speed and followed in her wake. It was a very dark night, with visibility down to 500 yards, so the early report the American radar had given us was invaluable. We now had to hope that our own less efficient radar would be able to assist us in holding the target throughout the engagement.

It made a good start, anyway. A few minutes later, we heard:

"Dogs from Wimpey. One target right ahead, 1,500 yards, and another at Green 20 degrees, range 1,700 yards, both closing. 18 knots. First attack will be to port."

I passed the bearings to the gunners at once, warning them to stand by for a port-side attack. We were coming down astern of the enemy ships, overhauling them fast, our presence still completely unsuspected.

At 0207, the enemy ships came in sight. This was the moment I always found most challenging: the moment when hands began to shake, when the stomach felt vaguely uneasy, when one had to try to look unconcerned about the whole business.

I put down my glasses and murmured into the telephone: "All guns.

Enemy in sight, fine on port bow. One F-lighter with an E-boat on either beam. Stand by."

The range closed slowly and still the F-lighter did not start shooting. Surely he must see us soon. . . .

"Dogs from Wimpey—Open fire!"

I pressed the gun buzzer, and I was just as surprised as ever at the immediate and deafening response. It seemed as if my pressure on a buzzer in fact pressed every trigger on board. And this time we were five boats, all concentrating on one target. Obviously the first he knew of us was when our shells began to hit. What a sight it must have been for him! Five streams of converging, relentless tracer, spread in an arc about him so that he could not possibly reply to more than two.

But reply he did, and desperately too. We in 658 were not surprised that he selected 657 and ourselves as his targets: we were the first two in line. It was a shock, however, to feel the thuds of shells hitting the hull and to see a blue flash at the pom-pom turret on the fo'c'sle, all from the first salvo.

There was a commotion over the telephones, and I heard the broad Yorkshire of Christon, our steward, reporting. "Preston and Brayshaw wounded, sir—but the gun's all right. Shall I take over?"

I shouted approval and told Corny the news. All the other guns were still blasting away at the F-lighter, and already his fire had slackened and flames flickered along his upper deck.

I noticed that 657 ahead had stopped firing as the bearing had moved well aft, so I pressed the buzzers once more to check fire, and watched the target as we swung in a tight turn in Doug's wake. The others followed round, and almost at once we were closing in for the second run. Christon was settled into the seat of the pom-pom turret, and Tony had Preston and Brayshaw in the charthouse, doing what he could for them. I moved a spare lookout up to act as loading number, and we opened fire again.

This time the E-boats appeared; it was a mystery to me that they had taken no part in the first exchange. Perhaps they had been so surprised that they had felt it wise to keep out of the way. Now, however, they both opened fire, and one suddenly swung towards our line and, moving very fast and firing all the way, it shot wildly between 659 and 655, almost ramming Pick's bows. Both these boats hammered him hard as he went but he disappeared into the darkness, leaving his comrades-in-arms to fight it out alone. We were never sure whether he had decided that he had already had enough of this particular battle, or whether his steering was out of action, or whether he really was trying to ram 655.

The other E-boat was very roughly handled by our three leading boats, and soon stopped firing and lay motionless with tongues of fire licking at the superstructure. The F-lighter, all fight gone out of her, also lay stopped, burning fiercely.

Over the loudspeaker came Pick's voice, unnaturally strained and distorted by R/T.

"Wimpey from Pick: I am damaged and am disengaging to the west."

I looked round and saw 655's stern as she made off westward. But Doug was turning again and closing in to the F-lighter to finish it off. It was rather like firing shots into a lifeless body: but the flames sprang higher as our shells struck home, and we were sure that this ship would carry no more cargoes to the battle front.

It seemed to lie low in the water, and was probably heavily laden; from the colourful display of rockets which shot skyward in graceful curves, we thought it might be carrying ammunition. A constant stream of fizzing shells radiated from the inferno, as though a spark from a bonfire had landed in the box of fireworks at a family November the Fifth party and provided an unplanned but simultaneous set-piece!

Slowly we turned away westward to find Pick and give him assistance. As we did so, the shore batteries opened fire, and we increased speed and began to zig-zag away. We had got well out of range and had settled down to our search for Pick when a vivid flash lit the sky, the boat shuddered as though hit with an underwater sledge-hammer, and we swung round to see a column of fire and smoke rising to 1,500 feet. The F-lighter had blown up.

We continued westward, and soon had a report from Pick that his damage was repaired. We all met up at first light and sailed triumphantly into Bastia.

I was very concerned about our two wounded men. Brayshaw, an ordinary seaman, was obviously in a bad way, with several severe wounds about his body, while Preston had been hit in the face with shrapnel and I was worried about his sight. As soon as we entered harbour, they were whisked away to the hospital with the Base M.O. in charge of them. What a difference from our experience at Bastia the previous October! But poor Brayshaw—a good seaman and a likeable lad—died during the day and all the pleasure went out of our success.

It was part of our job to accept that the lives of men must occasionally be bartered for enemy ships: but it was a necessity which was hard to bear and hard to forget, especially when the man was popular and a valuable member of the team.

Our damage, apart from dents on the pom-pom turret shield (which had been far more effective than we expected), had mainly been due to a burst of 20-mm. in the port waist. One shell entered the wing petrol tank, but luckily did not set it on fire. We always left the wing tanks full as long as possible, as liquid petrol in a full tank is far less dangerous than the explosive vapour in an empty one.

The vulnerability of the Dogs was emphasized by 655's experiences. Two 20-mm. shells had pierced her exhaust pipes, so that almost at once her engine room had filled with fumes and had to be abandoned until a motor mechanic, wearing a smoke-mask and with pure air pumped to him, managed to return and plug the holes. 657 had also suffered minor damage.

Doug made it an inflexible rule that all boats must fuel as soon as possible on return to harbour; and despite our exertions of the night, the damage and the ammunition stocks were made good, and by mid-day the whole flotilla was ready to operate again that night. The C.O.s held a conference, and as a patrol was required they decided that Doug should take 657, 663 and 659, leaving 658 and 655 available for the following night if necessary.

Stan Barnes was at the meeting and reported that the diversion had gone smoothly; but although his boats had made as much noise as possible, they had not been able to surpass the enormous explosion we had unwittingly added to the show.

Corny, Tony and I watched the boats sail at 1730, and then settled down to a quiet evening aboard. Corny had the unenviable task of writing to Brayshaw's parents; Tony had the log to get up to date from entries in his rough log, and I had some victualling accounts to check with the coxswain. The routine matters could not cease just because we had been in action.

Before we turned in, Tony and I went up on the bridge for a breath of air. The night was calm and dark. The boats had gone to a patrol area just north of the previous night's party. Would they see anything?

We knew the answer at 0400 next morning. It was still dark when I was woken by the bump of a boat coming alongside and the roar of engines near my head. I threw on a duffel coat and ran up the ladder to the upper deck.

Derrick grinned down at me from the bridge of 663 as her engines suddenly stopped.

"Any luck, Derrick?"

"Well—it was a bit frustrating. We bumped into a convoy of F-lighters with big escorts, and had a go at them, but 657 and 659 had some damage so we had to withdraw. We definitely sank an E-boat and almost certainly got one of the F's."

He yawned and stretched. "Your turn tomorrow, Rover. Hope you make it a hat-trick. Go and get your head down—you'll need all the sleep you can get!"

He was right. Doug and his three boats were dead tired after two hectic nights, so Corny was given the job of leading a small unit consisting of 658, 655 and PT 217.

We were on patrol south of Capraia Island very early, and settled down to a long night of patient search. It was a luxury to have the security of the PT's radar sweeping round us; there was a feeling that we could not ourselves be surprised by an unexpected attack, and more than that, we were far more likely to be able to spring a surprise on the enemy after early warning of a convoy's approach.

But four hours went by before the peace of the bridge was shattered by the shrill urgency of the W/T office buzzer. Corny lifted the voice-pipe cover.

"Bridge here—Captain speaking."

"Signal from S.O.I.S.,[1] sir. Reads 'Suspected enemy movements in Vada Rocks area. You are to proceed immediately to patrol southward from Secche de Vada to Piombino.'"

"Thank you, Sparks."

Corny bobbed down to the charthouse and consulted the chart with Tony. A minute later we were on our new course and were heading northward at 22 knots. It took two and a half hours to reach the new area, and we settled down again to search, moving slowly south-east about five miles from the coast.

It was almost 0400 and time to be thinking about going home when our usual warning—the click over the R/T loudspeaker—electrified us all into sudden alertness.

"Hallo, Corny, this is Doyle." The drawl was unmistakably the C.O. of PT 217 who was from the deep South. "I have several targets, range 4 miles bearing 085 degrees, course north, speed 12 knots. Over."

[1] S.O.I.S.: Senior Officer, Inshore Squadron—the operating authority at Bastia.

"Hallo, Doyle, this is Corny. Roger."

Once again Corny joined Tony in the charthouse. There was no time to delay. A few glances at the chart, a few quick movements as he stepped off distances with the dividers, and that was enough. Back on the bridge, he ordered: "Bring her round to north-east, Rover, and increase to 1,800."[1]

He picked up the R/T microphone. "Hallo, Pick and Doyle, this is Corny. Course north-east, speed 22 knots. Out."

We gathered speed and swung round to the new course. Corny explained his plan. He wanted to get ahead of the convoy and cut across its bows to make an attack from inshore, where the low clouds and land background would make us almost invisible.

After twenty minutes Tony's careful plot showed that it was just not going to be possible to get inshore, so Corny decided to approach from the west and attack direct. In the low visibility, if we reduced speed we should be able to get close without being detected.

Doyle passed more information, and as the range closed and the details came clearer on his screen, his messages told us that we were in for a warm night.

"We can make out at least five targets now, Corny—range 1,000 yards."

By the time we had closed to 500 yards, the convoy at last appeared in our glasses. There were six F-lighters in two columns, and one E-boat astern was the only escort we could see.

The almost unbroken line of ships seemed ideal for a torpedo attack, and Corny ordered Pick and the PT to spread to port and fire as convenient. Doyle fired one torpedo almost immediately, and breathlessly we waited. The range was only 300 yards, and he reported that it was running true. But no explosion came.

"Hell! the lighters must be running light," Corny exclaimed. "It's not worth wasting torpedoes."

He recalled Pick, and began to slide slowly round the enemy's stern. Meanwhile the PT had disengaged to the south-west at such a speed that the E-boat sighted her and immediately opened fire. This was ideal for us—a perfect diversion. Within a minute we had closed in to 100 yards from the E-boat on his "blind side".

I don't think he ever knew what hit him. Certainly the first he knew of our presence was the arrival of a full broadside from both ourselves and 655. Shells smacked into him and within thirty seconds

[1] 1,800 revolutions (about 22 knots).

he had stopped, with fires springing out from the engine-room and bridge. One brave man sent a last defiant spray of 20-mm. shells towards us, but one burst from the pom-pom silenced even this belated reply.

I swept round with my glasses. The F-lighters were no longer in two lines, but had scattered rapidly and were firing bursts of tracer in every direction. Over the west, smoke which the PT had made in her diversion was spreading towards the convoy and already obscured the first few ships.

The confusion was magnificent. The enemy did not know friend from foe, so we should be able to enjoy ourselves. Down in the radar cabin, Gunning was thoroughly enjoying himself. His accent grew broader and broader as he sent report after report up to the voice-pipe. Naturally he realized the advantages of the American radar set that everyone made so much fuss about, but he was jealous of his reputation and was out to prove that his set was by no means useless.

In fact, now we had lost the PT, it was invaluable. Corny could move about within the convoy, attack suddenly and then break off and creep to another target, leaving only fear and uncertainty behind.

In this way, we tackled first another E-boat which hardly replied to our attack, and then an unpleasantly aggressive larger ship which was pumping out shells of every calibre up to 88-mm. Howe down at the 6-pounder was as accurate as ever, and we watched Christon (still substituting while Preston was in hospital) pouring devastating pom-pom fire into its hull.

Very soon, though, the return fire got so heavy that we disengaged to the northward and, while doing so, Pick lost contact with us. Realizing how difficult it would to be rejoin now, he acted fast. He turned westward, informing Corny of his action over R/T, switched on his recognition lights for a split second (enough to let us know where he was) and began to attack an F-lighter on his way out.

Once again we were on our own. Corny picked out from Gunning's reports the best target for our present position, and we moved slowly in towards a single F-lighter. He was still unsuspecting when we opened fire at 100 yards, and he hardly replied.

We had a theory about F-lighter gunnery. We knew they carried an 88-mm. and several 20-mm. guns, and could therefore blow us out of the water if they had the chance. But their guns were protected by concrete emplacements—and far from helping them by reducing casualties, this only served to encourage their gunners to keep their heads well down in safety instead of firing steadily. Our own gunners had miserably inadequate cover, and were therefore never likely to shelter behind it!

Immediately we moved on to the next lighter, and found the same lack of fight. But there was at least one ship which intended to make us work hard for our results, and we could just pick her out as a good deal larger than any of the other ships in the convoy. As we finished a second run at the lighter, we felt the shudder of shell-hits and knew it was time to disengage.

We had been hit about the water line in the engine-room, and Last sent up a stoker to ask for extra assistance "as he had four feet of water in the bilges". It took only a few minutes to plug the holes, and soon the water was pumped out and we were out of the convoy heading for a rendezvous with Pick and Doyle.

We looked back. The blackness of the horizon was speckled with small fires, and tracer still wavered in every direction as the trigger-happy convoy beat off imaginary attacks. It had been a hectic half-hour in their midst, and we had no casualties and very little damage.

Our troubles were not over. The weather broke and our return voyage took four hours in the teeth of high seas and a howling gale. It was 0830 when we arrived, soaked to the skin and over-weary, at the entrance to Bastia harbour. But it was worth it to see 663's whole crew—officers and men—standing by to welcome us in. They had received the signals about the action, and had realized we would not be able to cook breakfast in the gale, so they had prepared a meal for the whole of our crew.

Their inimitable coxswain Nicholl took over completely as soon as we were alongside. The cook, with helpers, came aboard carrying an urn of tea and a large dish of bacon. Tommy told us to drop everything and to join them for breakfast in their wardroom. It was a heart-warming demonstration of true comradeship, and was typical of the spirit of the 56th Flotilla.

We sat down to breakfast and had hardly started when Doug and Cam arrived to hear our news. There wasn't really room for them, but they were found a seat and given a cup of coffee while Corny made his unofficial report on our night's work.

Next day an Intelligence report reached S.O.I.S. from the R.A.F. and other sources, that one F-lighter and an E-boat had been sunk, three others damaged, and (much to our delight) a 900-ton minelayer was aground near Vada Rocks, inshore of the position of the action.

This must have been the larger ship we saw towards the end of the action. We had bagged the biggest ship yet destroyed in this area by our boats.

The weather was too bad for operations for three days after this, and we had time to put our boats in order again. There was a great deal to do, replenishing ammunition and overhauling engines and guns, as well as the normal routine of maintenance going on as usual.

When the C.O.s sat down with Captain Dickinson (S.O.I.S.) and Commander Allan to review this hat-trick of attacks, there was much to discuss and to learn for the future. But one thing was clear. The 56th Flotilla had got off to a flying start; not only had we met the enemy three times in three nights, but we had come out well on top and almost unscathed.

There was a German E-boat flotilla in Leghorn or Baratti or Piombino which must be having a similar conference but with very different feelings. In three nights three of their boats had definitely been sunk and two others heavily damaged. Their morale could hardly be high!

Bobby Allan summed up the situation in a comment when forwarding Doug's action report: " . . . this was the first time that the newly constituted 56th Flotilla operated as such. After such a start it is satisfactory to note that their tails are nearly as high as the explosion they caused. The tactics were thoroughly aggressive and the results most satisfactory. . . ."

Aboard the boats much had been learned which was to prove invaluable. Such was the stimulus of action that in three days the new flotilla had worked up to a higher pitch than weeks of trials and exercises could have achieved.

Doug and his C.O.s felt they had proved two principles, too. One was that low speeds were far more effective during close attacks than high speeds, as the lack of bow-wave and wake gave the enemy less chance of sighting accurately, and our own gunners were conversely able to hold the target more easily at low speeds; the second confirmed their belief that once any action had begun, the results achieved depended on the crews, not the officers. What the S.O. and each C.O. did was to place the ship as close as possible to the enemy: from that point on the aim and continuous shooting of the gunners was all that really mattered, and finally accomplished the results.

We were lucky to be blessed with a fine crew.

## CHAPTER XIII

## FRUSTRATION

ABOARD 658, I had my first experience of a custom which was touching in its quiet sincerity and kindliness.

The coxswain organized a "sale of effects", and a message went round the flotilla. At the appointed time, a large crowd gathered on the jetty, and the coxswain auctioned Brayshaw's kit in order to raise money for his people back home. The generosity of the men was incredible. I saw a stoker, who normally drew less than a pound a week at pay parades, hand over two pounds for a pair of white shoes, and then throw them back in to be sold again. A large sum was collected, and sent off to England. The Navy has its own brotherhood and a tradition for open-handed generosity.

The nights in harbour enforced by the very bad weather (when we were certain not to be called out) had one very pleasant result. We began to see something of Corsica, with organized Jeep tours of the mountainous interior. A visit to the Field Hospital, where our pom-pom gunner Preston was under treatment, was a nightmare ride up a narrow, hairpin-looped road, with a precipice falling away on one side as it climbed tortuously higher and higher.

On our return from one of these trips we discovered a little fishing village several kilometres north of Bastia which boasted a very pleasant inn. Having once sampled its excellent company we returned frequently to Erbalonga until we became old and expected friends. It became traditional for us to sing there, and the Corsican peasants and fishermen would add their contribution by trying out "Tipperary" and "Pack up your troubles", which they vaguely remembered from the First World War.

Soon we were reciprocating with French songs, dimly remembered from school-days and now far more valuable than we had ever expected. Altogether, the evenings got very hectic. By the time we left, usually at about 2300, we had normally met the mayor, the policeman, the postman and all the other personalities of the village. Somehow or other, they all knew when we had had an action, and were full of admiration that we were fighting their hated enemies, the Germans. The Corsicans were tough and roguish, and nearly all packed a gun beneath the armpit; but their friendship and loyalty, once given, was sincere. It was easy to understand their reputation as brigands.

Apart from sinking a small patrol vessel in the very entrance of La Spezia harbour, our next few patrols were uneventful. One night we experienced the horrid discomfort of being illuminated by starshells from shore batteries, but we managed to shake off their attentions.

After every patrol the inevitable routine of fuelling had always to be faced, involving as it did the necessity of cooking dinner either ashore, or on another boat, or just postponing it till the power was available.

At our usual cruising speed, used on passage to and from a patrol, the normal consumption was 120 gallons of 100 octane petrol per hour. This was considerably increased at higher speeds, as the consumption curve rose steeply between 1,800 and 2,400 revs. After most patrols, therefore, our requirement was between 1,500 and 3,000 gallons, and above all we were anxious that every drop should be free of water which could cause a breakdown at the carburettors. Every drop of petrol was therefore filtered through a home-made contraption of half an oil drum, with a pipe inserted in the filler hole and a chamois leather (the most efficient means of separating any water, when wet with petrol), stretched across the hole. The flow was by gravity only, and this meant, with the frequent stops for washing out the chamois leather, that it would frequently take three hours or more to fill up. Every droplet of water which appeared on the chamois leather, however, justified the tedium of the system, as we could at least be sure that the risk of engine failure through contaminated fuel was not added to the unavoidable risks of action.

Naturally, we grumbled incessantly that no one could provide or produce a safe pump and filter which would render the whole operation both safer and more rapid, and so reduce the inevitable and unnecessary wastage of time which had to follow every night patrol. We felt that the R.A.F., or Coastal Forces at home, would never have had to put up with this state of affairs; in fact we built up envious pictures of bomber crews leaving their aircraft after each night's operation, to return to them only shortly before the next take-off time, with no cares of maintenance, fuel or ammunition to worry them.

At the end of a fuelling session, when the dip-sticks showed the correct tank reading, the shrill pipe would sound through the boat, "Open all vents and ports", to be followed after ten minutes by the sound of the 24-volt fans in the petrol compartments, and then, after a further suitable lapse of time, by the welcome sound of the "genny" being restarted. More fans operated, and at last would come the roar and splutter of the main engines starting up.

The regular pattern of our operations was interrupted rudely early in February when Corny fell ill and I was left as "caretaker" of 658. It was a new experience for us all to be without Corny. Up to now he had *been* 658, and 658 reflected his ideas and personality. To find ourselves without our acknowledged boss was rather like depriving a show jumper of his regular rider on the eve of a big horse show.

In the end, when we were next required for patrol, 657 was at Maddalena, and so Doug decided to take out 658 as leader of a unit of three. To have the S.O. aboard was a challenge which demanded extra efforts, especially as Doug was bound to give Corny his considered opinion on his boat, officers and men when he returned. Just as in life one has to live with people to know them truly, so, in our case, an S.O. had to patrol in a boat before he could really assess its efficiency and worth.

The patrol, with 659 and 640, was in the area near Giglio Island. It was full moon for the first time on any of our operations, and I was astounded at the distance of visibility. There was little need for radar on such a night, as the naked eye could see further than radar could possibly have probed. This meant that the patrol itself would not be as exacting as usual (we could hardly be taken by surprise), but, on the other hand, it would be virtually impossible to achieve any surprise during an attack. And so it proved.

It was Smith ("Torps" as he was usually known, although his job was to look after the electrics of the boat) who first sighted the convoy. It was four miles away and hugging the coast closely. As we were up-moon to them, it was almost certain that they had sighted us earlier. There were the usual six F-lighters in two columns, but ahead and astern were two large escorts. Doug estimated them at 2,000 and 1,500 tons respectively.

He tried the only possible tactic: to get round astern of them and then inshore, to get some background obscurity from the coast. But this was wishful thinking. As we passed two miles astern of the convoy, the stern escort challenged us, and opened fire almost at once with

88-mm. This seemed to be a pre-arranged signal, as every "F" in the convoy joined in, so that a hail of these very unpleasant 88-mm. shells began to fall around us. And we weren't even near enough to be able to hit back with any of our guns! Soon, the shore batteries also joined in, so Doug regretfully turned away westward and left the batteries and ships to pound hell out of the lighthouse on the Formichi de Grossetti rocks. We felt very sorry for its inhabitants.

We shadowed the convoy until it entered San Stefano harbour, and were happy to see that they were a "trigger-happy" bunch, who occasionally blazed away at nothing in particular. I could picture their discomfort after the reports of sudden attacks they must have heard up and down the coast.

But a similar experience several nights later, again in bright moonlight, convinced us that Jerry had strengthened his escorts and was taking no chances. This time, though, we spotted a new development.

Once again Doug took us out, this time with Peter Barlow (659) and two PTs, one of which returned with engine trouble soon after starting. We were just south of Leghorn, and the patrol had only just begun when first the American radar, then our own eyes, revealed a southbound convoy of F-lighters. Almost at once the PT fired two torpedoes (at extreme range) and retired hurriedly. Neither of them even ran truly, let alone hit.

Doug looked thoughtful and decided to do a bit of stalking. We closed slowly in to 2,200 yards and, turning on to a parallel course, reduced speed to seven knots to keep pace with the convoy.

Their reactions were immediate and astonishing. Two of the F-lighters separated from the rest and placed themselves between us and the convoy, about 300 yards from it. Whenever we tried to gain bearing, or to close, these two always adjusted their position to keep the same relative position in protection of their convoy. It seemed obvious that the new idea was to arm some F-lighters as flak ships, perhaps with extra 88-mm. guns. We had seen something similar in our own fleet at Sicily: tank-landing craft called LCGs with two 4.7-inch guns, manned by Marines; we were to see more of them later.

Doug felt we had to make some effort at an attack, so at 2338 when the range was 1,500 yards, and the leading "LCG" nicely up-moon, we turned our noses in and increased speed, opening fire with both 6-pounder and pom-pom. There was no delay in the reply. Every ship in the convoy let fly at once and once again we found ourselves in the middle of heavy and concentrated fire. A clatter sounded just for'd of the bridge, and we saw a hole in the Perspex wind shield, and holes in the charthouse roof. Tony swung himself down to investigate and came back looking a trifle blasé. His chart was covered with shell fragments.

By now we were disengaging again, but could only claim a few hits on the target. Our inability to get close in to the enemy on these brightly lit nights worried Doug, lest it should be construed as lack of aggression. He would not agree to suicidal attacks when we had no surprise and when the gun power of every ship in the enemy convoy was considerably higher than ours. Bobby Allan supported him in this, and added this remark to the action report:

> "*The fact that these aggressively designed boats manned by remarkably aggressively minded officers and men cannot get to grips with the enemy is giving rise to a sense of frustration. . . .*
>
> "*In this case the one E-boat never made any effort to give battle, keeping very close station in the middle of the convoy throughout the action. . . .*"

It is probably true to say that the frustrations of this first bright moon period and the absence of Corny resulted in a feeling of depression which spread through the whole company of 658 very rapidly.

But Corny arrived back next day looking much fitter, and studied the shrapnel holes in the charthouse with some interest. He had already had a talk with Doug and was pleased with the S.O.'s opinion of 658 now he had travelled in her twice. We did another patrol, somehow feeling much more at ease with the skipper in his usual place on the bridge; but on the return passage, we noticed severe vibrations down aft at speeds over 1,400 revs. Corny, the motor mechanic and I stood on the quarter deck while Tony stepped up the speed gradually from 1,200 to 2,200 revs, and the increase in "shudder" was considerable.

Back at Bastia, the Base staff came aboard and we took them out for trials. They shook their heads and stroked their chins, and decided we would have to be slipped for all the shafts and propellers to be checked.

"But where?" we asked.

They looked at each other.

"Well—we can't do it here or at Maddalena."

Corny shut one eye and studied the engineer officer with his most quizzical look. "Malta?" he suggested.

We left next day.

CHAPTER XIV

## VENI, VIDI, VICI—VADA!

THE passage to Malta was the most interesting and eventful we ever made. It began with the pleasant duty of carrying Captain Stevens and Commander Allan to Maddalena. Such was the regard we had for both of them that we thoroughly enjoyed their company, especially as they spent most of the trip on the bridge in spite of the very unpleasant sea.

When they had left us, at Maddalena, we reflected how fortunate we were in having men of their calibre and understanding "placed in authority over us". Since Captain Stevens had been appointed as Captain Coastal Forces Mediterranean (C.C.F.), in July 1943, the number of craft under his command had grown rapidly and their sphere of operations had widened greatly, so that to keep in touch with needs and conditions meant considerable travelling to the various Bases. He nevertheless insisted on visiting them in turn as often as possible, and was so much liked and respected that his visits were stimulating and genial occasions.

He always made a practice (so often neglected by senior officers) of showing interest in even the most junior officers, and knew many of our christian names. On his last visit to Bastia he had taken a Jeep party of junior officers (including Derrick and me) across the mountainous ridge of north Corsica and down to the picturesque west-coast village of St. Florent. In this way, he had provided both relaxation and an opportunity for getting to know us better.

Bobby Allan, too, was universally popular, and we had all been delighted when C.C.F. had brought the news that he had been awarded the O.B.E. in the latest list of decorations.

This time we were routed to Malta (after a little persuasion) via Ischia where there was an ML Base in operation. Ischia is a picturesque island—a twin to Capri—in the Bay of Naples; for us it had few attractions other than its natural beauty, but it did not take Corny long to arrange for us to move over to Naples for the day to collect supplies.

Naples was now in full swing as a big fleet centre, so "supplies" covered almost everything.

We split up and got to work. Corny made the Naval Stores his target, and arrived there with a list covering two long pages which the three of us had carefully prepared. On it was included everything we needed badly to keep 658 clean and efficient—from drums of paint to cleaning rags and from rope to extinguisher refills—all of which we normally found difficult to obtain in sufficient quantity. And we ordered on a flotilla scale. Naturally the supply petty officer's eyes went up when he saw the list; but Corny's persuasive tongue and the sad tale of our isolated flotilla in the wilds of Corsica did the trick. It needed the whole duty watch to carry the stores back on board, and there they were carefully stowed away in the bilges for distribution to the flotilla on our return.

At the NAAFI I was meeting with an even more popular success. Since we had delivered the January supplies of gin at Maddalena six weeks before, no reinforcements of hard liquor had arrived in Bastia at all, and our embarrassment at being unable to entertain our American friends had become acute, especially in view of the fact that their mess resembled the cocktail bar at the Waldorf Astoria in its variety, and their hospitality was traditionally open-handed.

I had therefore come to Naples well prepared. I had a document signed by the Senior Officer, 56th MTB/MGB Flotilla, and stamped with his official stamp, certifying that "not one boat in the flotilla had received a spirits ration in February, and that Sub-Lieutenant L. C. Reynolds R.N.V.R. was fully authorized to collect one bottle for each of the following officers:

Lt.-Cdr. J. D. Maitland R.C.N.V.R.

Lieutenant C. Burke R.C.N.V.R. . . ."

and so on, with every boat and every officer listed.

All this was extremely honest and true, although it is doubtful whether we would have persuaded any other Base but Naples to meet the order. But this was a large Base, and they were not used to MGB Flotillas. Perhaps it was just as well.

I walked out of NAAFI with three grinning matelots beside me trundling a barrow loaded high. Their expressions had nothing to do with the thirty-six bottles of gin which for me were the major success of the morning; what was much more important for them was the sight of crate after crate of beer—the first ration I had been able to get for them since Christmas.

The rest of the load was made up with cigarettes (thousands of them, at sixpence for twenty!), "nutty" (to sailors all chocolate is "nutty"), soap, toothpaste, and in fact all the luxury items we could not get from any other source. The messdeck was a cheerful place that evening. Three bottles of beer for each man—chicken-feed really—but so rare that every drop of it was appreciated like champagne.

In all sincerity we did not wish to be away from Bastia any longer than we could help, so next day we pressed on towards Malta. As we left Ischia, Corny looked meditatively at the outline of the Isle of Capri nearby, and sent for the motor mechanic.

Since the time when our boats had taken a major part in accepting the surrender of the island at the time of Salerno, Capri had become a leave centre for the American forces, and British personnel were not normally admitted. It seemed a pity to be so close to this renowned beauty spot and to be denied a close view of it. Besides we ought to check up on the stories 663 had spun of the wonderful scenery ashore.

Our course southward led, with a little licence, very close to the entrance of the harbour. Strangely enough, when we were only a few hundred yards short of it, each engine began to cough, peter out, restart, and generally misbehave itself in a very alarming, noisy fashion. Corny immediately rang down "cut wing engines", told Tony to hoist "Harry Two" and exclaimed "Hell, Rover—we'll have to put into Capri to see what's wrong with these damned engines. Get the harbour parties fallen in!"

With faces kept as straight as possible, we crept into the harbour and secured alongside the wall astern of an American destroyer. A U.S.N. port official came puffing along the quayside and shouted up at Corny.

"Say Lootenant—you can't stay here. What's the matter with your boat?"

Corny jumped down beside him, saluted, and said, "Lieutenant Cornelius Burke of the Royal Canadian Naval Volunteer Reserve, sir. Glad to meet you. I'm afraid we've got bad engine trouble, and my motor mechanic tells me we'll need three hours to put it right. I presume my men can snatch the chance to have a look at your lovely island? They're so often at sea they don't get much shore leave!"

The American looked suspicious, but his eye had spotted our row of swastikas—one for each aircraft destroyed and every ship we had sunk. It looked impressive and he softened.

"I guess that'll be all right then, Lootenant. But please be out of here before noon or I'll have my Chief after me!"

Within five minutes the first watch was on its way ashore already clad in their best uniforms and out to make an impression.

Corny and I also made the most of our chance, and just had time to ride up the funicular railway to look round the upper town. Each watch had an hour ashore, and at 1130 we sailed again, the crew happy and loaded with souvenirs, and an opportunity not wasted. No wonder the men would do anything for Corny!

We ploughed southward through troubled seas, and as night fell, a red glow appeared on the horizon right ahead. At first we thought it was a ship on fire, but when after two hours it was still on the horizon and burning brightly we realized our mistake. It was the volcanic island of Stromboli, which is in almost constant eruption, pouring red-hot lava down its northern side.

When we passed a mile off the turbulent volcano at 2200, every member of the crew was on deck to watch it. Sailors are normally fascinated by natural phenomena: after all, they live very close to nature and have every reason to respect the might of the sea and the wind.

We were in Malta for sixteen days, and spent twelve of them in the famous Number One dock getting our shafts right. Corny had to spend several days in hospital again, and I had the interesting task of taking the boat into dock, which I rather enjoyed. Once again we made the most of our dockyard visit, and emerged with many small details improved. One great achievement was to have new brass strips in place of the dull metal round the deck boards on the messdeck and in the galley flat (outside the wardroom). When they were polished, the appearance of the boat below decks was more like a luxury yacht than an MGB, and it all helped the pride we felt in our boat.

While we were in dock, though, we had our first major changes in crew. First Roberts the coxswain left to return to England for the torpedo coxswains' course, which would lead to an appointment to bigger ships. With him went Gunning, also for promotion. The crew knew that Corny was always willing to recommend his men for higher rating if they were worth it, even if it meant weakening the team for the time being. Some C.O.s did not go to the trouble of helping their ratings to the same extent, and this again led those on 658 to tell their pals over a beer ashore that they had the best skipper in Coastal Forces. They weren't far out.

Our new coxswain was named Hodges, and was a very different type from Roberts. He was fresh from England, where he had been in a very famous flotilla of British Power Boat (short) MGBs. At first both the crew and officers found his oft-repeated yarns beginning, "In my last boat . . ." very wearing; but he was a cheerful, irrepressible fellow and, although strict, was very popular with the crew. He soon settled down and did his difficult job very well.

We returned to Maddalena via Naples and Ischia once again, and I decided to "try it on" with NAAFI once more. It was now well into March, so they *might* be kind and repeat the spirit ration. After all, they weren't to know that we had not been able to deliver the first batch yet! They must have liked my face, or had a healthy respect for Coastal Forces, because I had no difficulty and once again returned triumphantly with three crates of gold dust.

When we arrived at Maddalena, we found the base buzzing with expectancy. After all our troubles during the last moon period, when we had not been able to get close enough to attack the large F-lighter convoys, S.O.I.S. and Commander Allan had been hard at work devising a new form of attack, which was being tried out for the first time that night.

"Operation Gun" consisted of a patrol in force by a large number of Coastal Force craft, with Commander Allan himself in overall command aboard a PT to act as radar ship, and with three LCGs (the ships mentioned previously, having two 4·7-inch guns manned by Royal Marines).

The general plan was that scouting forces (three units of two or three PTs) were sent to patrol in the north, south, and central areas. If they got any definite radar contacts, they reported by R/T to the "Admiral" (Bobby), and stalked the target reporting frequently. He then moved his LCGs and an escorting force of Dogs into an attacking position and, when ready, got to work.

As a plan it was fraught with great possibilities. Would it work? The next morning we had our answer. A signal arrived from Bastia reporting that operation "Gun" had been a great success, and that a complete convoy of six F-lighters had been sunk! Apparently the whole thing had worked like clockwork. A convoy had appeared at just the right time, Bobby had skilfully plotted his force into position, the leading LCG had fired star-shells, and then it had almost been a question of target practice. The gunnery of the Marines had been incredible; they only needed one sighting salvo, and in some cases they hit with their first shell after shifting target. The F-lighters did not seem to know what had hit them. They fired up at the flares, and obviously thought they were being attacked by aircraft, but the LCGs were using flashless ammunition, and at three miles were not seen.

The whole conduct of this operation, as well as its original conception and planning, was by Bobby Allan—and this brilliance explains why he was so respected by all under him.

Our arrival back at Bastia next morning was greeted with great jubilation. It took us a whole forenoon to distribute around the flotilla all the liquor, chocolate, cigarettes and so on that we had brought. We had also carried several bags of mail. Altogether, by providing all these good things on a far higher scale than was expected, we just about managed to counter the chipping that came our way for skulking in Malta. Secretly we were glad to hear that the dark moon period had seen few targets and only two minor actions, apart from the monumental "operation Gun" the night before.

We immediately began operating again, and after two quiet runs to Spezia and Piombino, we ran back into form with a hectic action.

Tim Bligh had arrived at Bastia with several boats of the 57th Flotilla, and Doug with most of 56th returned to Maddalena for a short rest and maintenance period. On April 7th, we sailed for the notorious San Vincenzo–Vada Rocks area, with Tim Bligh as S.O. in 662, 640 (Cam MacLachlan) and three PT boats. It was a bright moonlight night, and I for one was not very keen on the sort of suicide attack which might arise if we met one of those unpleasantly powerful convoys we had got involved with a month before.

However, within an hour our unit was depleted by the return of both 662 and one of the PTs to Bastia owing to engine trouble. Tim transferred to us and we were at once on our mettle to show him that he was lucky to be aboard 658, especially if any enemy ships were about.

We reached the patrol area and lay stopped eight miles off-shore owing to the extreme visibility in the bright moon. Almost at once, the leading PT reported a small radar contact close inshore, moving northward. 658 swung into action routine, and the old tension crept in. Corny and Tim went into the charthouse to study the chart, and when they returned, their plan was clear. The tactical position was very similar to that in our last action off Vada Rocks, but this time we had more room for manoeuvre.

"I"'s blinked astern, and we set off northward, to get ahead of the enemy and inshore of them just south of Vada Rocks. With such a brilliant moon, we could only hope for surprise if we could attack from close inshore. We crossed well ahead of the enemy, and successfully achieved the position we had hoped for.

Tim was anxious not to let the PTs get in the way if we had to attack with gunfire, so he ordered them to move astern of us. But when the target came in sight through our binoculars, it seemed to consist only of one large trawler and one E-boat. The range was three and a half miles at this first sighting and, while we closed, Tim decided that the trawler was large enough to attack with torpedoes. As MTB 640 and the two PTs spread to starboard to prepare their attacks, the two enemy ships suddenly altered course towards the shore and reduced speed. Obviously they had spotted us. We swung to port and tried to keep inshore of the enemy—but now we were only half a mile out, and the chart showed that this was a shelving coast.

Tim lifted the microphone to order the MTBs to fire, but before he could speak the loudspeaker clicked and we heard the PT skipper again. "Hallo, Tim. There's another convoy heading round the corner, coming southward from Vada Rocks. Looks like we've got to hurry."

Tim grimaced. "Roger! Carry out your torpedo attack as soon as you're ready."

Meanwhile, a white light began flashing the letter "P" at us from the E-boat. "Say, Tim, I reckon these jokers aren't sure about us yet, especially as there's this convoy coming southward. Shall we try a reply?"

Tim nodded. Corny picked up the lamp and flashed (purely arbitrarily) the letter "C". Immediately the E-boat returned the "C", so we handed back a "P" and this appeared to satisfy everybody. All the time the range was closing. They were playing into our hands.

It was our job to deal with the E-boat, leaving the others free for their torpedo attack. When we knew Cam had fired at the main target, we opened fire. The range was 150 yards. It seemed incredible when we thought that they had sighted us at nearly three miles!

The E-boat hardly replied to our fire. The pom-pom and three Oerlikons hit from the first salvo, and after only a few seconds it careered towards us, apparently out of control, blazing like a torch from end to end. It passed right under our stern, and the gunners soon ceased fire when they saw they were wasting ammunition on a stricken ship. The last we saw of that E-boat was over to the south-west, where

The author, Bastia, November 1943.

**Above**, in line ahead, leaving for patrol, and **below,** steering a straight course.

A/B Tom 'Nobby' Watt –
'Mr Reliable'.

**Below**, the ship's company
of 658 at 'stand easy'.

**Above**, 657's stern after mining.

**Below,** 658's twin Oerlikon.

**Above**, MGB 658 at Manfredonia, Italy.

**Below**, 658 alongside at Komiza, Vis (Dalmatia), August 1944. Note the typical schooner astern.

**Above**, the officers of MGB 658 at Ajaccio, May 1944. From left to right: the author Lt. C. Burke and Sub-Lt. C. A. M. Brydon. **Below**, after the battle. Elco MTB towing one of the flotilla back to Augusta after a patrol in the Straits of Messina.

**Above**, 658 looking from the 6-pounder, showing twin Oerlikon, single Oerlikon, ~~ra~~dar and twin Vickers. **Below**, E-boat surrendering off Ancona. 658 and Vosper ~~es~~corting.

**Above**, the engine room of a Dog-boat, looking for'd. **Below**, surrendered E-boats alongside at Ancona.

**Above left**, Lt. Cdr. Cornelius Burke DSC RCNVR; **above right**, Bill Last, P.O./M.M MGB 658, June 1943. **Below left**, Capt. Wuppermann, Senior Officer E-boats, Mediterranean, aboard 658. **Below right**, 'Mac', L/Seaman Maguire, 658's cheerful 'Killick', Malta, December 1943.

**Above**, the crew of MGB 658, Malta, March 1945.

**Below**, HMS *Gregale* seen from Hays Wharf.

'The Three Musketeers' – From left to right: Lt. T. E. Ladner DSC RCNVR; Lt. Cdr. J. D. Maitland DSC RCNVR and Lt. Cdr. C. Burke DSC RCNVR.

Victory! The E-boats surrender.

**Below**, "Peace at the last." A silent 6-pounder.

it lay stopped, on fire to the water-line, and (the most unkind cut of all) under fire from the trawler.

We shifted fire to the trawler, and on closer inspection changed our minds on what we should call it. It was more like a KT-ship[1] from its heavy armament, and was certainly pumping out an unpleasant variety of shells. But our 6-pounder had got its teeth in, and Howe was crashing round after round into the hull. Smoke was rising and spurts of flame began to show.

But suddenly the situation changed. We seemed to check way and begin to drag through water.

"Good God! We're aground!" Corny exclaimed.

At once a vision of the crew paddling Carley Floats right across to Corsica flashed into my mind: then I had a picture of the barbed-wire of a prisoner-of-war camp; but a glance over the side soon assured us. We were still under way, at least. But water was only pouring out of the port exhausts, so we were only running on two engines. Both the starboard engines had been put out of action by 20-mm. shells, and soon after the port inner also had to be cut, so our maximum speed was down to about 11 knots.

At once we disengaged to the northward, and came under heavy fire. We felt some shells hit us, but no one reported casualties, and we seemed to dodge all the 88-mm. bricks, anyway. A bit of cover was indicated.

"Get down aft and make smoke, Rover!" snapped Corny. I ran down the deck, slipping on empty cartridge cases and deafened by the blast of the twin Oerlikon firing over my head. When I arrived at the smoke apparatus I found the duty stoker there, waiting for the order. I shouted in his ear, and at once his gloved hands opened the valves, compressed air hissed into the container, and a thin jet of acid shot astern, turning into a dense white cloud of smoke as it touched the damp atmosphere.

I rushed back to the bridge. Over to starboard, Cam MacLachlan had fired his two torpedoes just before we had attacked the E-boat; but although his range was right and the approach steady, it soon became only too obvious that he had missed. He disengaged to the south-west, firing hard at the KT-ship (he too had changed his mind) and drawing some of the fire from us. The two PTs both fired their torpedoes very early and, finding they were unsuccessful, disappeared back to Bastia at high speed.

[1] KT-ship: a fast, well-armed transport of about 1,500 tons.

The situation as we withdrew behind our own smoke-screen was extremely ticklish. By now, KT-ship, shore batteries, and (we guessed) the south-bound convoy were all firing at us.

We used the old dodge of throwing overboard calcium flares to leave a blaze in the water at which the enemy could fire, and crept as inconspicuously as possible away, taking advantage of every whisp of smoke.

After a minute of this, with our fingers firmly crossed, there was a flash and the bridge was suddenly brilliantly lit. We sprang round, startled, and saw the ammunition pan of the port Vickers .303s burning fiercely. That pan held a 100 rounds, and there had obviously been a stoppage, and some cordite which had spilled out of a split cartridge was now ignited.

My mind reacted slowly. I was just reaching the conclusion that if I didn't act soon I might not be alive to do so, when Tony Brydon, standing nearest to the gun, jumped at it, and with his bare hands released the spring, plucked off the blazing pan and threw it overboard. The bullets were beginning to fly from it as he did so, but fortunately he was not hurt apart from burnt hands. Little was said at the time, but everyone on the bridge felt that if he had acted a second or two later it would have been too late for him and, indeed, probably for most of us.

But even when we had shaken off the attentions of the KT-ship and the batteries, and had enjoyed a first-class view of a three-cornered battle between these two parties and the south-bound convoy, our worries were not over.

We knew we had been hit several times, and I made a quick survey of bilges to check that we were not making water. There seemed no serious damage. Last soon had both port engines working, and we made 12 knots back to Bastia.

As we came alongside, the usual crowd was on the jetty to receive us, and we jumped down to chat there for a few moments, discussing the night's adventures.

Three minutes later, a rather scared quartermaster scampered up and stammered "Excuse me, sir, but I've an idea we're sinking!"

We all swung round and, sure enough, 658 was well down by the bows and already below the level of the jetty. Corny and I ran towards the boat and found the coxswain already organizing a bucket chain. The for'd bilges were full, and the messdeck floorboards awash already. For a few minutes it was touch and go. Relays worked feverishly at the hand pumps, more buckets were brought, and although the level dropped slightly the water still poured in. But where? The bilges had been dry under way—there was no hole there.

I suddenly had an idea. I sent for tools and began to unbolt the plate which gave access to the forepeak. We normally kept this closed, and so I had not been able to inspect it at sea. When the plate was removed, we could at once see the trouble. We had a hole bigger than a football just on the water-line. It was under the flare of the bows, so we had not been able to see it from the deck either. Apparently while we had been under way, the slight lift to the bows and the force of water flowing past the hole had prevented our shipping any water. When we had secured alongside, however, the hole was just at a level to enable water to enter, and as we settled so it poured in faster.

Everyone took a hand in that bucket chain. When our own crew flagged there were many willing volunteers from the Base staff and from the other boats to relieve them. They were a comic sight, and soon the drama left the situation and we began to see the funny side of it.

Arthur Francis sat with his legs dangling down the pom-pom loading hatch passing up bucket after bucket and giving a running commentary for the benefit of both those working below and those on deck.

"We 'ave just passed the three hundredth bucket . . . Alfy Tanner 'as stripped down to 'is swimming trunks and looks like a large goose-pimple. . . . Is it cold down there, Alfy? . . . Stand by below! The skipper's coming down, mind yer don't give him a shower. . . ."

The first outside help came from the American PT base. Always well-equipped mechanically, they brought round a large pump and gradually the water began to subside.

A little later, further relief arrived in the shape of a magnificently ancient fire engine shaped rather like Stephenson's Rocket and painted a vivid scarlet. It was the pride of the local fire brigade.

At the sight of this Francis could not restrain himself. He burst into song.

> "Fire down below,
> Fire down below.
> Pass a bucket of water, lads,
> There's fire down below."

As the hoses were coupled up, he shouted at the nearest Frenchman: "Eh, mate! We've got enough water down 'ere to last us for ever. Don't go and pour *more* down the 'atch."

And then an aside to the men below.

"Watch out down there! These Froggies are going to pump ship. I 'ope they know their manners."

In a very short while the bilges were pumped dry and two French divers were summoned. With the added incentive of a large tot of rum each, they were persuaded to put a large temporary tingle over the hole to save us from further embarrassment, in harbour at least.

That our reputation was firmly established by this time was confirmed by both Tim's report and Commander Allan's forwarding comment. Tim spoke highly of our gunners, and Bobby Allan remarked: "The gunnery was the high standard which has come to be expected of MGB 658. . . ."

## CHAPTER XV

## TEMPORARY COMMAND

NEXT day the Base medical officer sent Corny off again to Bighi Hospital at Malta to continue his treatment, and once more we were left leaderless. But at 1100 came the proudest moment of my life. A message came aboard asking me to go to see Commander Allan as soon as possible. I went straight away, and when I entered his office he stood up and came over to me. "Rover, would you like command of 658 while Corny's away? He wants you to have it."

I gasped and stammered: "Yes—of course, sir. But . . ."

"Then you are temporarily appointed, and you start by sailing to Maddalena tomorrow morning to get that hole and those engines of yours repaired. Good luck."

Before I realized it I was out of the office and walking, somewhat dazed, back to the boat. I broke the news to Tony, and—God bless him—he didn't seem either surprised or disturbed.

"Fine, Rover," he said. "I'll play so long as you don't chew *my* ears off at Captain's Rounds like Corny does yours!"

The voyage next day was very much routine, and one we had done many times before. But this time it gave me a great thrill, and I experienced all the weight of responsibility that a command entails. In fact I made the most of it.

As we only had two engines (and both of them were on the port side), our progress was slower and more ungainly than usual. But apart from this, as the sea began to get choppier and we ran into a stiff head sea, I worried a lot over the rather temporary tingle covering the large hole in our bows. Would it begin to give? I found myself drawn down into the forepeak to look at it twice, and was satisfied that it was not leaking; but if it buckled in the heavy seas, my first trip in command was going to be a very unpleasant one.

We had an incidental job to do on our passage south. I had been ordered to enter Porto Vecchio in the south of Corsica to pick up three "senior officers" and ferry them to Maddalena.

When we got alongside (without damaging either the boat or the jetty), our passengers turned out to be two Americans and a Frenchman, all colonels; one of the Yanks was the C.O. of a U.S.A.A.F. bomber squadron.

We headed out of the sheltered harbour at a fair speed, making the most of the smooth water. As we did so, the Air Force colonel told his companions—and everybody on the bridge—how he had travelled about Corsica by Jeep and train and plane—"and now here I am in an MTB. Gee, this is swell!"

We told him gently that 658 was a gunboat (and proud of it), and also that it would not be so "swell" when we turned south, nor in the Straits of Bonifacio, which were usually rough.

He guffawed and exclaimed: "Hell—I guess I've been bumped about enough in big kites to be able to stand a little bit of a sea in a boat!"

When we turned south, the wind had freshened even more, and once again I began to think about that tingle up for'd. We were pounding hard, and the bridge was getting wet; but although our other guests retired to the wardroom, the Air Force colonel still remained on the bridge, becoming quieter every minute.

I then played a very dirty trick on him. I pressed the W/T office buzzer and asked Sparks to get the cook to make some good strong "Ky" (ship's cocoa) to warm us up on the bridge. Ten minutes later Tubby Christon, our steward, came up with a trayful of cups and a jug of Ky that you could literally have stood a spoon in. It was greasy and strong and very sweet; in fact very sustaining when you were used to it. But when a cup was offered to the colonel, he muttered: "No, thank you," and turning to me said: "Cap'n—I think I'll go below if you'll excuse me." Christon escorted him below and showed him the heads.

An hour and a half later, when we were through the very stormy straits and threading our way through the islands in the approach to Maddalena, I went below to the wardroom to see how the passengers were faring. I was greeted with the unusual sight of every bunk raised and in use. The colonel, looking well and truly beaten, turned over restlessly and managed a wan smile.

"Say, Cap'n, I'm sure sorry, but I've filled your 'can' and don't know how to empty it!" We thought it was heroic of him to dispense with his pride and admit himself beaten, after his unfortunate forecast in the quiet of Porto Vecchio harbour.

I knew that Rear-Admiral Morse, who was Flag Officer Western Italy, was aboard the destroyer *Tumult* in Maddalena, but I had not bargained with a signal which ordered me to take our passengers straight alongside *Tumult* instead of berthing at C.F.B. as normal.

This was indeed a shock. I knew manoeuvring with only two port engines was going to be most trying, and with the gale at present blowing, it might be well-nigh impossible; it was hardly a suitable party-piece for me to demonstrate before an admiral on my first trip in command!

Nor did I manage more than a wan smile when I saw where *Tumult* was lying. The wind was howling exactly at right angles across her, so that it would send 658 racing away to leeward as soon as the way was off her.

Crossing my fingers, I decided on a bold approach, and taking a fine angle, I belted in towards *Tumult*, put 658's nose right up to her, and went astern at the last possible moment to take the way off. The bow-rope was swiftly passed, but it was now essential to get the after spring across to help pull the stern in. The second attempt with the heaving line was successful, but the seaman aboard *Tumult* took so long to carry it to a bollard and to begin hauling it in that all advantage was lost and the stern began to pay off at a tremendous rate.

I charged ahead again on the port outer with the wheel hard over, but as soon as I went astern to take the way off, the natural swing of the propeller thrust on the port side took the stern out again. Oh, for a starboard engine! It was no good.

"Cast off for'd—we'll come in again. And for Pete's sake get a move on with that spring next time!"

With a sigh of relief I saw a petty officer take the place of the seaman who had been so painfully slow. The second attempt proved immediately successful.

The officer-of-the-day aboard *Tumult* leaned over the side and yelled sympathetically :

"Bit of a bastard in this wind, eh?"

I couldn't agree more, but I shrugged my shoulders nonchalantly as if to indicate "Happens every day in Coastal Forces", and went to see our guests over the side.

Our repairs took nearly three weeks, and extended over Easter. We were given three new engines, and were the first Dog to try out the new floating dock which had just arrived at Maddalena. The bow was replanked, and by the end of three weeks we were as "tiddley" as we had been on leaving Malta last.

Operations had been going on successfully at Bastia during April, and the biggest event had been "Operation Newt", the second of Bobby Allan's LCG escapades. This time it was even more successful, and nine ships were destroyed, most of them laden F-lighters.

Corny rejoined us looking fitter than he had for a long time, and after one uneventful patrol came some interesting news. With 657 and 655, we were to go round the north of Corsica to Ajaccio for some hush-hush trials. Certainly it was a well-kept secret, as we had no idea what we were going to do until we arrived.

657 was carrying S.O.I.S. (Captain Dickinson) and Bobby Allan, and we regarded the trip in rather light-hearted fashion. We rounded Cap Corse in the early morning and, meeting a very severe line of squalls, decided to shelter for a while in the picturesque little harbour of Calvi. We could hardly have been closer to naval history than in this harbour. It was here that Nelson (who himself bore the title Senior Officer, Inshore Squadron, at one time) lost his eye in a landing-party action.

We soon discovered, when we got to Ajaccio, what we were required to do. We were given two assault landing craft (LCAs) each and asked to tow them at varying speeds. We tried our hand at three on one occasion, and nearly succeeded in swamping them. Naturally, we were very curious to know what would be the outcome of the trials we were doing, and made a number of guesses at the destination for the shipping which was collecting in Ajaccio. We knew the answers a month later, but until then the security was so good that none of us had any ideas based on solid fact.

We only stayed two days, however, and then moved south to Maddalena again, to find the base staff there enjoying the mother and father of all "flaps". We were ordered to take on board five weeks' provisions and extra ammunition, with such urgency that we began to think that something on the scale of Sicily was on the way.

But when we got back to Bastia again after sailing right round Corsica in a week, we found things running smoothly, with no apparent reason for any panic.

Then our hopes for something really big were built up when we were briefed for Bobby Allan's third LCG operation—called "Bash" this time. We were all prepared to see F-lighters pounded at long range by the stalwart Marines in the LCGs; but presumably because the enemy heard that 658 was in company for the first time, no targets at all were found on two successive nights. The LCGs, in their disappointment, lobbed starshell over the coastal channel to "startle a few rabbits", but all to no avail.

We had now gone six weeks without any contact with the enemy, and were beginning to wonder where the targets had been hiding. We found out the answer to this on 25th May when, with all six boats of the flotilla in company, we ran into a big convoy near San Vincenzo, all too adequately escorted by the flak trawlers and the F-lighter equivalent of our LCGs which, to put it mildly, had become our chief nuisances. Our own part in this action was marred by an unfortunate incident which could have been amusing in less severe circumstances, but was almost disastrous and taught us a lesson.

The target had just become visible from the bridge, and I was giving the necessary orders to the gunners over the loud hailer, when a continuous ring sounded on the buzzer from the engine-room. Under our code of signals, this could only mean "Help required immediately".

Corny snapped: "Off you go, Rover," and with my heart pounding, I dashed for the engine-room hatch, lifted it, and threw myself down the vertical ladder expecting scenes of fire, smoke, fumes and general confusion.

All was absolutely calm and normal, but there—only four feet from me—was the youngest stoker leaning nonchalantly against the bulkhead, his elbow neatly centred on the bridge buzzer as he read a magazine.

I thought of Corny's face when I left the bridge, and showered the culprit with a lurid flow of language before I started back again. As I emerged from the hatch, I realized we had opened fire and instinctively ducked as tracer floated over us from the enemy.

As soon as I could, I took over the gunnery control, but I had a very confused idea of the general situation, and after the brightness of the engine-room my eyes were unconditioned to the darkness. I was soon able to see that our gunners were scoring hits on one of the trawlers, and any amount of night blindness on my part could not have concealed the fact that much more tracer was coming our way than was either normal or pleasant.

I felt the faint thuds of small shells striking the hull, and waited with an anxious sinking feeling in my stomach for reports of damage or casualties. But none came. We discovered later that two shells had struck the for'd petrol space and had entered the wing tank which we had already filled with water. It seemed to disprove the old theory that shells never strike the same place twice.

655 had been badly hit, and her mast and all its rigging descended round the heads of those on the bridge. Pick and his Number One were both wounded, and the wheel was jammed in the wreckage. The navigating officer (Sub-Lieutenant "Kiwi" Clark-Hall) extricated the boat from its difficulties, and rejoined us shortly after. We had not managed to penetrate the escort, but each of the six boats claimed to have hit and damaged at least one target, so we felt it had not been a one-sided attack.

Next day a signal arrived from C.C.F. ordering Tim Bligh's flotilla (the 57th) round to the Adriatic. This meant saying an indefinite farewell to many of our friends, and especially, for me, to Gordon Surtees who had just left Tim to become Walter Blount's first lieutenant in 634. Gordon had been Norman Hughes' Pilot in the early days of the 20th MGB Flotilla, and had borne the brunt of the flotilla navigation since Tim had been appointed S.O. of the 57th, so his promotion was well overdue.

That evening we held a rather special party to celebrate this, and to say farewell to the 57th.

At this party, we founded an organization which had its effect on flotilla spirit in the months which followed; however lighthearted it was in conception, it made a more valuable contribution to our comradeship that we perhaps realized. We called ourselves the "Junior Dogs", and referred thereafter to all C.O.s as "Senior Dogs". The gap between C.O.s and their junior officers was a very natural one at this stage—in almost every case there was a difference of five to ten years in age; by now practically all the first lieutenants were the young pilots who had brought out the boats from home, and the new pilots had all arrived since Sicily.

We instituted at this party certain procedures and ceremonies for members of the club to follow. Whenever two members met socially in future they would be obliged to drink a toast to all other Junior Dogs—and do so in a certain formalized manner. It was a very gay evening and the first of many inspired by the excuse of the arrival or departure of a fellow Junior Dog.

The next day brought further cause for celebration. Corny came aboard during the morning, and found Tony and me studying the breech of the pom-pom, on which we had recently had an unusual stoppage. Silently he handed over a sheet of paper.

It was a memorandum from Captain, Coastal Forces and was headed:

*Honours and Awards.*

"*The King has been graciously pleased to approve awards to officers and men of the Mediterranean Station as shown on the following list . . .*"

My eye leapt down the page:

"AWARDS OF THE DISTINGUISHED SERVICE CROSS. Acting Lieutenant Commander J. D. Maitland R.C.N.V.R. Lieutenant C. Burke R.C.N.V.R. . . ."

That was enough to see for the moment. Tony and I, both very excited at our first contact with the business of awards, pumped Corny's arm and left him in no doubt of the sincerity of our pleasure. After all, he had undoubtedly earned it three times over already—at Sicily and in the Piombino Channel, quite apart from our series of actions in the past five months.

But Corny seemed very reserved in his feelings. He was obviously pleased, but mixed with his pleasure was a sense of discomfort. "You haven't finished yet—read on! It looks as though this batch is for the January hat-trick."

We read down the list. A/B Howe, our quiet, very reliable and accurate 6-pounder gunner, was awarded the Distinguished Service Medal, and Tommy Ladner, Herb. Pickard and Peter Barlow (who had been the three other C.O.s in that series of actions), with our motor mechanic Last and our pom-pom gunner Preston, were all mentioned in dispatches. There were also awards to members of the crews of all the other boats of the flotilla, so it looked as though their Lordships at the Admiralty had looked with favour on the events of January 21st, 22nd, and 23rd, 1944.

We soon found on talking it over that Corny was very sensitive about awards. He had seen a good deal of unpleasantness over them in his service in Coastal Forces at home, and was very anxious that the fine spirit in our flotilla should not be upset by them now. Already he and Doug felt that Tom Ladner deserved a "gong" every bit as much as they did. Tom had seen a considerable amount of action with Hichens at home, and had not been decorated apart from one "mention" for a

Channel Islands operation. Besides, 663 was an excellent boat which was maintained with relentless efficiency and probably had the best record for reliability in the flotilla. It always seemed ready for operations, and had hardly missed a patrol or action since the flotilla was formed.

But all doubts were forgotten when we celebrated our awards by a joint party with 663. That afternoon, after making sure that bad weather would definitely not allow us to be called out on patrol, the two boats were berthed alongside each other in a distant corner of Bastia harbour, and a magnificently spontaneous party and entertainment began.

Derrick and I had arranged for the crew's monthly ration of beer to be available, and also supplied several jars of the local vino, especially the general favourite "Cap Corse", a heady aperitif which was very popular. But the main part of the programme was a concert arranged by the two coxswains, conducted on the lines of a broadcast over the loud hailer. The turns were provided alternately by the men of 658 and 663.

Our Leading-Seaman Maguire (who left us the following week to become a coxswain in a 7th Flotilla short MTB, and later won the D.S.M. himself) was the star turn as a crooner. He was a great favourite on board, and soon there was a shout for him to sing "Begin the Beguine", which was his most popular piece. There was also a seaman from 663 who gave an excellent impersonation of Winston Churchill, his speech containing many topical allusions to the officers, men and activities of the two boats.

The flotilla was sent back to Maddalena for stores soon after this, and Corny was packed off to hospital, this time to Algiers, for more treatment. He was having a gruelling time with a kidney complaint, and should really have spent a month or more in bed; but he insisted on returning to the boat whenever he knew it was due for operations.

Once again I was temporarily in command, and after a few days I was faced with an awkward situation in dealing with defaulters. One of the crew, a young seaman of eighteen, had gone to sleep whilst on watch as quartermaster (the duty man on guard to see all was well throughout the night). Although this was a serious offence in the eyes of the Navy, we all knew that the lad wanted a shake-up more than anything else, and I was sure Corny would not want the case sent ashore to the C.O. of the Base. As a sub-lieutenant and officially only Number One, I could not deal with it myself, so I arranged for Peter Barlow, the C.O. of 659, to come aboard to take defaulters for me.

Peter was a very popular fellow, and had a very enjoyable "party piece" with which he frequently entertained us at wardroom parties; he would take off (and adapt with topical allusions) the style of the stammering comedian Oliver Wakefield, who never finished a sensible sentence.

Next morning all was prepared: the wardroom was converted to a courtroom by the removal of the table, and the coxswain stood by with the culprit in the wardroom flat. Peter came over, and I briefed him about the sleepy seaman, who was a rather foolish youngster but by no means a bad lad.

Peter nodded, and the coxswain brought in a very sheepish ordinary seaman. The charge was read, evidence heard, and the time came for Peter to pronounce the sentence. He fixed the seaman with a penetrating eye, and began sonorously: "N-n-n-ninety days cells . . ." There was a pause. The Coxswain's head jerked up, his face full of astonishment; Tony looked hard at me, and I looked at Peter; the miserable seaman, several shades paler, hung his head and presumably visualized a diet of bread and water. ". . . is what I *could* send you to!"

Peter's face remained expressionless, but Tony, the coxswain and I had the greatest difficulty in selecting suitable focus points for our eyes as Peter continued to harangue the hapless defaulter who had seen no humour in the perfectly timed hesitation. And although this became an oft-repeated and much enjoyed story in the wardrooms of the flotilla, the effect of Peter's lecture was salutary: we never had trouble with this youngster again. The amusement was strictly reserved for the less involved participants in that defaulters' session.

During our stay at Maddalena we lost Tony, who was appointed first lieutenant to Cam MacLachlan in 640. We had become such a team that his departure was a real blow: but Corny had strong views on opportunities for promotion, and felt he had to help Tony on his way up the ladder. It was eight months since he came aboard, and in that time we had had almost as many actions as uneventful patrols.

658's new Pilot was Mike Walker-Munro, a Scot and an Old Etonian. Mike had been "spare officer" in the flotilla for some time, and had been out with Doug on many operations in 657. He was a delightfully mannered young man, and was often the butt of good-humoured banter from the Canadians. He soon showed that this did not worry him, and retaliated cleverly by frequently and intentionally misquoting the more picturesque Canadian expressions.

When we returned to Bastia and operations, Corny was still not back from Algiers, and Doug took 658 out on two quiet patrols. He was free to do so because 657 had gone south to Bizerta to be fitted with S.O. radar from a PT boat at the American Base there. Apparently Doug had set his heart on obtaining one of these sets as soon as he had realized the enormous difference that efficient radar could make to our operations.

He had therefore worked hard on the PT boys at Bastia, and with their willing co-operation and especially that of Stan Barnes, their S.O., had come to a gentleman's agreement on the matter. The story goes that the only payment at this stage was one bottle of Scotch, which seemed to us lease-lend at its best. Later, many more British boats were fitted with this excellent apparatus, and presumably the financial aspect was sorted out.

In any case, this was one of the best examples of the unselfish co-operation which marked our friendship with the United States Navy.

I was sun-bathing on the upper deck one afternoon, stretched out on a mattress and with only a towel round my middle, when Derrick came aboard.

"Have you heard the news, Rover?"

"What news?"

"The Allies have invaded France at Normandy. They have got ashore and it looks as though they are established!"

I whistled. "That must be some party. Is this the beginning of the end, d'you think?"

CHAPTER XVI

## "FOR WHAT WE ARE ABOUT TO RECEIVE . . . "

BUT another D-Day was soon to occupy our minds and leave thoughts of Normandy in the background.

On the morning of the 15th June the veil was drawn aside from the secrecy which had been shrouding the tremendous activity of the past few weeks. Alongside the jetty at C.F.B. was a quaint craft, rather like a Noah's Ark, which had been found adrift north of Cap Corse one morning a few weeks before. She had presumably gone adrift from a tow or mooring off the South of France, but she was brought into Bastia, christened "The Ark" and more officially H.M.S. *Dickinson* (after S.O.I.S.). She had been converted into a very useful "NAAFI" boat, but for a few days she was turned into something with a more serious purpose.

It was to the Ark that officers of the flotilla were summoned, and as we entered her large messdeck we found a distinguished company of senior officers standing beside a large chart of the particular part of the enemy coast (i.e. Elba and the nearby mainland) which we regarded with almost proprietary pride.

So this was it! We were addressed by Captain Errol Turner R.N. who introduced himself as S.N.O.L. (Senior Naval Officer Landings), and he briefly sketched for us Operation Brassard, the aim of which was to attack and occupy Elba. With the Eighth Army now speeding north from Rome, the strategic value of holding Elba was immense, and would assist the advance to Florence and Leghorn considerably. An important and unusual feature of this landing was that although the Royal Navy was to provide the craft and escorts, the actual landing forces were to be Free French, carrying out their first major commission in Europe. Their leader was a hitherto little-known general named Lattre de Tassigny, who was later to achieve great fame and become France's first military man both in the war and in her post-war troubles.

The general plan was that a large force of French infantry were to be put ashore (a high proportion of colonial troops, including the fearsome Goums from Morocco, were to be used) by LCIs, and LCAs which would be towed by MLs. A large minesweeping force of MLs was to precede the invasion fleet, and LCTs would follow in with tanks and heavier guns when the beachhead was established. For support, the rocket LCTs and the LCGs, with the River Gunboats would also be used. Our task was to provide close escort for the convoy, and cover for the anchorage.

We now understood all our towing exercises at Ajaccio the previous month, which had been solely designed to check whether, in emergencies, we should be able to tow comfortably. It did not prove necessary, as each LCI and ML took along two LCAs.

The landings were scheduled for 0400 on the 17th June, and the two days before saw the arrival at Bastia of an armada of coastal craft and landing craft of every type.

On the morning of D-1 (we were due to slip at 1630) I had a summons to see Bobby Allan in the Base, and there he told me that although he thought I was competent to take 658 to sea, he simply could not give me the responsibility of a first operation on such an occasion in view of my youth, and he was therefore going to send Lt.-Cdr. W. O. J. Bate, the Number One of the Base, in command. He made it clear, however, that for all intents and purposes I should be doing all the donkey work, as "Woj" did not know our routine in any way, and would be relying on me throughout. Woj himself confirmed this when he came aboard that afternoon and was most helpful in easing a slightly awkward situation.

However, Woj was still in the Base and I was still very much a working Number One, when I was startled, at about noon, to see a group of senior officers approaching, escorting with it a gaggle of be-ribboned and red-tabbed Army officers, wearing those high stove-pipe hats that hitherto we had only seen in pictures of General de Gaulle. It was obviously a visitation, and it was obviously bound for us!

Fortunately the quartermaster was smartly dressed in whites (our infallible rule) and so (to a reasonable extent, but not so infallibly) was I, and we were able to make a decent show of piping this high-priced selection aboard. Captain Dickinson presented me to General Lattre de Tassigny, and asked me if we would be good enough to take him out on a tour of inspection of his troops, now all embarked in landing craft and anchored ready for the start in Bastia Bay. Feeling sure we had been selected for our reputation as a "tiddly ship" (and hoping it was not simply because we had been the only boat alongside in a single berth) my breast swelled with pride as, with these distinguished passengers on our bridge, we sped out to the anchorage. The crew reacted marvellously too; in no time they appeared smartly turned-out in spite of the fact that a few minutes before they had been working ship in overalls and dirty khaki. In fact, they put on an air of nonchalance as though generals were an everyday assignment.

Captain Dickinson whispered to me that the general would want to address his troops—how was our loud hailer? With this, I went hot and cold all over. Our loud hailer was the most temperamental creature on board and received more care and loving attention from A/B Smith the wireman than any other piece of apparatus. On its day it was a first-class worker; but when in a bad mood it could screech and howl like a banshee and distort every word spoken into it beyond recognition.

I had, after long experience as gunnery officer, worked out a routine in dealing with these tantrums so that now, as an efficient nurse can with a single glance control a difficult child, I was able to guarantee at least 95 per cent success if I used a carefully timed plan. Would this be possible? I could not tell. Offering a silent prayer, I warmed up the set, blew into it to produce that so familiar blast and crackle which indicated success, and quickly switched it off again.

As we passed each ship, the general stood high up on our searchlight platform (it no longer held a searchlight) and was cheered by his troops. Eventually we stopped in a central position and, switching on the microphone, I handed it to the general. One of my techniques was to "coo" into it so that I practically took it by surprise, and this had to be done across the face of the mike and not directly into it.

Imagine my horror when, after standing impressively still and silent for several seconds (each one bringing nearer that screech I so much dreaded), the general drew the mike to his lips and began to pour voluble and highly accentuated French into it. I saw Smith looking at me (I must have turned pale) but nothing untoward happened. All went well. Finally, after hurling some battle cry (of the same type as "God for Harry, England and St. George" on a somewhat similar, if reversed, occasion) into the bewildered microphone, he handed it down to me with a flourish. Before I could switch off, the little beast had its last laugh. There was an almighty screech at an ear-piercing pitch which was cut off as if strangled as my fingers found the switch.

I patted it affectionately, put it in its holder, and turned to invite our visitors to our wardroom for the return to harbour.

All this preliminary excitement was forgotten when we slipped at 1630 to set off on the long, roundabout approach to Elba. It was well before sunset, and in fact one group had set out two hours earlier. Elba, as ever, stood out sharply against a clear eastern sky, and looked far less than 30 miles away. The convoy was an amazing sight, quite one of the most ungainly that could ever have sailed. The LCI in itself is a peculiarly shaped vessel, and with two LCAs dragging astern like recalcitrant puppies on long leads, its beauty was in no way enhanced.

As night fell and we turned in on the final course, the vague darkness gave the mass of shipping an eerie aspect. It was so unusual to be one of dozens of craft. We had our scares, too. The minesweepers were clearing a half-mile-wide channel ahead of the convoy and any mines they cut were naturally bobbing about in the fairway. Mines which are adrift are theoretically rendered automatically safe; but in practice the safety device is often jammed by corrosion. In any case no one would ever want to try out the theory! So after sighting one mine about 20 yards on the starboard beam, we posted a lookout lying right in the bows and bent our knees ready for the shook. After ten minutes of this strain, the lookout turned and screamed out: "Mine right ahead—twenty yards!"

There was no time for an order. Hodges, our new coxswain, was very quick and spun the wheel to starboard. As soon as he had, I yelled: "Now midships!" Once again he reacted immediately and spun it back again. I dashed to the port side of the bridge, and there, so close that I could not see all of it from the bridge, was the drifting mine swirling down the port side with great ugly horns bumping down the side.

I swore softly and thanked my lucky stars that I had remembered (in the heat of the moment) that the swinging stern would surely have caught the mine had we kept turning away. Woj was in the chart-house at the time poring over the chart and therefore did not suffer the same agonies of apprehension. In fact, it was fairly soon obvious that Woj (who had been ashore for many months) could see very little through his binoculars on a dark night. The bulk of the watch-keeping therefore fell to Mike and me, although in this "invasion party" there was no question of any of us getting any sleep.

By 0200 all the craft were in position, and we were startled to see some tracer flying away over to the eastward at the other end of Elba. We had some nasty moments thinking that the whole plot was discovered, but fortunately the firing soon petered out and all was quiet. We learned afterwards that two PT boats had run into F-lighters evacuating the Pianosa garrison.

At 0350 the three rocket ships were to open fire. They were LCTs carrying bank after bank of rockets which were detonated electrically from the bridge, and which were reputed to paralyse completely all life within the sectors at which they were aimed. I checked my watch, focused my glasses, and waited.

Suddenly three simultaneous pink flashes lit the sky, and the first salvos streaked upward. My glasses were trained on the centre one, but for an instant I saw nothing, the glare was so intense. A sheet of flame enveloped the hull. Hundreds of rockets soared towards the beach. Seconds later came the "sssswsh" and roar of the rockets detonating. It was a noise like a thousand giant Chinese crackers.

Before we could recover from our astonishment at the frightening violence of the first salvos, the second batch were on their way. 4,000 rockets were fired in four minutes.

"What price Stromboli?" I breathed, fascinated. "You wouldn't think anyone could be alive after all that flash—and the back-blast must be colossal! Still, I'd rather be on board firing them than be on the beach watching them land!"

We could not see them, but we knew the LCAs were moving in to the shore directly after the first rockets. And at once we could see that *this* landing was not going to be unopposed. Already tracer swung out from the shore and criss-crossed over the approaches. The flashes of big guns lit the night in momentary brilliance.

"Good God, Rover," said Woj, aghast, "they must have known we were coming. Just look at that flak!"

Our R/T was tuned in to a special invasion wavelength. Almost immediately we heard reports from the beach liaison officers and instructions from S.N.O.L., which helped us to piece the progress of the action together.

"More smoke off Red beach, please. . . . All my troops ashore. . . . Three of my LCAs badly hit. . . ."

The LCIs followed the LCAs in, and although dense smoke was now blotting out even the gunfire from our vision, their R/T reports sounded grim.

"Amber beach impossible. . . . Heavy fire from village. . . . One craft sunk, all others hit. . . . Beached but had to withdraw. . . . Suggest we try alternative landing on Green beach. . . . Amber and Red beaches both covered by cross-fire from batteries. . . ."

As daylight came, we heard S.N.O.L. ordering the LCIs and the next wave of LCTs in to land at Green beach.

Now we could see something of our bombarding forces. For us, the whole thing was frustrating. All we could do, unless aircraft or enemy ships appeared, was to sit tight in our privileged grandstand four miles off-shore, and applaud the efforts of the gallant men and ships doing the real work. We were immune—or so we thought.

But as soon as the daylight brightened and our position was spotted from the shore, the familiar and ever awesome sound of heavy shells arriving shook us suddenly out of our security. This was no place to stay. We started up with a crash of exhausts and followed Doug a little further out. I spotted the position of the battery by the flash, and was watching it intently through my binoculars when Mike pulled my arm.

"Look, Rover—the LCG is going in to try to knock it out."

I lowered my glasses and looked round. The frail landing craft—one of the ugly ducklings of the fleet—was steaming straight for the point which housed the battery. Defiantly, her for'd 4.7-inch gun belched flame and smoke as she fired her first sighting shot. In reply, a flash came from the battery and the bows of the LCG lifted as a near miss raised a waterspout just ahead of her. She did not flinch, but went steadily on. It was the tournament lists of the Middle Ages all over again: single combat, with the rest of the contestants eagerly looking on, waiting their turn.

For fifteen minutes LCG 8 steamed directly towards the battery, her ensign streaming proudly and her guns firing continually. I trained my glasses on the battery once more, and acted as unofficial spotter.

"Good shot, Number 8! That one exploded right by the gun flashes. . . . And another, slightly left and high. . . . Now she's shifted a hefty chunk of rock! . . ."

Salvo after salvo crashed into the sea around the LCG, but she seemed to ignore them and sailed relentlessly on. Surely she could not risk so much and get away with it! But she did. Just before we were ordered away to Bastia, a cheer went up from a group of our seamen who had been spotting the fall of shot round the battery.

"She's got it, sir—right bang on the nose!" True enough that battery was destroyed and did not fire again. It had been a near thing, but the LCG had put up a stirring display of courage and accurate gunnery.

We escorted a batch of empty landing craft back to Bastia, fuelled, and prepared to leave again. We were to patrol in the Piombino Channel to intercept any ships trying to evacuate men or to bring reinforcements to the island.

When the time came to sail, the weather had closed down and we were faced with a choppy sea, heavy rain and low visibility. Dark low clouds scudded rapidly across the sky, and eerie flashes of lightning lit the surface occasionally and showed up the dirtiness of the night. I felt restless and unsettled, and somehow I had a premonition that something was going to happen. More than anything, I missed Corny. And I was not the only one on board who felt the same.

There were four boats in the unit: Doug was leading in Pick's boat (655), and 633 with a new skipper was second in line; while Tom (663) lay third to allow the two MTBs to be together, leaving 658 as "Tail Arse Charlie", a very unusual position for us.

By 0100 we had passed along the south coast of Elba, and were searching up the east coast, when Doug's familiar voice came over the R/T.

"Hallo, Dogs, this is Wimpey. Possible targets close inshore. Tommy, stand by to light. Will probably attack with torpedoes first."

Once again the old tension spread. On went tin hats. The gunners twirled their turrets to check the power. The engine-room staff laid out their emergency repair set. The coxswain took over the wheel and Peacock, the new leading seaman, moved to the starboard Vickers guns. A/B Smith checked the loud hailer for me, and stepped back to the port wing of the bridge. 658 was all set.

Woj was self-possessed (he was an experienced Coastal Force C.O.), but obviously worried about his difficulty in penetrating the inky blackness of the night. Mike dodged down to the charthouse to check our distance off shore, and as he did so the R/T crackled again.

"Hallo, Steve. Flag Four![1] Pick is just firing."

In the silence which followed I heard the "w-w-w-whoosh" of the torpedoes leaving the tubes. I jerked my glasses up, and focused them on the dim shapes just visible inshore. "Damn! they're turning!"

[1] Flag 4: Fire torpedoes.

"Hallo, Tommy, let's have some light."

Without any pause came the thump-thump of 663's pom-pom, and the little groups of tiny flares lit the coast in their ghostly unreal glow.

"Hell! there's something pretty big there, Woj. Destroyer, I think." As I said it, my finger was pushing the open-fire buzzer.

The flotilla swung into line ahead and turned to port, every gun blazing but with the pattern of the tracer complicated into intricate designs as it crossed the fire from the destroyer's guns. I climbed up on the step I used to give me extra height and quickly checked each gun. All were firing steadily. In return more and heavier shells were coming our way. I didn't like being last in line!

There was no time to analyse the situation (there never is when the boats are moving fast on different bearings), but it had just flashed through my mind that the fish must have missed when there was an explosion from inshore. This hardly interested me as at the same time my glasses told me that the destroyer was really moving fast now and getting alarmingly close.

I yelled out: "He's trying to ram us, I think!" Every starboard gun poured out its hail as the range closed, and as I put down the glasses I had a vivid picture of this long, low craft with the stream-lined funnel characteristic of Italian destroyers hurtling across our stern. Woj was desperately keeping station on 663, and I was concerned only with gunnery—we could do nothing to prevent him "crossing our T in reverse". When he was right astern only our 6-pounder could fire, whereas all his guns were firing on the beam with a maximum broadside. And he was very close—so close that he didn't go by "all in one piece." I watched the bows, then the for'd turret, then the bridge and the funnel slide past one after the other.

"For what we are about to receive!" I thought. And then it happened. A spout of tracer came ripping along the decks. The bridge filled with noise and light. My mind was utterly confused: no noise now, just complete bewilderment. I found myself on the deck, and struggled to my feet, trying hard to think straight.

I still held the loud-hailer mike in my hand and I looked at it stupidly. I had felt a heavy blow on my back, and when I put my hand to my face, which was stinging, it came away wet and sticky.

I looked round the bridge. There was at last some other movement. "Thank God," I thought, "they're not all dead!" Hodges the coxswain was kneeling by the wheel, still clutching it and trying to turn it. "I can't move the wheel—it's jammed." He said the words in a matter-of-fact way, addressing no one in particular but making a simple, automatic report.

I called out: "Are you all right, Woj?" and a faint voice answered. "I think I've got it in the leg, Rover—can you fix the wheel?"

At last I realized what was wrong. One of the shells had brought down the wireless aerials and recognition lights from the mast and they were festooned round the wheel and jamming it. I pulled these away and shouted for Mike. He was already beside me. At the time of the burst he had been in the charthouse, but he was rapidly taking in the situation.

"What's the course, Mike?" I had no idea of the course we had been steering, and could see no other boats without my glasses. Even the destroyer was no longer visible, but I didn't grumble about that. I looked at the compass and saw that we were swinging wildly. How long had we been out of control? Where were we heading for? In no time Mike gave me the course to steer, and I hastily scanned the blackness ahead for signs of the other boats.

I could see nothing. My heart sank. But suddenly the loudspeaker spoke.

"Hallo, Woj, this is Tommy. Are you all right?"

What a difference that voice made. We still had to find Tom, but he was there and he was looking for us. We were no longer on our own, but restored miraculously to membership of a group.

I picked up the R/T microphone, pressed it, and replied. "Hallo, Tommy, this is Rover. Yes, I think so. We're a bit shaken but would like to pick you up. Over."

Back he came immediately. "I am making smoke and I can see you. Can you see me now?"

I picked out a smudge of white against the depth of the night's blackness and sighed with relief.

"O.K., Tommy. I can see you now; will rejoin fast." I rang up full speed (2,400 revs.) on the indicator and felt the boat surge forward. Simultaneously, a starshell appeared over our heads and we were bathed in golden light. Was this the destroyer looking for its damaged prey?

In the eerie light of the flare, I took my first real look round the bridge. Woj, the coxswain and the killick were all sitting or lying on the deck and were all wounded. Over in the port wing of the bridge—

a yard behind me as I stood in the gunnery-control position—was a lifeless heap that had been Smith. Little Nobby Watt from Y gun appeared at the back of the bridge.

"I'm afraid Jameson's dead, sir; and McEwen and Orme at X gun are both wounded."

"Have a look at them, Mike—I'll try to sort out the bridge when we've got to the others." We were fast overhauling 663, so I slowed down, got into station and handed over the wheel to an A/B. Woj had a mass of shrapnel in the thigh and back; the coxswain's legs were peppered, and Peacock's face was bleeding.

I had them helped below and did what I could for them in the charthouse. While I sorted out bandages, I remembered the thud on my back, the stinging on my face, and the blood. Surely I must have been wounded: and yet I was not even in pain.

On the upper deck aft, Mike was having a more gruelling time. Jameson was undoubtedly dead. A 20-mm. shell had hit him in the back. McEwan (a cheerful little orphan from Liverpool) had his foot hanging by a slender thread from a shattered ankle. Mike could see no way of dressing the wound as it was, and stifling his nausea he went below for a razor, amputated the foot, wrapped it in a towel and bound up the stump.

McEwan was conscious all this time, and extremely calm: he saw Mike throw his gruesome parcel overboard and remarked: "That was my foot, wasn't it, sir?" His pal Orme was also in a bad way, and we could not safely move either of them. Nobby Watt volunteered to look after them, and spent the whole four hours of our return to Bastia supporting and caring for them, and releasing the tourniquet on McEwan's leg every twenty minutes. He was magnificent.

Everything still seemed against us. The wind rose and a nasty sea was running, with spray soaking everyone on deck. We wrapped the wounded in blankets and tarpaulins and prayed for the weather to ease up.

Those four hours were nightmarish. As soon as it was light enough I made myself look at Smithy. He could not have suffered at all. He must have been hit by two or three shells at once. The plywood door at the back of the bridge was splintered and holed, and as I studied it the truth suddenly dawned on me. No wonder I was not in pain. It was Smithy's blood over my face and bespattered over my "mae west"—and the thuds on my back had almost certainly been splinters from the bridge structure. In giving his life, Smithy had unquestionably saved mine. He had been a fine shipmate, and the most popular rating on board. He was sadly missed.

I covered him with a flag from the flag locker (which was also in splinters), and set about checking the damage to the boat. The engines had not suffered at all, as the main damage had come from the devastating burst of 20-mm. which had ripped in from astern. There were holes everywhere in the superstructure, but a hasty inspection of the tiller flat revealed no under-water damage there.

We limped slowly back through the mounting seas until at last the ancient walls of Bastia came into view. On the quayside, waiting patiently for our arrival, was the Base Surgeon with two ambulances. He jumped aboard even before the lines were secured, and I led him to McEwan and Orme. In no time his stretcher-bearers had got them into the ambulance and away, and he quickly despatched Woj, the coxswain and Peacock after them.

But I was most profoundly grateful for his help in removing the bodies. I felt I could not face the job after the strain of the past seven hours. There had been five of us on the bridge when the shells hit; I was the only one unhurt. It was a sobering thought.

When Derrick, Tom and Doug came aboard to offer their sympathy and assistance, I heard that 655 had also been hit badly, and suffered several casualties. But not all the entries were on the debit side. At least one ship—probably a loaded F-lighter—had been sunk by torpedo.

Intelligence later confirmed that our action interrupted the only major attempt at evacuation and that it was not repeated. Our tactical duty had therefore been accomplished.

Corny returned from hospital later in the day, and took our sad news very much to heart. He felt very keenly that on this occasion he had not shared our misfortune, whereas when he was in command we had always had good luck. He was left with a feeling of owing us a debt: but we did not feel that way, and only reflected on Woj's bad luck in being wounded when only a temporary C.O.

Two days after the action we held the funeral of the three ratings who had been killed. Doug asked me to make all the arrangements, and we performed the full ceremonial for the first time. It was the only formal naval funeral I ever attended, and although I was in charge of the firing party and all the preliminaries, I was deeply impressed.

Almost the whole Base embarked in the boats of the flotilla, and aboard 658 we carried Captain Dickinson, Commander Allan and representatives of every boat.

The firing party was drawn from 658 and 655—shipmates of the dead men—and they drilled in the morning to perfect their movements. Bobby Allan took the service and it was intensely moving. As the volleys rang out, the flag-draped bodies were slipped into the sea. There followed two minutes of absolute silence.

The return into Bastia was very slow and very dignified. Ensigns flew at half-mast, and the silence spread and remained, cloaking the Base in its folds. Death had touched more than three men: their sacrifice made clearer the purpose and deeper the resolve of those who were left.

## CHAPTER XVII

## TWENTY-ONE

IT was an indication of the spirit of the flotilla that the night after the funeral we were among the three boats which sailed to maintain the blockade around Elba. Once more we waited silently off Port Baratti, our thoughts back eight months to the night when, in this exact position, 658 had first proved herself in the acid test of battle.

But we had no repeat performance. The fight for Elba finished that night. The garrison surrendered, and this minor skirmish in the arena of total war was over. But for the men of the small landing craft and the MLs which led them in, it had not been minor: it had been the bloodiest, most bitterly opposed landing that men had yet been asked to undertake. Nor did the gallant fierce French colonial troops regard this as a mere stepping stone. Hundreds of their comrades lay dead, but they had played their part in the liberation of France as surely as if they had landed directly on the shores of Normandy.

Our patrols resumed their old pattern, and with more settled weather began to intensify once more. On 27th June we sailed with two other boats to intercept some enemy minelayers which Intelligence reported to be busy off San Vincenzo. By the time we got there, there were no signs of any ships, but we patrolled up and down the coast for seven hours before Corny gave the word to leave.

658 was leading, with Cam MacLachlan in 640 close astern. We increased to eighteen knots, and settled down to the long passage back to Bastia. The night was calm and peaceful, and I established myself in the most comfortable corner at the back of the bridge, sitting with my back against the mast. Corny was on watch and I was just dozing off when a gigantic hammer crashed against our keel and sent a shudder through every timber of the boat.

I jumped to me feet, instantly awake but confused with sleep. What had happened?

Corny was looking aft, a stunned expression on his rugged face.

"It's 640, Rover. She's hit a mine. I think she's gone altogether." A pall of smoke hung astern of us. "Hard a'starboard, coxswain. Put a man in the bows, Rover—this may have shaken a few more of the bloody things from their moorings."

"Look, Corny, she's still afloat—but . . . Good God! What a mess!" I stared aft. Her bows had vanished.

At once the crew moved into action. The dinghy was launched, scrambling-nets lowered, and the coxswain unshackled the towing gear down aft.

We turned and gingerly nosed towards the wreck. Her stern was well out of the water, but she was very low forward, and there was nothing at all for'd of the charthouse. No bows, no pom-pom, no messdeck, no wardroom—all had been blown clean away. A small group of men stood on the starboard side of the bridge, their feet covered with water. I could hear Cam checking the crew.

Corny picked up the megaphone.

"How bad is she, Cam? Any chance of a tow?"

Cam's voice, thin from between his cupped hands, floated towards us.

"No such luck, Corny. She's dropping quickly by the head, and that bulkhead won't hold much longer. I guess we'll have to sink her."

" O.K., Cam. Any idea how many are missing ? "

"Eight, so far as I can tell. They're not on board, anyway. I guess they were blown clear."

We swung round and came alongside, and began helping 640's men aboard. My thoughts were all for Tony. He had shared with me the close intimacy of our tiny wardroom for many months, and the bond between us was very close. He was nowhere to be seen. Was he one of the eight?

I was just going to call over to Cam when a quiet voice beside me said: "Reporting back aboard, Rover!" I wheeled round to see Tony standing there. He had been in charge aft and had stepped over the stern when all his party was aboard.

"Thank God you're safe, Tony. How about the Pilot?"

"He was in the charthouse, I'm afraid, and he's not there now, so he doesn't stand much chance. All the others who are missing were up for'd, poor devils."

We drew away from 640, and prepared to sink her with gunfire. Before we started, the PT boat which had been last in line came up on our far side. Her skipper shouted over.

"Say, Corny! I've just picked up Sub-Lieutenant Rogers and two ratings. They're all right, too!"

It took us ten minutes firing with pom-pom and Oerlikons to set her on fire and leave her obviously sinking. It was a cold-blooded and melancholy task. The gunners, tight-lipped and grave, were conscious of the eyes of 640's ratings upon them. Their home and their belongings were destroyed before their eyes. Five of their pals had died, and there had not even been the comfort of retaliation.

Corny turned 658 towards Bastia and increased speed once more. We made Tony and Cam turn in, but I noticed that none of 640's crew would go below. I didn't really blame them. I felt safer on the upper deck myself.

It seemed that 658's proverbial good fortune was holding. *We* had travelled over that mine just a few seconds before it hit 640. In fact, almost certainly we had primed the mechanism of that mine as we passed, leaving it poised to attack the second boat in line. One more click in the delicate device may have meant our stern instead of 640's bows.

This was our first experience of mining, or we would not have wondered so much at the second boat being the victim. It happened in almost every mining incident our boats were involved in. It happened again later to us. It seemed to fit the perverted, cunning nature of a weapon (used by both sides) which ignored the human element completely and struck impersonally and cold bloodedly.

Naturally, this tragic blow following so closely on our casualties at Elba had some effect on the general atmosphere. The crews had been under the strain of frequent operations with the additional tension of action constantly recurring, and were in danger of becoming stale. The zest had gone for the time being and perhaps this was realized more rapidly than we expected by C.C.F.

We had no time to sum it up for ourselves, as Doug greeted Corny next day with a signal which obviously bore good news.

"Say, Corny—how would you like to trot down to little old Malta again and then move round to the ro-mantic islands of Yugoslavia?"

It was true! Our flotilla was ordered to leave Corsica and to move as fast as possible round to the Adriatic, where the Yugoslav Partisans under Tito were already pushing the Germans northward.

There was one more patrol to carry out before we left Bastia for good on 1st July, and there was an important personal landmark to be noted, too. I was delighted when we were briefed for a patrol on the night of the 28th June, as on the next day I would reach my twenty-first birthday, and with any luck this would mean that we should be free to celebrate it fittingly without the fear of being called out.

The patrol itself was simply an anti-E-boat cover for some shipping at anchor off the main port of Elba, and although we were on our toes, there was little likelihood of the enemy showing up. We only had 663 with us, and at midnight, as we lay stopped, wallowing in a gentle swell, Corny and I became suddenly alert as the R/T loudspeaker crackled and Tom's well-known voice came over.

"Hallo, Rover, this is Tommy. Congratulations on your majority and many happy returns from us all. Over."

Corny grinned and handed me the microphone to acknowledge the message. Then he moved over to the port side of the bridge, picked up the loud-hailer microphone, and announced, "This is the Captain speaking. Just one minute ago the first lieutenant achieved the great old age of twenty-one, and I know you will all join me in wishing him every success in the future on this auspicious occasion."

We were back at Bastia by 0600, and as it was certain that we were not required for operations that night, Corny and Tom gave Derrick and me leave for the day. We began with a delightful swim from the seaward side of the breakwater before breakfast, and as we lazed in the sun on a great cube of rock we planned our day carefully.

Everyone was very helpful, as we obtained without any difficulty the use of the Base Jeep, and set off to drive the forty miles down the coast to the hospital where our wounded ratings were being treated. We felt very much like day trippers as we munched biscuits and sweets and looked out for the first time on the delightful coastal scenery of Corsica south of Bastia. A wide plain stretched before us, with lagoons and sandy coast on our left and the gradual ascent to the distant mountains sweeping away to the west. In the breeze of our own movement in the open Jeep, the hot sunshine was exhilarating, and we sang as the miles peeled away behind us. We were like schoolboys on the first day of the holidays.

We found our men in an American hospital, and they were in good spirits. Orme was doing quite well, and spent most of his time looking after McEwan, who would be bedridden until the stump of his leg healed. They were in a ward entirely occupied with sailors, all of whom had been wounded during the Elba landings; they considered themselves a very special group among the American soldiers and airmen, and certainly the staff of the hospital seemed to make a great fuss of them. We took many messages and small gifts with us from the crew of 658 and in return the two stout-hearted sailors sent their greetings with cheery and often rude replies. There was not much wrong with Britain if she could turn out men like this so cheerful in pain and discomfort, in spite of being in a lonely hospital hundreds of miles from home.

We got back to 658 by noon and, as I stepped aboard, Tony ran up the "gin pennant". Soon friends from every boat began to flock aboard, and we entertained them on the bridge. Good humour, good talk, and good liquor flowed easily and naturally. It was a rather special lunch-time party, but typical of its kind in many ways. Every subject under the sun (literally) was discussed, but in the end "shop" always won. Where would we be based in the Adriatic? How long would we have in Malta? When would the war end? How was the Normandy fighting going? Would the Russians get to Berlin first?

And more trivial things too. How good (or bad) was the new Pilot of so-and-so's boat? How much longer would we have to wait for mail? How was 663's pet guinea pig getting on? (It was mischievously christened Uncle Tom and was kept in a box made by Derrick called "Uncle Tom's Cabin". Tommy Ladner naturally couldn't stand it, and when it died and was given a naval funeral, stitched in canvas, some weeks later, he was heartily glad.)

The last of our guests left at two o'clock, and we snatched a quick lunch. Then it was time to sleep, catching up on the previous night, so that we would be fresh for the evening's celebrations. By now our plans were fairly well laid, and most arrangements confirmed. Tony had prevailed on a kindly Number One from one of the boats to sit in aboard 658 for the evening so that he was free to join us. We had fixed the previous week to have our dinner party at a tiny restaurant high up above Bastia, looking down over the sea from the mountain-side. On our exploratory visit the proprietor, a little Corsican of Italian descent known to everyone as "Papa", had promised us a magnificent meal if we could help him with supplies, and now his eyes sparkled when he saw the eggs, tinned butter and other delicacies we brought with us. Corny and Pick were chiefly responsible, as their food parcels from Canada could always be relied upon to produce something out of the ordinary.

There were ten at my party, transported in a Jeep and a fifteen-hundredweight truck. While Papa was busy preparing the meal, we sat on his terrace and sipped our drinks. Marie, his charming young daughter, was always at hand to bring out another bottle of wine, and when we finally sat down around a majestic oval table lit with candles we were extremely mellow and appreciative.

After 658's amateur cooking, Papa's meal was like a dream of the Savoy. Course followed course unendingly: as one finished, we wiped the plate clean with very white bread (specially baked) and drained our glasses. Magically the next would appear, be served on the same plate, and melt delicately in the mouth. The omelettes were the pride of the evening. Papa had really let himself go. He had used two dozen eggs, and each was as light as a feather. The vegetables were cooked in butter; the fruit was surmounted with delicious whipped cream.

And then we sang. Papa, Mama and Marie came and joined us on the balcony, and, it seemed, so did most of the population of Marino de Sisco. There were speeches—speeches by everyone: Derrick swore afterwards that my own lasted three hours, with interruptions for singing and refreshment. At the end, there was still the tortuous drive down the steep hairpin bends of the road to Bastia. In daylight I had been terrified: but now, in deep blackness, the road held no terrors. It was negotiated at speed with confidence and the nonchalance only found in a man who has wined and dined well.

My twenty-first birthday was memorable for yet another reason. Next day we said our farewells and left Bastia for the last time. We had grown attached to the place over the past nine months. The Base staff were quite the most helpful and cheerful we ever met—every one of them showed his understanding of the urgency and importance of our operations, and the dependence we put in his technical skill, whether it was with the engines, the W/T, radar, electrics or guns.

And above all, the spirit of the Base had been achieved through the inspiration of Bobby Allan himself. We were all devoted to him: he had proved himself a great leader both at sea and in harbour. When we left he submitted a report to C.C.F., which summarized the work of Coastal Forces from Maddalena and Bastia for the first six months of 1944. It began:

> "Having been in Coastal Forces for four and a half years, I am inclined to think that the last six months have been in every respect the happiest that have ever been known, not to me personally, but to Coastal Forces in general.
>
> "I attribute this largely to the magnificent spirit in the flotillas attached. The 56th Flotilla under its all-Canadian leadership infected us all with a spirit of New World camaraderie and almost embarrassing keenness. . . ."

As we left Maddalena, after a brief stop for fuelling, the C.O. of the Base there also sent a farewell signal:

*"For V56.[1] The Canadian Flotilla is so essentially a part of us all here that we lose much of ourselves in your departure. Good luck, and may the spirit you have shown bring continued success to your work in new areas."*

[1] V56: Senior Officer 56th MTB Flotilla.

## Chapter XVIII

## ROUND TO THE ADRIATIC

ON 3rd July we were back in our old familiar berth at Hays Wharf, opposite H.M.S. *Gregale*. The target for our overhaul was two weeks—then on to the Adriatic; and there was a devil of a lot to be done. Every boat had armour plating fitted on the doors at the back of the bridge: the boats at home had had it for months; for us it came just two weeks too late. The sides were already partly protected, so we felt quite snug now.

For the first time in twelve months, the whole flotilla was in Malta together: it was obviously an opportunity to enjoy ourselves while we could. And a change of great significance had taken place in the social life of Malta. The first Wrens had arrived.

Time was short, and the chairman of the Junior Dogs Club called an Extra-ordinary General Meeting to lay plans for an immediate campaign. We decided that we must take the offensive straight away in order to establish a bridgehead at the Wrennery.

That afternoon, I rang up the First Officer W.R.N.S. (familiarly known as the Queen Wren) at her office. I explained very politely that the officers of the 56th MGB/MTB Flotilla were holding a dinner party and that we should be delighted to entertain half a dozen of her most beautiful Wrens if any of them would like to come. She was charmingly co-operative, and promised to pass on the invitation and let me know. Before she rang off, I asked her if she would care to come herself, but although she seemed to enjoy the gesture, she excused herself pleasantly on the grounds of a previous engagement.

The whole affair went splendidly. We borrowed a flat in Sliema, persuaded the Maltese chief steward at *Gregale* to provide the food and cocktail snacks, laid in stocks of beer and concocted a large bowl of punch. We were not disappointed when we went to pick up our guests, either. The Queen Wren had done her job well. We had six gay and attractive English girls to share our pleasure—almost the first English girls we had talked to for eighteen months. We felt we deserved a good time.

When the Wrens had to leave, we escorted them back to the Wrennery, making plans for the rest of our leave. And then began the second half of the evening—a cocktail party for the Senior Dogs. By the time it finished, R.A.F. types and the submariners from Manoel Island were almost outnumbering their Coastal Force hosts. It just seemed to grow. It was that sort of party.

But if we played hard, we worked hard as well. Each boat in turn went up on the small dock in Msida Creek and was given thirty-six hours to paint bottom and sides, and overhaul shafts and propellers. Corny had been working with Doug and one or two engineer officers on a new design for a gun cradle for our single Oerlikon mountings which would convert each mounting to take two guns. These cradles had now been cast, and we took them out to test them.

There was no doubt about the increase in fire-power, but in our case the vibration was very severe, and Corny felt that to throw away accuracy for increased killing power was false economy. We therefore did not fit the new cradles, but Doug was able to accept them, possibly because 657 had more effective deck strengthening beneath her Oerlikons, which stopped undue vibration.

Her gun-power was now impressive. On either beam she could pour out shells from a pom-pom, 6-pounder, four Oerlikons and two Vickers .303s. We were glad she was on our side.

Before we left Malta, we spent a good deal of time finding out more about the conditions we would meet in the Adriatic. In Corsica, we had been too busy with our own problems to bother about understanding the rather complicated political and military situation on the other side of Italy. Now it was time to do some homework and catch up.

In the early days after the Germans had advanced into the Balkans, the British had had great difficulty in finding out what was happening inside Yugoslavia. First they had helped General Mihailovitch's Chetniks, but later it was decided to transfer the assistance to Tito and his Partisans, who were already hard at work fighting the Germans. Brigadier Fitzroy Maclean was sent to establish contact, and after many initial troubles supplies began to trickle into Yugoslavia, mainly distributed from Vis, a tiny island about twenty-five miles south of Split. Most of the Dalmatian Islands had been taken by the Partisans by this time, and the Germans were confined in the major ports, necessary to them as the only means of supplying their armies; the overland routes were threatened continuously by bands of Partisan guerrillas.

But the Germans soon became aware of the new supplies flooding in, and took the obvious course: they re-occupied the islands one by one and strengthened their garrisons along the coastal area. At once it became important to hold Vis, so that supplies could continue to flow, and so that there would be a Base available from which strikes by all three services could be made, and a full invasion mounted if this should ever become necessary.

Our boats had already been using Vis as a base for operations before this decision was made—they had hidden, camouflaged, in creeks by day and patrolled by night. Now they were joined by Commandos, units of the Royal Artillery, and a squadron of Hurricanes.

The Germans realised that Vis was an irritating thorn in their side, but had not the necessary confidence or strength to take it by force. Soon it was too late for them to do so. So the situation at Vis, where we would be operating, was unique: it was an island fortress containing about 4,000 allied servicemen and 8,000 Partisans, but surrounded on all but the seaward side by islands held by the Germans.

All this was in our minds when we left Malta on July 21st and sailed north-eastward for the Adriatic. The first call (for fuelling) was at Augusta, and how very peaceful and different was this Augusta from the one we had known a year before. Then it had been a major supply port for the Army battling in Sicily; now it was a deserted backwater of the war.

As we left Augusta at dusk for the long trek to Brindisi, the signal lamp flashed from 657. Tony Brydon, who was now "Spare Number One" of the flotilla, was travelling with us on passage, but I got to the lamp first and began to take the message.

Tony wrote it down. It read:

"*Congratulations, Tony, on award of D.S.C. for Vada Rocks action. Also Tim Bligh. Corny is mentioned in despatches.*"

Tony's face was a picture of incredulity and delight. It was pure chance that he should write the message down—and nobody could have been more surprised than he was.

When we arrived at Brindisi the Junior Dogs honoured their first recipient of an award at a ceremonial meeting, when Derrick pinned a large cardboard D.S.C. on Tony's chest. It was thoroughly deserved.

Brindisi was packed with boats, mostly lying alongside the Italian seaplane tender *Miraglia* which had become the Base-Ship for Coastal

Forces. She was an ideal ship for the purpose, having excellent arrangements for loading torpedoes, and good repair shops; but her administration was surely the strangest expression of compromise the Navy could produce. She still had an Italian commanding officer (after all, we were "co-belligerents"!) and skeleton crew aboard, but as a Base she was run by British officers and men.

Lt.-Cdr. Freddie Warner (whom we had not seen since 636 was sunk) was the C.O. of the British half, and gave us a warm welcome. He had to be extremely diplomatic to please both the Italian owners and the demanding Coastal Force skippers of the boats alongside.

Some of the Dog-boats we now joined were those we had never met before for various reasons. The 60th Flotilla had worked with us at Sicily, and we now rejoined Tim Bligh's 57th Flotilla, although all his boats were "in the Islands", as it was always put. We looked forward to joining them and meeting old friends, especially (for Derrick and me) Gordon Surtees in 634, whom we had last seen in Bastia at the foundation party of the Junior Dogs.

Altogether, in the forty-eight hours we spent at Brindisi, we felt ill-at-ease and uncomfortably green. We were unquestionably regarded as "those chaps from the other side" and, with the disadvantage of having to learn a new set of conditions, we were obviously going to have to prove our worth. The reputation which had preceded us cut little ice, so we kept quiet and prepared ourselves for the new job.

By continually asking questions, we began to piece together a picture of the sort of targets we could expect. At first, the Germans had used only local sailing craft and small auxiliary vessels like caiques and schooners; when our boats had met them it had soon become obvious that they were poorly armed and not designed to withstand attacks from powerful naval craft. Tom Fuller, the bearded Canadian who had brought 654 out from home in our convoy, had led his flotilla in a series of very glamorous and successful operations against them, and had captured and towed triumphantly back to Vis schooner after schooner full of valuable supplies. The Partisans (and the Germans) had been impressed, and relations with them had become quite cordial.

But for several months now the situation had been changing. The juicy plums of the early days had withered to tough bitter prunes in the shape of heavily armed escorts, F-lighters, E-boat flotillas, and schooners mounting 40-mm. and 20-mm. guns, so that in many cases they were now at least as powerful as our boats.

In all this one particular factor was still on our side. The crews of the "impressed" ships were of poor fighting quality. Many Italian seamen had been forced to serve in them against their will, and frequently there was only a mere stiffening of Germans in the crew to maintain discipline and strengthen morale. F-lighters had begun to appear more and more on the Dalmatian coast. We held their heavy guns in healthy respect, and after our experiences on the west coast we knew how formidable they were, but felt that given any advantage of surprise or cover we could deal with them.

And to add to this was the knowledge that at least the major unit of our flotilla (Doug, Corny and Tom) was so perfectly balanced that its team work could hardly be approached by any other trio, and the crews of the three boats, being aware of this harmony, were confident of success if we could meet the enemy in reasonable circumstances.

On the morning of the day that we were due to sail for Manfredonia (the stepping-off port for the Islands), Corny came aboard with Doug and they went straight down to Corny's cabin without a word. I noticed that they both looked worried and I wondered what was wrong.

Ten minutes later I knew. The quartermaster came up to me on the upper deck, saluted, and said: "The C.O. would like to see you in his cabin, please, sir."

The news was dumbfounding. Corny had been to the M.O. (he was still under orders for regular checking) and after an examination had been informed that he must enter hospital once more with suspected pleurisy—of all things.

Doug looked at me.

"I can't get Cam MacLachlan up from Malta in time before we go over to the Islands, Rover—so you'll be in command. Tony can come back to you as Number One, and we'll just hope that Corny won't be too long."

This time it was the real thing. I wasn't going to be a mere chauffeur, driving the boat from port to port. I should be taking 658 on patrol—into action probably—and thirty-four men and a boat worth many thousands of pounds were to be entrusted to a subbie who was four weeks over twenty-one. I tried to analyse my feelings. Pride came out on top, with humility close behind. Doubt crept in; but on reflection, confidence in 658 and its proved company soon removed it.

There was not long to wait. Within six hours we sailed for Manfredonia, and, stopping there only to fuel, we were off across the

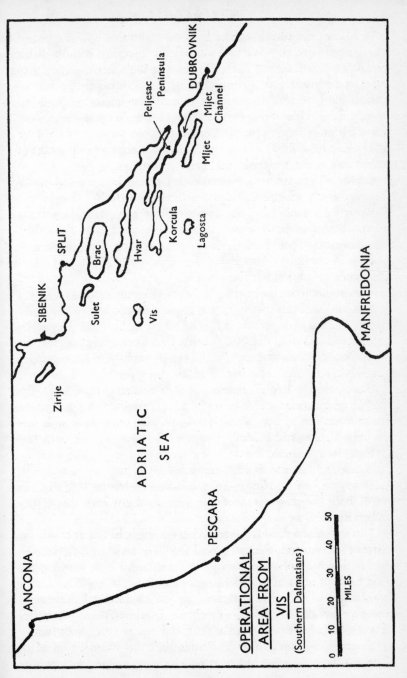

ANCONA

PESCARA

MANFREDONIA

ADRIATIC
SEA

Zirije

SIBENIK

SPLIT

Sulet

Brac

Vis

Hvar

Korcula

Lagosta

Mljet

Mljet
Channel

Peljesac
Peninsula

DUBROVNIK

OPERATIONAL
AREA FROM
VIS
(Southern Dalmatians)

MILES

0   10   20   30   40   50

Adriatic to the Islands at first light on 30th July. We first entered Komiza at noon that day, and were deeply impressed with the beauty of its setting. The tiny harbour nestled at the western end of Vis at the foot of steeply dropping hills. Bare rock was partly clothed in scrub and low trees, and brightly painted little houses crowded close to the quay. Here at last was deep clear blue water. It was enthralling. But ten miles away were the Germans.

Half an hour after we berthed, Doug sent a message asking C.O.s to meet him at the operations room at the Naval H.Q., overlooking the harbour. Feeling very self-conscious, I joined Tommy and walked along the jetty with him. We gathered in a small room and found Doug talking to a young lieutenant-commander with straight rings. Doug introduced him straight away.

"Gentlemen, I would like you to meet Lt.-Cdr. Morgan Giles, the Senior Naval Officer, Vis. He's got something for us to do right away, so I guess he'd better tell you about it."

Before he began his briefing, Lt.-Cdr. Giles shook hands with each of us, and we immediately got an impression of a strong personality and a likeable man. I fancied that he looked rather hard at my single stripe and my youthful face (people told me I really needn't have bothered about shaving, even at this time!) but he made no comment.

When he outlined the operation we were to join, I realized that I wasn't going to have a routine patrol or two to get acclimatized to being in command. This was a good deal bigger. We had arrived just in time to take part in a "false-nose" job on quite a large scale. It meant we should be out for three nights in a row, and that for a considerable time we should be operating in daylight, too, escorting landing craft to and from their beaches.

I was glad that my first patrol was sprung on me like this. I escaped the worst nagging pangs of anticipation, and found myself busy checking with Tony that the boat was in top-class order in all respects.

When we sailed, Doug sent over a message that our R/T call sign would be "Rover", and that I should be "Tail-arse Charlie" at the end of the line behind Tommy in 663. For a moment my memory flashed back to our last real patrol, when we had held the same position and had received the wrath of the destroyer: I dismissed the thought rapidly and turned to other more immediate things.

We had several new men aboard, and especially a new coxswain. Hodges had not returned to us after being wounded off Elba, and Petty Officer Lamont had relieved him, and was still an unknown quantity. Both Howe and Preston, the key gunners who had done so well on the 6-pounder and the pom-pom, had gone ashore, and in their places were little Nobby Watt and a very solid character named Duffill. I knew they were both absolutely dependable but, naturally, they had to settle down, and it wasn't quite the same as having the old tried guns' crews we had become so accustomed to.

On the passage to the patrol area that first night, I felt something of the loneliness of command. I felt a definite heaviness and depression of my spirits, and sat in my cabin, alone with my active imagination, thinking of all the things that *could* happen even on my first patrol. I soon pulled myself together and realized what an enormous drawback this gift of imagination was. When we reached the patrol area, I was quite calm, and had adjusted myself to my new view of the proceedings.

I no longer had to be good at obeying orders and creating routine efficiency: now it was my job to make decisions and to expect efficiency. It was undoubtedly pleasant to feel that independence.

In any case, I soon began to feel the confidence I needed to put me at ease. I found that whenever any seed of uncertainty cropped up, the simple application of experience provided an answer. What had Corny done in similar circumstances in the past? What would he do now?

We met nothing that first night. I was glad, really, as it gave us all a chance to shake down. We were patrolling to cover the landing on Korcula (an island forty miles east of Vis) of the observation officers who were to play a vital role in the big operation planned for the third night.

There was one pleasant change from our old Corsican routine: whereas passage to and from patrols had made operations very long and tiring there, the distances were generally much smaller here. After all, the Germans were on our door step—or we were on theirs. But this did not make entirely for an easier time. The length of time spent in the patrol area, under real strain, was correspondingly much longer, covering virtually the whole period from dusk till dawn.

We were back in Komiza at 0700 and, as every boat was needed again, a queue developed for fuelling. I could see at once that this was not going to be funny. Fuelling had been bad enough from the old *Grete* at Bastia, but here, there was no space to reserve a special jetty for fuelling, and the boats had to take the petrol by gravity-feed from "bowsers" (Army petrol lorries), alongside the main jetty. This meant either an obvious slackening in safety precautions or a great deal of discomfort aboard those boats lying close by but not actually fuelling, as generators and electric circuits could not be functioning during fuelling. Most boats solved the problem by going out to buoys in mid-harbour when fuelling was in progress at the quay.

At a further briefing, we heard details of Operation "Decomposed Two". We were to escort a force of LCIs and lighters to a point on the south coast of the eastern tip of Korcula, and there land a Partisan company and eight 25-pounders with their Royal Artillery crews. At dawn, these guns would fire over the island of Korcula and bombard the twin towns on each side of the narrow straits which separate the island from the mainland of the Peljesac peninsula. Two R.A. officers had carried out a reconnaissance of the enemy positions in Orebic and Korcula dressed as peasant girls, moving about the area picking grapes in the vineyards. They had reported excellent targets, and it was known that Korcula town was an important calling-in port for coastal shipping.

But there was still a further night's work to be done before the main job, and we spent this in the company of Charles Jerram (667)— another fellow-member of our original convoy. We escorted a group of landing craft to a "half-way-house"—a cove on the island of Lagosta between Vis and Korcula, where they were to lie up, thereby reducing their passage time for the next night. After that we patrolled off Peljesac, but nothing disturbed the peace of a lovely night. At about 0530, I was sent back to Komiza in advance of all the other boats to pass on some additional intelligence. This had been provided at the last minute by one of the small parties of gallant men who remained for days at a time on the scantily protected hillsides of the occupied islands, to spot and report the passage of enemy ships.

As we ploughed back to Komiza, I stood on the bridge and eagerly searched the horizon. I dreamed of meeting a solitary unarmed enemy ship, but such pipe-dreams seldom come true and the only advantage we gained was to get an extra hour's sleep.

We were off again at 2000, this time on the real business, and the landings were successfully made with complete surprise before dawn on 2nd August.

We had been ordered to remain close by while the bombardment was on in case any enemy ships appeared; in fact we soon discovered that we were perfectly safe, as all the enemy fire was directed at a decoy ship which was designed for that very purpose. LCI 254 had a magnificent canvas funnel at a rakish angle, and two large canvas gun turrets. When the bombardment was ready to begin, the dummy

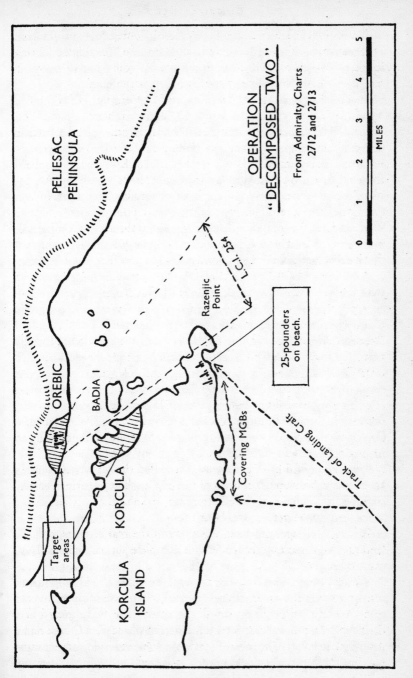

OPERATION
"DECOMPOSED TWO"

From Admiralty Charts
2712 and 2713

PELJESAC PENINSULA

OREBIC

BADIA I

KORCULA

KORCULA ISLAND

Target areas

Razenjic Point

L.C.I. 254

Track of Landing Craft

Covering MGBs

25-pounders on beach.

MILES
0  1  2  3  4  5

destroyer sailed out into full view of the battery at Orebic—but at its extreme range. As soon as the 25-pounders opened fire, the LCI began to let off fireworks, which simulated gun-flashes, from behind each turret. Soon the Orebic batteries replied, but at that range they had no success, and only helped the Forward Observation Officer (hidden on a nearby island) to plot their position more accurately.

For half an hour the batteries shelled the "destroyer", obviously believing that she was doing the bombarding; meanwhile the eight 25-pounders rained shells down into the two target areas. At a pre-arranged time they shifted target to the enemy anti-aircraft batteries, and the Hurricanes from Vis were able to roar in and unload their light bombs practically without opposition.

Eventually all the 25-pounders and infantry were safely re-embarked, and we sailed quietly away. There had been no casualties in our force, and we felt the planners had done a first-class job. But we still had to get back to Vis. It was broad daylight, we were fifty miles from the Base, and the convoy was making only about six knots. There was one enemy air-strip within range, but no fighters arrived and we sailed wearily but unscathed into Komiza at about 1800.

At last, after three nights and a day at sea with little chance for real sleep, we were assured of a night off. The first pipe was "Hands to bathe" and within a very short time almost every man on board was splashing about in the deep clear water or diving from the boat's side. We had been warned of the presence of swordfish, so had a lookout posted while the swimming was on. No one particularly fancied the idea of swordfish, although we were a bit hazy about their size and method of attack.

Soon the non-duty watch were making their way ashore. We had been ordered to give the men a few warnings about Partisan peculi-arities, and they soon proved necessary.

For one thing, the Yugoslavs were touchy about security, and our men were advised not to be too nosy as they walked about the island. And the womenfolk had been absorbed into the Army until the Germans were defeated, and had thereby virtually renounced their sex. They were treated as men, wore Army uniform, marched in the same formations, and were included in every combatant unit. Hand grenades hung from their hips, and rifles were slung over their shoulders: the penalties for forgetting their new status were heavy and strongly deterrent. The men of 658 looked solemn and breathed sighs of regret. I hoped we would not fish one of them out of the harbour that night: rumour had it that one amorous matelot had finished up that way.

The last warning was on the local hooch. In common with most Mediterranean countries, Dalmatia had its own specially distilled brand of poison, with a very high alchohol content. Here it was called racchia; after one sip I decided I would give this one a miss. It burnt the throat, tasted like methylated spirits, and left a headache which seemed to throb like a two-stroke engine. But, naturally, this was an experiment the serious drinkers in the crew had to make. They had the benefit of further proof within two hours.

I had decided to stay aboard to write letters, feeling too tired to explore the surrounding countryside. I had been over-anxious on my first patrols and had stayed on the bridge for almost the whole night on each occasion, and now I wanted only to rest.

Just as I had settled down, enjoying for the first time the privacy of the tiny cabin provided for the C.O., there was a commotion on deck and I went up to investigate. The trot-boat was alongside, and lying in the bottom of it, struggling and shouting, but held down by two stokers, was one of our young gunners. The coxswain was at the gangway.

"Looks as though he's been trying this racchia stuff, sir. They tell me it sends 'em berserk if they're not used to it."

I called down to the two men in the boat: "Can you help get him aboard? We'll shove him in a Neil-Robertson stretcher to stop him damaging himself, and take him off to hospital."

The coxswain gathered several of the toughest men, and between them they struggled with the frantic seaman until he was securely lashed in the bamboo and canvas stretcher which was normally used for lowering casualties down vertical hatches. Flecks of foam circled his lips, he still swore and shouted senseless strings of words, and his eyes bulged. Obviously he knew nothing of what was going on.

Then came the task of getting him back into the trot-boat, obtaining a Jeep from the Base, loading him like a cargo in the back, and driving him out to a British field hospital about five miles inland.

There the duty M.O. greeted us cheerfully.

"Oh, yes! we're used to the effects of racchia. You leave him up here for the night, and we'll pump him out and let you have him back in the morning. He'll be very sorry for himself too, I can assure you—the after-effects are most unpleasant!" He was right.

On the drive back to Komiza, I gained some first impressions of this tiny Dalmatian island. The hills were predominantly of bare limestone, clothed only patchily with scrub and occasional groves of olives and other small trees. Very little was cultivated, and I saw no animals. Food must be a problem, I thought. The people looked alert and intent: they had a determination in their faces, and they were organized for war—total war in this case. There was no room for passengers on this island: Tito demanded—and received—an all-out effort from all his people. I noticed the slogans painted on walls; the two most common were "Smyrt Fascismu" (Down with Facsism) and "Zivio Drug Tito" (Long Live Tito Our Leader). This was my first sight of the energy of a Communist system. It was impressive in its single-minded enthusiasm but left me with an uneasy feeling that I was witnessing a force too ruthless to be well-balanced.

But we were lucky in arriving at Vis at this stage, when the Navy's relations with the Partisans were at their smoothest. It had not always been so, nor did this state of affairs continue.

Gradually, as the Germans were driven from island after island in the next few months, political and diplomatic considerations began to over-ride the military "rapport" we had achieved, and so, para-doxically, as more military successes were recorded Yugoslav relations with the Allies became worse.

In August, however, there was only mutual respect; we saw them as men of granite, well-trained, well disciplined, ruthless and aggressive. They knew that our boats were more effective than anything they could produce, and they admired the results we obtained in action with the enemy.

The scene at the waterfront in the evening was frequently more like a comic opera than purposeful, lethal war. A band of Partisans would come marching down the street, singing in tuneful harmony, with rifles and machine-guns slung nonchalantly over their shoulders. The usual sprinkling of girls were there, looking very masculine, with packs as big as any of the men. They would embark in one or two of their schooners (called "Tigers") and we would watch the graceful craft glide out of harbour, the soft put-put of an auxiliary motor hardly audible over the inevitable singing. The departure would grace any opera: the destination and the intent were frequently far removed from the world of entertainment.

In the next three days, we patrolled twice more among the islands to the north of Vis, but found no shipping moving at all. 657, now equipped with the American S.O. radar we had so much admired in the PT boats, was an absolute godsend, as her set could see round corners, behind peninsulas and islands, and lay bare on the screen the secrets of the night-darkened sea. We could be certain, therefore, that we were not missing opportunities, but were just in one of those periods of dullness when full energy had to be used to keep up to scratch.

The period was not without its excitements, however. Everybody on board (except the quartermaster) was fast asleep one night, when I was suddenly conscious of a clatter on the wardroom ladder, and the next moment the light snapped on in my cabin. I sat up and stared at the bearded officer who stood in the doorway. Slowly recognition came. It was Lieutenant Baker, S.O.O. to SNOVIS.

"Come on, Rover, out of it! There's a suspicious vessel off the harbour, caught in the searchlights, and we can't identify it. Get out there and bring it in if you can."

I threw on a coat over my pyjamas and a pair of shoes, shouted into the wardroom, and bounded up the ladder. As soon as I reached the bridge, I rang the alarm buzzer and the boat burst into life. Tony was shouting down the after hatch, and Last emerged dressed only in shorts. Within seconds the jarring note of the starters was followed by the explosive bursts of the exhaust gases and water shooting out of the pipes against the hull of the boat alongside. The smell of the gases crept over the bridge, and scantily dressed figures appeared. Almost immediately came the "toot-toot" on the engine-room buzzer to show that Last was ready to use the engines. Tony shouted through his megaphone: "Let go everything!" and we were off—as Corny would put it—"in a cloud of heifer dung!"

So far so good. A quick get away—now for S.O.O.'s suspicious vessel. I wound the little handle by my side twice every few seconds, and, as if in answer, the throttles were opened and 658 was soon creaming along at her top speed.

The searing gash of two searchlights crossed at right angles out in the blackness of the night, and there at the intersection was a ship, sparkling brilliantly like a moth shining with reflected light outside a window.

I focused my glasses and stared at it. The strange light was very confusing. I had no idea of the range, and no means of telling it except by closing fast. The vessel was very indistinct in outline, and could have been anything from a destroyer at three miles to a motor boat at half a mile. Which was it?

I had to be sure to keep our quarry in the light and 658 in the dark, so I steered right up to the beam which cut across at right angles, and then ran parallel just to one side of the beam until I could tell—with some relief—that it was only a motor boat about 30 feet in length. There were two men in the cockpit aft, and no flag was flying.

What was the next move? Diplomacy or "brute force and ignorance"? I turned on the loud hailer and boomed out: "Stop your engines or we shall sink you."

The motor boat went straight on, the two men waving and shouting at us. Of course, they couldn't understand plain English! Obviously we had to make our actions speak for us. I manoeuvred across her bows, forced her to stop, and sent the Pilot and three armed men to board her. They had no trouble. Mike stood over the occupants with a revolver significantly pointed, while Peacock made fast a line thrown from our stern.

I tried to talk to the two men, but got no further than discovering from their frantic gestures that they were fishermen, and that they were very frightened. We towed the boat in and handed over our charges to S.O.O. and a Partisan interpreter, and went back to our bunks.

In the morning S.O.O. came down to give us details. They were only fishermen who had strayed from their normal grounds, and had nearly died of fright when the searchlights caught them. Our approach had been so effective that they had not seen anything in the blinding glare, and the first they had known of our presence was when our loud hailer boomed at them. One of them confessed that he thought the Day of Judgment had come and that Jonah was summoning him into the whale!

## Chapter XIX

## THE BATTLE OF THE MLJET CHANNEL

CORNY was waiting for us on the jetty when we came along-side two mornings later after yet another uneventful patrol. Everybody was glad to see him. I heard one of the seamen say to his pal as they went below from harbour stations: "The bloody skipper's back: I bet we find some bloody Jerries now!"

For myself, although I had settled down to the command and gained confidence I felt no disappointment at reverting to my work as Number One. That was the way with Corny—he made everyone feel the importance of his job and knew when to give that word of praise and encouragement that marks the true leader by his under-standing of men.

Straight away we went down to the wardroom and talked over with him what we had done. I wanted to hear *his* news, but he in-sisted on hearing 658's first. He had not had pleurisy, anyway; but the hospital had continued his old treatment. He had finally more or less demanded his discharge and got back to us as soon as he could. As Doug and 657 were in Manfredonia, Corny lost no time and took out a small unit that night. He soon made his presence felt, asking questions, checking the routines and generally getting himself back into the picture.

But we drew blank once again, and felt worse about it when we got back to harbour and heard that Tim Bligh had met an enemy convoy further north off Vir Island, near Zara.

With Tim's boats resting that night Corny was anxious to try out the Vir area himself, and off we went northward to try our luck. But it seemed that the Germans had wind of the presence of the 56th Flotilla, and were determined to annoy us by staying at home.

Doug arrived with 657 on 17th August, and plans were laid for the "Three Musketeers" to operate together again for the first time in several months.

There was an incidental job to do before we began our patrol. Two Royal Marine Commandos had to be put ashore on the north-west end of Mljet Island as spotters, reporting on any passing enemy ships. 657 put them off at the right position, and we moved into the Mljet Channel for our patrol. The channel was very narrow, and ran between the Peljesac peninsula and the island of Mljet.

Almost at once our luck seemed to change. We had hardly settled down to patrol routine when the R/T crackled and Doug's calm drawl came over as we had heard it so many times before off the west coast of Italy. Was this it? Was our patience to be rewarded?

"Hallo, Dogs, this is Wimpey. I have a possible target. Four small ships moving fast up Mljet Channel. Am steering to intercept. George 22."[1]

We had a chart on the bridge. As I followed Doug round and cranked the rev counter handle to increase speed with him, Corny bent over the little chart table. A moment later he straightened himself and scowled.

"Looks like E-boats, Rover, and I don't think we can catch 'em." We knew only too well that the E-boats could always outstrip the Dogs.

Doug increased speed until we were running at maximum revs, but from the bearings and ranges he passed it was obvious that we should never catch them. In the end they crossed our line one and a half miles ahead, but as it was a cloudy moonless night, we did not even sight them. Our first smell of the enemy in the Adriatic had done nothing more than tantalize our appetites. Still, as the E-boats had neither altered course nor speed, it was probable that they did not suspect our presence, so the rest of the patrol was not jeopardized. We were lucky that they had no radar to enable them to see beyond visibility distance.

We took this "near-miss" with bad grace and ill-humour, and retired into the Mljet Channel again to sulk under the Peljesac shore. But we didn't sulk for long. An hour later, Corny was in the charthouse studying the chart and enjoying a quick smoke when 657 began to creep astern towards us.

At once the atmosphere stiffened. A word down the voice-pipe brought Corny back to the bridge. Doug raised a megaphone to his lips and hailed us. "Hello, Corny and Tommy! Can you hear me?" A reassuring shout came from 663 and Corny waved.

"Say, fellers—I think we're in luck. There are three targets at range three miles just entering the channel and running down towards us.

[1] George 22: Speed 22 knots.

Come to action stations and get into cruising line to port. I shall wait as long as I can before attacking."

Aboard 658 there was no need to press the alarm buzzers for action stations. Everybody on deck had heard the S.O. and it took only a few second for all the guns' crews to report "Closed up to action stations", and for the engine-room and W/T office to confirm their readiness.

Two rapid engine telegraph orders and we were in station on 657's port quarter. The unit's position was ideal; we were close inshore in a shallow bay, so that even if the convoy was hugging the coast it would have to pass outside us. This would give us the advantage of visibility because we were hidden against the dark background of the shore while they were silhouetted against the lighter skyline to seaward.

Even though we expected it, we jumped when the bridge loud-speaker suddenly gave us our orders.

"Hallo, Dogs, this is Wimpey. Target range two and a half miles, three ships surrounded by several smaller ones. Course 115, speed 6 knots. Out."

The convoy was approaching from our right, and Doug's plan was that we should wait until they had almost reached us, and then to move out of our bay and slide between them and the coast, attacking them as we ran along on the opposite course to theirs.

Mike Walter-Munro made a rapid calculation. "About twenty-four minutes before they're abeam, sir," he reported.

"Thank you, Mike."

Five minutes later the R/T emitted a brief "Target now clearly eight or nine ships". It looked as though we were going to be busy. Our night-glasses scanned the even darkness ahead, waiting for the first all-important sighting.

One always tended to disbelieve the invisible eyes of radar until one actually saw the target it had detected many minutes earlier.

Suddenly Corny spoke. "Here they are—three in sight, right ahead." I murmured this information into the loud hailer, and the gun barrels moved slightly as if in acknowledgement.

Still Doug waited. My mind hammered "They'll see us, they'll see us. . . . We're sitting ducks. . . . Why doesn't he start . . . ?"

But all remained silent and the dim shapes became visible, crossing ahead of us so slowly that they appeared almost motionless.

I saw the pom-pom gunner wave one hand, indicating he had the target in his sights. The others would have to wait until we swung round to attack.

At last came Doug's signal. "Here we go, Dogs. Speed 8 knots, fine Seven Order. Attacking on port bow. Tommy—light please! Range is 500 yards."

I clicked over the switch on the loud hailer. "All guns. Stand by. 663 is about to illuminate target bearing Red One-O, range 500 yards."

It took less than five seconds to say. As I finished, the peaceful darkness of the night vanished. From astern came the vicious thump of 663's pom-pom, and the blackness was torn aside by her starshell. Before us, suddenly revealed, lay the convoy.

The starshell, like fading rockets, dropped steadily down, each group replaced, as it died, by the next above.

Corny moved the telegraph handles, and we moved slowly off, swinging gradually round to starboard.

My heart seemed to beat in time with Tommy's pom-pom. My hand shook as I raised the loud-hailer mike again.

"All guns. First group of targets bearing Red Six-O. Open fire."

The first crash of the broadside always took me by surprise, even though I ordered it. Each time its noise and concussion seemed fiercer. Each gun had its own rhythm, and the beats mingled like savage jungle music at the climax of a native dance. Smoke drifted over the bridge, and the hot, pungent smells of gunfire descended and penetrated to the back of my throat. It was dry enough already.

I did not need my night-glasses any longer. I watched the tracer curling away towards the first group. The range was about 300 yards by now, and after one burst the guns had begun their destruction. My heart swelled. The three main guns had selected one target each from the first group, just as though we were on a practice shoot. The pom-pom shells were the easiest to follow. They flashed and sparked against the hull of what looked like an F-lighter. Further to port, two large schooners were receiving the full attention of both our twin Oerlikon and 6-pounder, and all Tommy's guns. The 6-pounder especially made a satisfying sight. Every second 658's stern shook with the recoil of this ancient piece, and great spouts of flame rose wherever its shells struck home.

It took the enemy about twenty seconds to recover from the rude disturbance of their peaceful passage. Then it was our turn to duck.

The stuttering flashes from the decks of the schooners and the lighter blossomed into streams of brilliant multi-coloured tracer. At first, I thought that all of it was aimed at 657 and 663. Almost at once I changed my mind: it seemed all of it was aimed at 658. Shells cracked alarmingly overhead and tracers flicked by, hissing and ricocheting when they hit the water.

My American-style tin hat shut out so much of the din that I was quite calm by now. But Corny was shouting and I could not hear him, so I pulled it off and substituted my normal one. I suddenly felt more at home. Corny was yelling: "Shift target now, Rover."

I pushed the buzzer, and obediently the guns ceased to bark. As soon as I knew they could hear, I gave the new orders.

"All guns shift target right. Group of small craft. Open fire."

The change took only the few seconds the words take to say. Immediately, our shells began to spatter around the smaller enemy boats. But although we were only crawling along at eight knots, we were past them in no time and suddenly came upon the last ship in the enemy line. It was keeping poor station and paid the penalty of all stragglers: as each of us passed we pounded our broadsides into it. Streams of pom-pom, Oerlikon and 6-pounder took only a few seconds to transform it into an exploding inferno which quickly sank.

I rang the "check fire" signal and a strange silence cloaked the bridge. We had passed down the whole convoy and had engaged eight ships on the way.

"I think I felt a hit, Rover," said Corny. "Check up, will you?" We were swinging out into the channel round the stern of the convoy, and the three gunboats stopped to see how things were going. While Corny sized up the situation, I had a quick look round the deck. We were apparently undamaged there; but in the engine-room it was a different story.

The bridge indicator from the engine-room clanged and its pointer stopped at a new reading. The leading seaman sprang to it and reported "Cut port outer, port inner, and starboard inner, sir!" he reported.

Corny swore softly. "Only one engine left! Now we'll need some luck."

Down in the engine-room, although we did not know it, Petty Officer Bill Last, the chief motor mechanic, was working as though his life depended upon it: indeed it might well do so—and the lives of everyone on board, too! He was stripped to the waist and his tanned body, glistening with sweat, was smeared with oil and grease. He had clambered over the two port engines and was inspecting the damage. A jagged hole in the ship's side showed where the shell had entered.

"Looks like a 40-millimetre, Bert!" he shouted to his leading mechanic. "Bloody great holes in the water intakes—we won't get those going tonight. Let's have a look at the starboard inner."

A hasty inspection revealed that only minor repairs would be necessary. "You get a bit of rubber tubing on there, Bert, and I'll nip up to tell the skipper what's going on. We'll need to use the distilled-water tank under the bridge."

A few moments later he was climbing up to the bridge and giving Corny his report. "I hope we'll have the starboard inner going in a minute, sir, but the two port engines are out for the night, I'm afraid."

"Well, do your best, Last," said Corny. "You can see we've still got a lot of homework to do down there." He pointed to the fires flickering down the channel which alone revealed the results of the first run. Last grinned, and ripping up the deck boards disappeared into the storage space beneath the bridge, trailing a hose behind him. It wasn't long before the starboard inner made reassuring noises, and we were able to report to Doug that we could now continue on two engines. He had had a fire under his twin Oerlikon platform, and this was now safely extinguished.

Ten minutes had passed since the first run ended and every man on board had been busy: each gun's crew had checked and replenished its supplies of ammunition from the ready-use lockers, and the 6-pounder and pom-pom had begun bringing up more from below. We had had no stoppages so far, and the gunners were elated and in high spirits. All but the starboard Oerlikon had been engaged, and they had all had the satisfaction of seeing their shells exploding on the target. I leaned over to the gunner at the starboard Oerlikon. "Your turn this time, I think. Don't forget—shoot low."

We moved off, and Doug, who had watched the whole convoy on his radar screen, passed a stream of ranges and bearings which kept us in the picture despite the poor visibility. As we closed on the tail end of the enemy line we realised that their gunfire during the first run had started an extensive bush fire on the Peljesac shore. That meant we had to attack from seaward this time so that the enemy, and not us, would be clearly silhouetted against the blazing hillside.

So our starboard gunner was again disappointed and we prepared to attack once more on the port bow.

This time we were running down the convoy on the same course as theirs and so would pass them much more slowly. As we closed up to the first group of smaller boats we could distinguish an E-boat and two landing craft. They opened fire and sprays of 20-mm. tracer poured from them.

The coxswain's lip curled. "Call that shooting?" he growled. "I don't need my tin hat if they can't get nearer than that."

I waited for Doug's order. "Dogs from Wimpey—open fire!"

At 200 yards we sailed relentlessly and slowly past, pouring out a deadly hail of fire which silenced all reply in a few seconds. When I sounded the "cease fire" signal, all three were left as burning, lifeless hulks.

The "big three" at the front were stronger meat. They were in line ahead, and I studied them through my glasses. The two schooners ahead looked large, and stood higher out of the water than usual targets. By contrast, the F-lighter, which was nearest to us, was low and sinister in its compact mass. They made no attempt to alter course or to evade the issue, but opened fire when we were still about 600 yards away.

We waited yet again for the S.O.'s signal; I clicked on the loud hailer. "All guns. Our target is the middle one. Accuracy is going to count here. Shoot low. It's up to you!"

This time Doug opened fire first and we followed suit. He had loaded some starshell, and the gunners had no difficulty in selecting their target. I had my eyes glued to our own target, but I had vague impressions of 657's attack on the leading schooner and of 663 pounding away at the low F-lighter.

I looked aft. The 6-pounder crew were steadily passing ammunition from hand to hand and I could feel the jerk as every round was fired. Good lads! They were the men who could win this fight, not Doug, or Corny, or me. By putting 658 in a good firing position, we could give them the opportunity to win it—but they had to do the shooting. If they couldn't shoot low and hit, then we had wasted our time and we should all pay the price. I thought of my gunnery instructor. "The quick—and the dead." He had known.

As soon as schooner number two realised he was receiving our complete broadside, he opened up at us with everything he had. I picked out a 40-mm. for'd and a multiple 20-mm. aft, and told the pom-pom and twin Oerlikon to knock them out. The noise was deafening and incessant, and the smell of smoke, hot metal, grease and cordite mingled with the ever-present tang of exhaust fumes.

Suddenly I found myself cheering. Watt at the 6-pounder had been crashing shell after shell into the schooner's hull and now he changed his aim to its high poop-deck aft. A vivid flash was followed by the boom of an explosion. Ammunition spouted skywards like a set-piece of fireworks at the Crystal Palace.

Corny shouted: "That was an ammunition locker, I reckon." I nodded. It was time to check fire as we were now well ahead of our target. I directed the guns to schooner number one. It was still firing, however, and tracer skimmed over and across us as we drew further ahead.

The coxswain continued his scathing commentary on German gunnery and training methods. "I reckon they don't do any drill, sir; perhaps they haven't got bastards for gunnery officers like we 'ave!" No one really listened, but it raised a smile and it relieved his feelings to natter.

Their fire began to slacken as we drew ahead, and I breathed hard and swallowed. "That wasn't too pleasant, was it?" said Corny. "Check the guns and see if we have any damage." We increased speed and followed Doug out ahead of the convoy. Each gun reported all correct, and I sent the leading seaman to have a rapid look round below decks.

"Hello, Dogs, this is Wimpey. I'm going to get well ahead, to give us time for reloading. Well done so far. Let me know when you're all set."

More ammunition was brought up from below, and the task of reloading empty Oerlikon drums began. We heard Tommy ask Doug for time to clear a pom-pom stoppage, and within twelve minutes all boats were ready to move in again. Once again Doug gave us a word picture of the enemy convoy, and Corny told me to pass on the information to the gunners. In this way everybody on board knew what we were doing, and we found that the resulting confidence was invaluable.

One of the large ships had stopped. The other two (the schooners, we thought) and another smaller craft were continuing down channel towards us. This meant that we could again make use of the bush fire (which our own shells had stoked up again) to silhouette the targets. This time it was the starboard gunner's turn, and as I warned him to stand by to open fire he grinned up at me to show that he was only waiting for the word to go.

We moved in at eight knots, and were astonished to see the leading schooner challenge us with the letter "H". Corny's brow knitted. "I wonder if she's expecting more escorts to join?" he muttered.

Our reply, from 400 yards, was made by twenty guns which poured a continuous hail of ammunition into her. After a few seconds she swung away to port towards the shore, completely shattered, and all her gunfire stopped.

Immediately we shifted target to the second schooner. Fire soon spouted up from her high poop-deck. By this time, we were also getting lit up by the shore fire, and Doug pulled us out again to find a better attacking position. As we did so there was a startling explosion, and Doug's voice came over: "We just watched that one disintegrating on the sunflower."[1] It was the schooner we had left on fire.

Down in the engine-room the starboard inner engine was still giving trouble, over-heating badly; finally Last had to stop it. He came up to the bridge and with a sad face—almost angry with himself—reported that we should only have one main engine running for the rest of the night.

When Corny passed this news on, the S.O. immediately ordered 658 to take up "Fleet Number Three", and told Tommy to move up ahead to become second in line while we dropped back to third place. We heard Tommy's voice on the R/T. "Hello, Wimpey, this is Tommy. But yes!"

I grinned at Corny. "They'll be getting swollen headed in the '63 boat—we'll have to think of something to take them down a peg." We had operated with 663 for eighteen months, and only once before had she been ahead of us in the line.

Once more over the R/T came Doug's drawl. "Hallo, Dogs, this is Wimpey. Two of these jokers are still holding course, so we'll wait inshore of them till they come up."

We got into the attacking position, and a quarter of an hour later the first schooner loomed into sight again, still with a smaller vessel tagging along. Corny muttered to me: "I wonder how he feels, Rover? He can't turn back and run for it; he's got to go on. He's had three attacks and he's waiting for the next. It's one hell of a situation."

When they got to 300 yards range, we opened fire, and once again it was returned heavily. These schooners could certainly take some punishment! But they had by no means our accuracy or fire-power by now and in a very short time were both silenced. The smaller boat was well ablaze and stopped, and the large schooner had a deck fire, and turned sharply inshore under our stern.

Doug's radar screen now showed only stationary ships. Not one

[1] Sunflower: R/T code for radar screen.

was moving in the original direction, and he therefore decided to move back along the channel to "mop up" the remains.

We were most concerned with the large schooner and, sure enough, we sighted it close inshore about half a mile away. As soon as we stopped, the schooner, which must have spotted or heard us, turned sharply for the beach and disappeared from sight. We hunted along the coast twice, but still could not see her.

Doug ordered us to search with the remains of the pom-pom star-shell, and so Duffill began banging away with short bursts along the cliffs until eventually, with the help once more of burning shrubs, we spotted the elusive craft beached at the foot of a cliff. At once all guns opened fire, and when the target was well alight 663 was sent in to finish it off. It continued to burn fiercely with periodic explosions, and blew up finally an hour later.

We then continued along the channel until, after some searching and assistance from the radar, we found a stationary target which on closer inspection turned out to be an oil tanker which had been abandoned. Doug debated whether to take it in tow, but eventually decided to sink it. This took two runs to accomplish. On we went again, closing the shore near the position of the original attack, but the radar screen was blank and nothing seemed to be left afloat along the whole length of the Mljet Channel.

We had now been continuously in action for nearly five hours, and Doug considered the victory complete. He turned for home.

We limped back to Komiza, with Last nursing our one sound engine to give us about eight knots. On the way, Doug sent a signal to SNOVIS asking him to arrange an R.A.F. sweep over the area at first light. Two Hurricanes were sent, and found only one ship afloat, which they destroyed with rockets. Apparently it was the F-lighter we had "lost" after the second attack. It must have found a secure little hiding place, as we had looked hard enough for it.

Although the return was slow and we were dead-tired, there was a jubilant air in the boats. None of us had ever been in so long an action, and aboard 658, Corny, Mike and I talked over every stage of it and every feature of the ships we had fought.

The two schooners had put up a very game fight. They had had a quadruple 20-mm. on the raised platform aft, and one or two 20-mm. for'd; and there had been at least two 37-mm. guns midships which had only fired single shot.

Within two minutes of berthing alongside, the post-mortem was continued in 657's wardroom with all the C.O.s and Number Ones joining in. During the night, the three Dogs had sunk at least two schooners, one E-boat, one oil-tanker and one Pil-boat; four others (including the F-lighter the R.A.F. had finished off) were either sunk or damaged; and no ship of the convoy passed the point in the channel where the last attack was launched, or completed its voyage. Our boats had suffered not a single casualty, although both 657 and 658 had been hit many times. 663 had emerged completely unscathed after five hours of attacks.

Later the Partisans brought in fourteen prisoners they had picked up among the islands, and these were interrogated and revealed some interesting facts. The schooners, they said, were of about 300 tons each, one carrying ammunition and the other foodstuffs. They had only just completed long refits in Split, and were sunk on their first voyage after recommissioning. They had sailed from Korcula and were bound for Dubrovnik. The crews of the schooners (one of the prisoners was a German petty officer coxswain) did not know much about the other boats of the convoy because they joined after dark.

In forwarding Doug's report to the Commander-in-Chief, Captain Coastal Forces made the following comment: "This action may well be regarded as a 'peak' performance of the 56th MGB/MTB Flotilla, with all its R.C.N.V.R. commanding officers under the magnificent leadership of Lt.-Cdr. J. D. Maitland, D.S.C. That he was faultlessly followed and supported by Lieutenant C. Burke, D.S.C., and Lieutenant T. E. Ladner is clear from the action report, and to one who knows them is almost to state the obvious. As the S.O. stated in his report, this was teamwork of the highest order. . .

"In the light of the reports from Intelligence, it is thought that this action may be described as the shrewdest blow that the enemy has suffered on the Dalmatian coast, and well may have speeded his evacuation of the Islands."

## Chapter XX

## MINES TAKE THEIR TOLL

A S soon as we had got our breath back, we were sent to Manfredonia for repairs. The shipwrights and engineer officers came
aboard and shook their heads over a large hole in the engine-
room. The deck-shelf which ran the length of the boat beneath the
rubbing strake (at the gunwale) had been shattered, and this would
obviously weaken the rigidity of the boat and cause serious trouble in
a bad sea. Many Dogs had already been weakening midships after
eighteen months of battering in all weathers, and it had been decided
to put in steel braces to maintain the strength there: in our case 658
would have to have the longest possible steel brace to prevent her
breaking her back as soon as she began to plunge into a head sea. This
was fitted and seemed comfortable when we put it through a series of
trials, and in a short while our engines were repaired.

Next day we were about to return to the Islands, when a signal from
Brindisi caused one of those completely unexpected turn-rounds for
which the Navy is renowned. Obviously Intelligence obtained some
special information, and after (one imagines) great deliberations at
enormously high level, signals were despatched which summoned every
Dog-boat of every flotilla to gather at Brindisi. Boats arrived hot-foot,
were sent to fuel, and given sailing orders to leave next morning.

The news was momentous. The Germans were planning a withdrawal from the major islands of the Adriatic. This was something new.
Up to now, they had never given an inch without fighting for it: now
they were being forced to concentrate their strength on the mainland.
It might well be the beginning of the end.

The purpose of our patrols was therefore to ensure that any enemy
ships withdrawing men and materials from the islands to the
mainland were given an uncomfortable passage. The 56th were
despatched to patrol between Corfu and the mainland. But Corfu was
150 miles from Brindisi, so we should be away for a long time. Tim
Bligh and the 57th were given the island of Cephalonia to blockade, and
that was nearly 250 miles away!

Doug was in Corsica chasing radar spares from the United States Navy once again, so Lt.-Cdr. Basil Bourne, S.O. of the 60th Flotilla, travelled with us in 658, with 663 and 657 in an unusual order behind us. We cut down speed on passage to conserve petrol, and took twelve hours to reach the patrol area soon after dusk. The most unpleasant part of this operation was the need to penetrate the very narrow gap into the inshore channel, especially as coastal batteries were plotted on our charts and completely covered the gap.

We managed to slide self-consciously through, holding our breath and talking in whispers, before the moon was up. But we knew we should have to return through the same gap in bright moonlight before dawn. Suppose they already knew we were in, and were quietly waiting for us to return? It was an uncomfortable thought.

We patrolled for ten hours, and saw nothing. Just before first light, we crept out again, but no hornets buzzed round our heads. In view of the nervous tension we had generated and exhausted, we felt this was worse than two ordinary patrols.

Tim's force not only had the very long passage to and from Cephalonia, but also met the promised evacuation and destroyed four I-lighters and two schooners, taking fourteen prisoners. In all they covered 535 miles and were at sea for forty-seven hours. It was one of the longest coastal force patrols of the war. Gordon came over from 634, and his only complaint was that the "flap" had meant going to sea when his ship's side was newly painted, and most of the paint had been stripped off. This had made him furious.

No one suggested that we should return to Corfu for a second night, and that evening we moved back to Manfredonia. Awaiting us there was a signal which routed us on to Ancona, which had fallen into Allied hands only a short while before. A Base at Ancona would put Venice and possibly even Trieste within striking distance of our patrols, and C.C.F. had lost no time in sending the newly raised Mobile Base up there by road. In command was Lt.-Cdr. Norman Hughes, who had been our S.O. at Sicily, and the engineer officer was another great friend of ours from Bobby Allan's Base at Augusta, Lieutenant (E) Taylor, whom we all knew as "Chum".

We found Ancona rather pleasant after Manfredonia and Brindisi, with well-organized welfare services; this was commonly the case in a town which was near enough to the front line for troops to be sent there when resting. Norman had established the Base along a stretch of quay close inside the southern entrance to the harbour. The major disadvantage of the position was that it was sandwiched between the fuelling tanker and a huge ammunition dump in the castle-like arsenal. It would not be healthy in air raids. But this was not considered as serious as our second discovery. It took a quarter of an hour to reach the dockyard gates when going ashore!

At Ancona we were nearer to the main front line than we had been since Sicily, the present battle being centred round Rimini, about fifty miles up the coast. A big push was just beginning, involving the Canadians and the Eighth Army, and the famous artillery barrage was pounding away at the enemy.

To assist it, our old friends from Bone, the destroyers *Loyal*, *Lookout* and *Laforey*, were moving up the coast each night to bombard the enemy's flank from seaward. Minesweepers were keeping a channel clear for them, but Jerry had been laying mines from low-flying aircraft and from E-boats, and so we were immediately detailed for a series of patrols to deter the E-boats. That was all very well, we thought, but what about the low-flying aircraft? Suppose they dropped mines behind us? We still had to get back.

No one had the answer to that one, and we weren't very happy to see an ML towed back to Ancona with her bows missing. In 658, we thought back to the sight of 640 and began to wonder if we would always be as fortunate as we had been then. The crippled ML once again added mines to our list of worries, especially as the Adriatic got shallower and shallower from Ancona northward and was reported to be thick with mines.

Twice we sailed up the channel and patrolled steadily along the stretch opposite Rimini. It was fascinating to have a seaward view of the tremendous barrage. Huge flashes rent the darkness and small red balls of tracer trundled slowly across the gap, looking inocuous at this distance.

On the third night we stayed in harbour and Corny obtained permission to visit the front line with his brother-in-law, who commanded a Canadian unit at present resting after hard fighting.

While he was away the first heavy blow struck at our flotilla. At 0400 that morning a hand shook my shoulder, and I stared up, suddenly alert, into the eyes of the Base duty officer.

"657's been mined about sixty miles up the channel, Rover. 633 is standing by her but you are to get up there quickly. The weather's freshening, so 633 will probably need some help."

As I thrust my feet into my sandals and pulled on trousers and duffel coat, my thoughts clicked into focus. Of course—Doug was still away in Corsica, and Freddie Mills, his first lieutenant, was in command of 657 for the time being. And Tony was out with them as spare Number One. . . . Had he been lucky again?

"Is there any news of casualties?"

The duty officer handed me the signal from 633 which contained all the news they had received.

"657 mined aft. Still afloat. Am attempting to rig tow. Position..."

Aft, eh? Well, Tony may have cheated the devil again—and probably aft was the least dangerous place to be mined from the point of view of casualties.

We plunged northward through grey choppy seas—and eventually spotted two small blobs right ahead soon after first light. As we closed we could see that they were under way, but when I saw 657 I gave a whistle of astonishment. Her stern was completely missing, and the after bulkhead of the petrol compartment was exposed and appeared to be holding. The tiller flat, stokers' and P.O.s' messes and the after ammunition store had vanished, and the deck above them was curled upwards as though a giant smoothing plane had taken a large shaving against the grain and left it jagged and forlorn, pointing skywards.

I manoeuvred 658 close to 657 to see if she needed any further assistance, and to find out about casualties. It was not easy to get close as she was yawing from side to side, completely uncontrollable as both her rudders had gone. At each limit she brought up with a shudder as the tow came taut and vibrated under the strain before it eased again while she charged off on the other tack.

At last my fears for Tony were allayed. I breathed a sigh of relief as I saw him on the fo'c'sle with a small party of seamen watching the tow. Freddie, too, was safe, and waved from the bridge as we came near.

I raised the megaphone and shouted.

"Hallo, Freddie! Bad luck. How are you off for casualties?"

"Nice to see you, Rover. Five missing I'm afraid, including Jock Gardner the motor mechanic and Hales our steward. Nobody injured otherwise, but we all got a bit of a shock."

"How's Tony?" I shouted.

"Oh! He's quite convinced he's immune from mining after this second go. He's in good form!"

I increased speed and went ahead to talk to Steve Rendell, the Canadian skipper of 633. Steve was from Vancouver and had been

Doug's Number One in 657 until the spring, so he was probably feeling the blow rather hard. He was obviously worried about his tow, and it certainly looked as though it was bound to part if 657 kept up her constant yawing.

The coxswain had already rigged our towing gear, and it was all set for passing if the need arose. Within half an hour it did. The tow parted with a twang, 657 slid round rapidly into the trough, and began rolling crazily in the heavy swell.

In a few seconds I had laid 658's stern close to her bows, and saw with pleasure that already Tony and his men had heaved in the useless end of the tow, which had parted near their end, and had got it un-shackled and ready for our hawser. Over went our heaving line— first time—and as it was seized and heaved in by one of their men, we bent on our stern line first, then the hawser to make sure nothing parted.

Leaving Mike at the controls, I went down aft to superintend the careful easing out of the hawser without damage to our propellers. All was under control though. I heard our coxswain shout to Collins (the coxswain of 657):

"Don't forget to return our bloody stern line when we get in!"

In a flash Collins replied:

"That's all right old man—we don't need one now—we haven't got a stern!"

Slowly we went ahead and nursed the tow gently taut until the weight was taken up and the strange sluggish feeling gave the helms-man much more trouble. The coxswain took the wheel and had his work cut out to counteract the quarter swell and the yawing tow. However we built up from five to eight knots and all seemed well, with 657 still afloat.

Tony semaphored that water was slowly gaining in the engine-room, but the hand pumps were able to cope with most of it. We finally reached Ancona at 1000 and slipped the tow before going alongside 657 and taking her into her new—and last—berth in the "graveyard" alongside the remains of the ML crippled in the previous week.

This was the melancholy sight which greeted both Corny and Doug when they returned from their respective journeys next morning. For us, the loss of 657 was a very sad business, as we had been together so much throughout all our commission. And we could ill afford to lose men of the calibre of Jock Gardner, Doug's motor mechanic, who had been awarded the D.S.M. for fine work in many patrols.

And our period of sadness was not yet over. We did not know it, but there was another—even closer—blow to fall.

About a month later, and quite unexpectedly, Tommy Ladner left 663 and became C.C.F.'s S.O.O. at Malta. He had been actively engaged in Coastal Force operations for almost four years continuously, and felt it was time he went ashore. He had therefore stepped down, and tried very hard to pass 663 over to Derrick. But Derrick had not been considered to have sufficient seniority, and the command had been given to Lieutenant Bill Darracott, who had been Tim Bligh's very distinguished first lieutenant in 662 and already wore a D.S.C. and bar.

Tommy's going was a great shock to me, and a sad blow to Derrick. I admired him immensely, and felt we had lost a magnificent leader. After Corny, I would have chosen to follow Tommy Ladner whenever things looked bad and, indeed, I remembered his thoughtfulness and help when we were in trouble off Elba several months before.

Seamen will tell you that ships have a personality of their own. They will describe one which was a real bastard and another which was always a delight to sail in; they will ascribe feelings of pride or sorrow to their ships and attribute to them the jealousy of a proud woman. We all believed our boats had feelings; and certainly 663 was to prove it in the only way she could.

Nine days after Tommy left her, on her first patrol with her new C.O., 663 hit a mine and was so severely damaged that she had to be sunk. She had laid down her burden. Derrick told me the details when the survivors were brought into Ancona at about 0600. I had been warned by the Base duty officer who knew our close liaison with 663, but once again we had no details about casualties. I spent two hours of torture. Derrick was my oldest friend in the Navy; Tony Marriott another constant visitor and good friend. How had they fared?

They were both on the bridge of 649 when she came in, and when they had made the necessary arrangements for the wounded and the other survivors, we gave them breakfast and tried to help them out with a few items of kit. They had lost everything except what they were wearing.

They had been patrolling with two other boats off Venice all night, and had started for home with the wind freshening behind them.

663 was last in the line. Suddenly, the deck lifted under them and everyone on the bridge was blown clean out of it. Derrick travelled in a standing position and came down fairly softly on all fours on the starboard ammunition lockers. Petty Officer Nichol, the coxswain, came down above him and found himself draped on the Oerlikon depression rails. Bill Darracott landed like a sack over the guard rails and dangled there unconscious. The bridge lookout was never seen again.

A mine had detonated beneath the bridge and had torn away the forward end of the engine-room. The boat folded in the middle, held rigid only by the steel straps which had been fitted a month or two earlier as part of the general strengthening of Dog-boats. Without them she would have split in two. As it was, bows and stern were well out of the water, and the deck amidships was about a foot under water. Things looked bad for the engine-room crew.

Derrick mustered the crew and found that two of the stokers were missing, as well as the bridge lookout, and eight men were wounded. The number of missing would have been greater, but Billingham, the leading seaman, had climbed down into the flooded engine-room, found two men trapped there with their heads in a pocket of air, and led them out through the submerged hatch. It was the act of a brave man: nothing is more eerie than the death noises of a stricken ship, and the engine-room must have been a dark and fearsome place to enter.

Peter Hughes, the S.O. of the unit for the night (he was a quiet South African lieutenant, very well liked and rather older than most of the C.O.s) took off all the survivors while Derrick and Tony went below to destroy the radar and W/T. The noise of grinding frames and pounding waves filled them with awe and they finished the task as quickly as possible.

It took several minutes of concentrated firing from two boats to leave her burning to the water line and slowly settling. Not one of the survivors had had to go into the sea: everyone had walked calmly across to 649 and there had been no signs of panic or even of undue alarm.

In one month the pattern of our lives in 658 had changed completely. No longer did we have 657 and 663 to maintain that closeness of spirit we had found so vital in our operations. It was never the same again. Only six weeks earlier we had fought together an action in which the most outstanding feature was impeccable team-work and understanding. Now we were left alone.

We soon found that C.C.F. had acted with speed and decision in re-arranging the available personnel after the depletion of our flotilla. Doug Maitland, who had led us for almost a year of eventful action, went to become S.O.O. to the Senior Naval Officer, Northern Adriatic (S.N.O.N.A.)—our old friend Captain Dickinson who had been relieved as S.O.I.S. at Leghorn by Bobby Allan.

In Doug's place, Corny was appointed as senior officer of the 56th Flotilla, and became an acting lieutenant-commander. As soon as the news came through he took me into his cabin.

"I've talked over your position with C.C.F., Rover, and he is going to appoint you as 'spare officer for flotilla duties'. That duty—and he agrees—will be to command 658 with Tony as Number One." He looked at me keenly and went on: "You can't be appointed in command yet, as C. W. Branch[1] would probably object on the grounds of your youth—but, except for the command money, you will be skipper. I'd like to live aboard if you don't mind—I'm very attached to the old '58 boat, y'know!"

At the same time, we lost Mike Walker-Munro, who had been a fine shipmate and had shared some of our most unpleasant experiences, and received in his place Doug's old Pilot, Sub-Lieutenant Louis Battle, always known as "Eager-Beaver Battle" by the Canadians, a name well earned by his energy and efficiency.

To complete the turn-round, Doug's coxswain, who hadn't been with him long before 657 was mined, came to us. Petty Officer Ron Collins would have made a good officer. He was content to be a good coxswain, and that was very agreeable for us. He had his own business in civvy street, and it always amused me to think that after the war I might well be reduced to asking my coxswain to give me a job!

Till the end of our commission I never had to worry about victualling accounts or anything of that sort. Collins was a valuable asset and I was glad to get him. As so often happened, our good fortune with him was countered by our misfortune in losing Bill Last, our re-doubtable motor mechanic, who went ashore to the Base at Malta where he could relax a bit after three years or more of operations. Young Burrows, who had qualified as a P.O. motor mechanic some

[1] The Admiralty Department responsible for officers' appointments.

months before, moved up to become "Chief" of the engine-room, and we received a new leading M.M. in his place.

When we returned to Vis a few days later, we felt different in every respect: different in company and in spirit. We needed to start afresh, and this was a difficult time to do it.

## CHAPTER XXI

## RADAR, REFIT—AND ROME!

WE found the whole pattern of war in the Islands had changed completely in the four weeks since we had left for repairs. The Germans had evacuated the islands one after the other, and Partisans with the help of a British force called "Land Forces Adriatic" (L.F.A.) had been assisting them to move more rapidly and taking considerable toll of the German garrisons in their withdrawal.

L.F.A. included the 43rd Royal Marine Commando, and already relations between this unit and our boats had become cordial. They were cemented firmly within a day or two.

There was still a German garrison in the island of Brac, and the first night of our return saw us sitting quietly off the coast, hoping that the noisy battle going on ashore would mean that soon a nice fat target such as an unescorted German transport would appear, making a hurried exit heading for the mainland. But though guns crashed and machine-guns stuttered only a quarter of a mile away, no one noticed us and there was nothing for 658 to do. We could not even join in the fight with a few judiciously placed bricks from the 6-pounder, because we did not know how the battle was going on ashore.

For over a week we operated among the more northerly islands, working in two sections so that each boat had every other night in harbour.

One night all the boats were rested. A poker session was in full swing in 658's wardroom when suddenly a beard followed by Lieutenant Baker (S.O.O. to S.N.O.V.I.S.) appeared in the doorway.

"Hallo, S.O.O.—come down for a drink?"

"No—sorry, Corny. How soon can you get a unit out? We need two boats for a flap patrol."

"Give us a quarter of an hour, then. It'll be 633 and 655 as 658 and Peter Hughes were out last night—I'll travel with Cam in 655. Shall I come along to the operations room for the dope?"

658's wardroom rapidly cleared. It sounded as though they might meet something again, after a rather dull patch. We had been carrying a Canadian Naval Press Relations officer for the past fortnight; he had been out on five fruitless patrols and was getting wrong ideas about the work of Coastal Forces, although it was just as well to impress upon him that it was not all blood and glory, but often boredom and unrelenting concentration.

Although it was 2300 when S.O.O. interrupted our poker game, at 2318 Tony and I were watching the two boats leave. They were back at 0530, and the duty quartermaster came down and woke me.

Corny was ready at the gangway as Cam brought 655 alongside us, a broad grin on his face.

"That was a nice little job, Rover. I wish they were all like that. Only six hours out, two hours on patrol, and we sank three I-lighters.[1] No damage or casualties. I'll just go along to see Morgan Giles, then I'll be back. How about having some Bovril and sherry ready?"

When he returned, he found Cam and Steve Rendell already nestled in corner seats, sipping their steaming cups of this very popular beverage. It had almost become traditional in our flotilla that if boats came in during the night the C.O.s should gather over Bovril and sherry to talk over the night's activities.

"They wouldn't start telling me any details till you got back, Corny," I complained. "So come on, let's hear what you've been up to."

Corny was very modest about the whole affair. Everything had gone right. Conditions were good, they had arrived at just the right time, the enemy were unprepared—in fact the operation from beginning to end had been blessed with the best of good fortune. To cap it all, "Charlie Charlie" (C.C.F.-Captain Stevens) was in Vis and was vastly pleased to have the opportunity to see his boats both leave and return from a successful patrol. Corny had made a good start as S.O.

I got more concrete details out of Cam and Steve. The boats had been ordered to patrol off Rogac Cove, a bay on the island of Sulet. The sudden "flap" had started after S.N.O.V.I.S. received a signal from the Commandos that the Germans would be evacuating the island during the night.

The boats arrived to find three I-lighters in the bay. They must have just left the beach. Corny promptly waded in attacking at close range. Apart from a little sporadic 20-mm. fire, the I-lighters did not fight back: and almost immediately the first lighter blew up and showered itself over our two boats.

[1] A lighter similar in design, but smaller than an F-lighter.

When 655 turned into the bay for the second run no sign at all could be found of the two remaining lighters. Incendiary shells from 655's Oerlikons lit the shore but still nothing could be seen. A further check was made with pom-pom starshell, and as the bay was manifestly clear of any shipping, and the two lighters could not possibly have escaped unseen, it was assumed that they had sunk after being hit hard in the first run.

There were two unusual and interesting sequels to this action. The first was the arrival next day of a signal from S.N.O.V.I.S. for Corny. It read:

"*The Royal Marine Commandos today occupied Gromote and Rogac. They have sent the following message: 'Complete combined operation. Royal Navy and Army in right place at right time. Well done Royal Navy, thanks and congratulations from all ranks. 43rd R.M. Commando.'*
*It appears that the three I-boats you sank last night contained almost the entire garrison of Solta. Well done indeed.*"

Two days later, more details were revealed when two Poles were brought to Vis for interrogation after deserting from a labour squad attached to the German garrison at Sulet. They had been part of the force of two hundred men with mules, guns and equipment, who had embarked in the three I-lighters and begun the voyage to the mainland at Split. They had seen the MTBs' attack, and watched two of the lighters blowing up: the third (theirs) sank more slowly and they were able to swim ashore and hide in a slit trench in the confusion.

From their hiding place they had watched two E-boats come over from Split at first light to take off the remaining survivors. From the numbers they saw on the beach, it seemed that at least one hundred and twenty men must have been killed in the MTBs' attack, and all the equipment had certainly been lost.

After this achievement, we felt happier. True, 658 had not taken part in it but Corny's rapid success was a tonic to our rather shaky confidence after the unsettling events of the past few weeks.

Now came further news destined to change our routine a great deal. We were to sail to Ancona at once to be fitted with the S.O. radar gear which we had been awaiting eagerly for months. We should be out of action for at least a week.

This was our first chance to explore and get to know Ancona well, and we soon found that it was a pleasant town to be based in. In the middle of the town, down under a square rather like a large public convenience in the West End, were the Public Baths. There was no swimming pool—only rows and rows of baths, and they soon became the true centre of Ancona's service life.

We would pay a few pence, wait in a comfortable armchair, chatting or reading a magazine, and then have the luxurious relaxation of soaking in delightfully hot water, which in no time would banish all cares from the mind and all aches from the body.

Doug (now a very important person ashore) had a pleasant flat in the town, which was used by most of the flotilla when a headquarters ashore was needed. He did not seem to mind. For the first time in any of our Bases we could enjoy our limited recreational time with well-organized amenities, and we began to take full advantage of them. We visited the theatre, the concert hall (an Italian orchestra was giving symphony concerts every weekend), and the cinema, and in all of them the Army welfare service provided good programmes.

The men were delighted with what they found, too. A huge NAAFI building just outside the dockyard filled many of their needs, and Jack was able to enjoy his run ashore in Ancona more cheaply and easily than in any place since Malta.

When our radar was fitted, it was necessary to get 658 out of the water to finish the job and, as there was no floating dock yet in Ancona, we sailed south to Manfredonia to get it completed as quickly as possible. The little pontoon dock there was rather eccentric, and was prone to flooding unexpectedly, thus causing a pronounced list to starboard. It took a little while to get used to this, as it did not feel very safe to be high and dry with the deck twenty feet above the dock and to know that the mechanics in charge of the dock were not within easy call to put the list right. Fortunately for my peace of mind, the arrival of Tim Bligh's 57th Flotilla distracted my attention from the dock and soon gave me more pleasant things to think about.

We soon discovered that Tim's boats had just fought a magnificent action off Vir Island in which, over many hours, they had sunk six F-lighters and at least five other small craft.

In spite of the fact that this successful action was not fought by 658 or by any boats of the 56th flotilla, we all derived very great pleasure from the thought that at last the Dog-boats had, on their own, proved themselves the masters of their old enemies, the F-lighters. It did not matter which flotilla had done it—it had been done, and we were full of admiration for Tim and his men for doing it.

Next day we went out to do our radar trials, feeling very naked without our mast, and eyeing the dome (which seemed to loom over the bridge) with some uneasiness. The results were excellent, and at once we felt the confidence that high-performance gear gives. Now we were ready to sail back to the Islands and could expect to be able to seek out the enemy even on the darkest night.

But Fate had other ideas for us. Instead of our sailing orders for Vis arrived a signal ordering us to Brindisi for engine change and minor refit. Our engines had run for 600 hours, and apparently our turn on the rota had come up, and so although we were completely operational and ready to sail, it had been decided to fit us in for overhaul at Miraglia.

I was disappointed, as we were all keen to see our radar in use among the islands, but nothing could be done. Corny left for Vis to lead the flotilla, and I took 658 southward again to Brindisi. On the way the thought suddenly struck me that this might be the opportunity for getting in a short spell of leave.

After all, we had been in the Med for eighteen months and I had hardly been away from the boat in all that time, so I felt there might be a chance.

When Tony took over the watch I went below and took out an atlas. An idea was germinating, but I didn't know if it would be possible. Derrick and Tony had just gone off from Ancona to spend ten days survivor's leave in Rome. Could I join them there?

I stepped off the distances with the dividers. Brindisi to Bari—70 miles. There was a railway marked from Bari to Naples—would it be functioning? Otherwise it was 150 miles, and the Apennines to cross into the bargain. Then another 150 miles from Naples to Rome. If I could wangle a week's leave, I reckoned I could get to Rome in forty-eight hours, and it shouldn't be too difficult to get back. Unless there was any official transport for part of the way, I would have to hitch-hike, but I knew several people who had already done that successfully, although not for as long a trip as Brindisi to Rome.

The more I thought of it, the more the idea of Rome and a spell away from the boat appealed to me. I was feeling stale: I needed a change. I soon convinced myself.

I waited till our refit was well under way, and then broached the subject with Freddie Warner, the C.O. at Miraglia. He had no objection, so I packed a bag containing my best blue uniform and a few essentials, put on khaki drill with a battledress top, and walked out to the coast road just before lunch.

I was soon bowling along in an Italian greengrocer's van towards Bari, but after thirty miles I transferred to a more stylish conveyance, riding with a colonel of the Royal Marine Commando in his Jeep. When I arrived at Bari railway station, I found I should need a leave pass and permit to travel in order to get a place on the Naples train leaving at 2000.

This was a very small obstacle. Was I not my own commanding officer? I walked into the waiting room, rummaged in my bag for paper and pen, and wrote myself out an imposing document which (I hoped) would see me past most barriers.

I took this back to the ticket office. The official gave it a perfunctory glance, and pushed it back with a ticket to Naples. I was through. The R.T.O. on the platform suggested that I should contact Major Green, the O/C of the train. I shared a very uncomfortable compartment with several army officers, and the long cold night passed restlessly away. I had no coat, and only the fortification of the hip-flask of brandy I had thoughtfully provided, prevented me from freezing completely.

The train crawled into Naples at 0600, and I made a bee-line for the Transit Mess for a shave and breakfast. Over my bacon and egg I made enquiries about my route. I wanted to visit the Allied Force Headquarters at Caserta, partly to see the magnificent palace in which it was housed and also to deliver a parcel to a young Wren there on behalf of an officer from one of our boats. I discovered that a duty truck left Naples for Caserta at 1000, and that I should probably be able to get a "hitch" from Caserta up to Rome.

That short drive was about the most uncomfortable I have ever had. The 15-cwt. truck was covered, it had board seats, and there were twelve of us wedged in it. The atmosphere was stifling and redolent with garlic, and I began to wish I had not started. But we got there, and I was not sick. That alone was an achievement.

I was directed to the Naval H.Q. section, and climbed wearily up several flights of a magnificent stairway, whose beauty I was in no fit state to appreciate. I paused to shift my heavy bag to my other hand, wiped the perspiration from my streaming face, and was about to move on to the next floor when I became aware of another's presence.

I looked up, and saw before me an admiral in full immaculate uniform eyeing me up and down as he studied this khaki-clad, travel-stained and bedraggled sub-lieutenant. I tried to stand to attention, but did not put down my bag; I was still so surprised to see him that I forgot to count the number of gold rings on his arm. I knew he had more than me.

I stood by for a large-size reprimand, knowing that I hardly conformed to the rig regulations for a place like this. Still I had put my head in the lion's mouth—I would have to grin if it bit me.

"What ship are you from?"

Even as he spoke I realised who he was. I had seen a photograph of him in *Union Jack*, the Forces newspaper published in Italy. I had not done things by halves. This was Sir John Cunningham, the Commander-in-Chief, Mediterranean.

"Motor Gun boat 658, sir—56th Flotilla."

"Ah!" he said, and to my astonishment he smiled and disappeared through the door. I breathed again, and spent the next ten minutes listing all the things "Ah" could have meant.

I delivered the parcel, and walked up the road until I came to the junction of Highways 5 and 6—each leading to Rome, but one via Monte Cassino where the Germans had put up such stern resistance and held up the Army's advance for months during the previous winter. This was still closed to traffic.

After half an hour, with no one taking any notice of a dusty khaki figure beside the road, my spirits began to flag and I wondered if my leave was going to be wasted. Would I have to go back to Naples and arrange something from there?

But my luck was in. Up screamed a boxed-in Jeep containing two young infantry majors.

"Jump in, sailor—where d'you want to go?"

"Rome, please."

"Certainly. Anything to please the Navy. Take the gentleman to Rome, James!" They were going on leave themselves and were in high spirits. "You don't know how lucky you are—you've chosen the only vehicle in Italy which would get you from Caserta to Rome within three hours—road blocks and all!"

I had no idea if this was an idle boast, but soon began to suspect that it was not. The driver seemed very skilful, and drove very fast. As we went, the two majors pointed out places of interest, and obviously knew the route very well. The journey passed rapidly, and before tea I was dropped at a central point in Rome, and received an invitation to dinner at their hotel.

I found the Naval leave hotel, produced my home-grown leave certificate and settled into a room. At the reception desk I found that

Derrick and Tony were still booked in, but they were not in their rooms.

When I had bathed and changed, I went down to the bar, and waited there. The trip to Rome was worth it just for the pleasure of seeing their faces when they came in through the swing doors and saw me sipping a drink straight ahead of them.

They had two days of their leave left, and were then to make their way to Naples and Malta to wait for new appointments. Both of them were dressed in khaki battledress, having lost all their naval kit aboard 663, and were looking forward to having a shopping spree at Malta.

For two days with them, and then for a further three days alone, I revelled in the freedom of independence; I put away all thoughts of boats and fuel and engines and guns and men; instead, I concentrated on enjoying myself, and succeeded with very little effort.

I had my first taste of grand opera, and the magnificence of the Opera House and the production of Tosca took my breath away. I toured the galleries and the ancient churches. I stood in St. Peter's Square and gazed at the great cathedral, then spent hours in the cathedral and gazed out at St. Peter's Square.

It was five days of escape: escape to the restfulness of an ancient and cultured city, to the pleasures of good food and drink, to new faces and to a bed more than two feet wide. I took a bath every day and break-fasted as late as possible.

And then came the problem of getting back to the boat. The first step was easy. By this time I had made some contacts, and the trip to Naples was very pleasant, in a staff car with two attractive young nurses for company.

From Naples, I arranged to travel beside the driver on the routine truck to Foggia (the huge airfield near Manfredonia) and so had the experience of travelling by road across the Apennines, and in daylight this time. The scenery was magnificent, but my frame did not appreciate the journey, and I was glad to lift my aching body from the front seat when we arrived at Foggia, to transfer to another 15-cwt. which took me on to Manfredonia and then Brindisi.

I found Tony pleased with the refit and the boat ready for trials. Two days later, we sailed for Ancona.

I felt fit and the boat seemed in good shape. We were ready to do our bit once more.

## CHAPTER XXII

## ALARUMS AND EXCURSIONS

O N the passage northward, I browsed through a batch of signals delivered just before we sailed. I came across one to C.C.F. from C.-in-C., whom I had met on the stairs at Caserta; despite the doubtful impression made by Sub-Lieutenant Reynolds, it read:

> "*I have observed with pleasure the conduct of the Light Coastal Forces operating from Bastia and in the Adriatic during recent months. The constant harrassing of the enemy's sea routes has had a direct bearing on the success of the armies fighting in Southern France and Italy, and highest praise is due to the officers and men whose uniform vigilance, daring and skill have been responsible for the destruction of many tons of enemy shipping and escort vessels, as well as to Base personnel who have maintained our craft in fighting conditions.*
>
> "*It is requested that you will convey my appreciation and congratulations to all concerned.*"

Knowing that Coastal Force operations had not always been regarded favourably by the powers-that-be, this tribute from the C.-in-C. made good reading. Perhaps if the potentialities of the boats had been appreciated earlier, we should have had much less trouble with the serious shortage of spares and supplies which had proved such a handicap in the not-too-distant past.

In Ancona, we picked up scraps of news straight away by inviting Ken Golding, the new C.O. of 633, down for a drink. Steve Rendell had heard that he was to return to Canada for leave, and Ken (whom we already knew quite well as C.O. of a Vosper MTB) had relieved him.

But Ken's other news was a great surprise and delight to us. When he had arrived in Malta, Derrick had been given command of 655, and with Johnny Mudd (Peter Barlow's old Pilot) and Tony Marriott would soon be joining us after a complete refit in Malta and the fitting of S.O. radar. It was great news for the Junior Dogs.

Corny was over in the Islands, and we sailed to join him almost immediately. This time the phrase "in the Islands" was literal, as Vis was no longer close enough to the scene of operations, after the fall of all the southern islands, to be of any value. Our boats were therefore working from a sheltered anchorage called Veli Rat at the north end of Dugi, the outer island of the group near Zara.

As we made our landfall, I searched anxiously for the landmarks which would fix our position. The margin of error was very small here. The islands a little to the north were still held by the Germans, and so was Zara, the main port of the region. There was every chance of meeting the Luftwaffe and enemy ships in daylight here, so even this pleasant passage could not be regarded light-heartedly. And there were always mines to think about. Our chart of the area was literally covered with shading which denoted minefields, and although there was a swept channel into our anchorage this was no guarantee that some unsporting German had not slipped out in an E-boat and mined the narrow entrance overnight in defiance of the off-side rule.

I was soon reassured. Our new Pilot, "Beaver" Battle, had lived up to his reputation as a very efficient navigator. The Maknare Channel lay right ahead and Veli Rat lighthouse came into sight on the starboard bow. Soon I could see the masts of Hunt-class destroyers in the bay, and gingerly I felt my way through the narrow gap into the otherwise land-locked anchorage.

All round the low, smoothly-rounded hills of the limestone islands rose in a bleak barrier, all bare rock or scrub, and at first sight very uninviting. And yet they were not ugly. Their very bleakness, stark against blue sky and deeper blue sea gave them a certain air of aloofness, of isolation, which had its own beauty.

Veli Rat was definitely overcrowded. Three Hunts—the *Wheatland*, *Lauderdale* and *Eggesford*—lay at anchor looking sleek and peaceful. Each had several boats alongside. On the far side of the bay a signalling lamp winked and ordered us alongside. The signal came from S.N.O.V.I.S. (Lt.-Cdr. Morgan Giles), but his headquarters ship was a new one to me. She was an LCI with additional superstructure and a large radar device mounted in place of a mast. On her side was painted LCH 315—officially "Landing Craft, Headquarters", but translated by the Partisans at first sight as "Landing Craft, Horse" owing to the stable-like appearance of her upper works.

I reported to Morgan Giles, was warmly welcomed, and returned to see Corny being rowed over in a dinghy from one of the boats along-

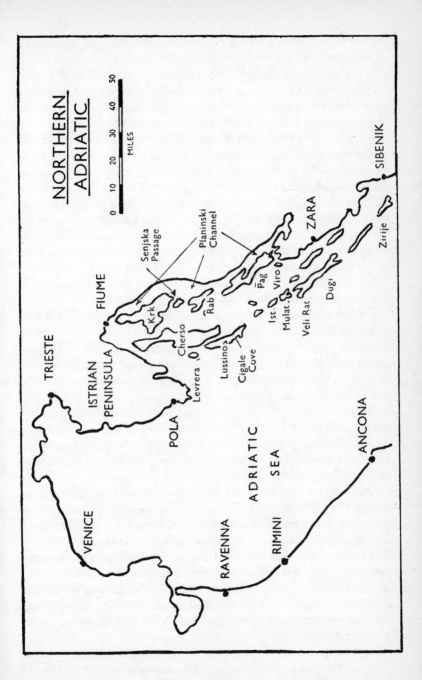

NORTHERN ADRIATIC

TRIESTE

ISTRIAN PENINSULA

POLA

FIUME

Krk

Cherso

Levrera

Lussino

Cigale Cove

Senjska Passage

Planinski Channel

Rab

Pag

Ist.

Viro

Mulat.

Veli Rat

Dugi

ZARA

Žirije

SIBENIK

ADRIATIC SEA

VENICE

RAVENNA

RIMINI

ANCONA

MILES

0    10    20    30    40    50

side *Eggesford*. We received him with ceremony, and he looked genuinely pleased to be back aboard.

"How's the radar, Rover?" he asked.

"Going like a bomb, Corny—we picked up some boats at seven and a half miles on the way over, and the charthouse repeater is a marvellous idea—you can pop down and see the situation in no time."

Eager to try out our new gadget, Corny took us out that night. We gloried in the new experience which made navigation (almost) foolproof and watch-keeping so much less strain.

As we searched up the coast we came across several drifters fishing with nets, using giant flares. It seemed a very ingenuous activity in the midst of total war. We stopped to search them to make sure they were not concealing any sinister purpose, but were soon satisfied. The fishermen were obviously scared stiff to find themselves under the guns of three aggressive-looking gunboats.

We soon got into a routine to overcome the difficulties of operating without any Base or even harbour.

When we returned from patrol, we would go alongside an LCT and fuel from 40-gallon drums; it took a long time, but it was the only fuel available. If we were not required for patrol, we would spend the night alongside one of the bigger ships, rather than anchor ourselves. For one thing, we could save our generator by taking electrical power from our temporary parent ship; also we always avoided anchoring if possible as we were only provided with a slender wire for the purpose, which never seemed very substantial, especially in bad weather.

And bad weather was on the way. We had been warned about the Bora in Ancona. The Bora was a freak wind which blew up very rapidly from the north, and with very little warning could reach gale force almost immediately as it funnelled down the Adriatic. In the mid-winter months, these gales sometimes continued for a week or more, although more often they would die down after several hours.

We were treated to a full demonstration almost immediately. We were berthed alongside LCH 315 for the night, and I had settled down to sleep when I was disturbed by a violent rocking of the boat. At first I thought it must be caused by the wake of another boat going past, and ignored it; but within five minutes it was bad enough for both Tony and me to crawl out of our bunks to have a look on deck to check lines and fenders.

I was staggered at the sight. From dead calm a few minutes earlier, a wind of gale force was blowing. The sea, even in this landlocked anchorage, had reacted immediately, and we were bumping up and down severely and crashing hard against the side of the LCH every time the ropes tightened. It was pitch-black, and for a moment my sense of direction deserted me completely. I looked anxiously round, and could see nothing except the occasional flash of torches on other boats nearby.

It was obviously impossible to stay alongside the LCH in this, so I gave the orders for engines and one watch on deck. Corny appeared on the bridge and offered to take her (he was still officially in command); almost at once he moved the telegraphs and 658 slid astern. We were just in time. As we left, a black shape loomed out of the darkness and came crashing in against the LCH exactly where we had been only a few seconds before. It was a minesweeper, dragging anchor and completely out of control.

"I think the only safe bet is to get alongside one of the destroyers," yelled Corny above the violence of the wind. "I wouldn't like to try to get out of that narrow entrance in these conditions, and there's nowhere to go if we did!"

The nearest destroyer loomed ahead, a Dog-boat already alongside. It was H.M.S. *Eggesford*. Corny crashed 658 against her and quickly the lines were passed and secured. Then we had the job of doubling and trebling them to withstand the force of the severe jerking and strain they would have to take. We did not sleep well that night.

Daylight revealed a sorry sight. Two BYMS (wooden minesweepers) and an ML lay broadside on to the beach, fast aground and heeled right over. Corny disappeared to talk to *Eggesford's* C.O., and re-appeared looking more cheerful.

"*Eggesford* and *Lauderdale* are going to move into Mulat Cove at 1000, and it should be comparatively sheltered there; so all four of our boats can get over there and lash up to them until this Bora blows out. It might be anything up to a week, so keep your fingers crossed!"

We made the move successfully, although it was very rough crossing the Maknare Channel and we got very wet, and then 658 settled down to ride out the storm firmly tied up to her foster-mother. Ken Golding brought 633 alongside on the starboard side, and *Eggesford* swung at her cable looking like a disdainfully elegant swan with two rather ugly cygnets in train. Tony put out every line he could muster, and was astonished when he counted them to find that he had rigged thirty-three altogether. They were all needed.

Although it was unlikely in such weather that we would be disturbed by any attack, there were known to be some German explosive motor boats (E.M.B.s), and human torpedoes based on Lussino Island only thirty miles away, which would relish such sitting targets as anchored destroyers. *Eggesford* therefore made a practice of lobbing small explosive charges overboard every five minutes, which were reckoned to be an effective deterrent to any little men in the water.

Every five minutes throughout that first day, 658 lifted a few inches, shook, and dropped down again. We began to worry about the effect on our propellers: we should have hated to start up engines and find that they had all dropped off! By the evening, Corny decided on action. He scribbled a mild protest to the *Eggesford's* skipper, and suggested that the charges might be dropped off the bows instead of the stern. The quartermaster took it over and was told to wait for an answer.

Several minutes later we heard the quartermaster descend the wardroom ladder and knock at our door. As the signal was handed to Corny, a terrific wallop beneath us seemed to lift the boat clear of the water, and he read: "Certainly. Was that one better? We'll drop them over the bows from now on. R.P.C.[1] you and your officers at 2030."

It was a beautifully timed gesture, and we congratulated the *Eggesford's* officers on it when we visited their comparatively spacious wardroom that evening.

The Bora continued for five days with hardly any break. We used the time to get the boat in first-class order, and to settle in our rather changed guns' crews with some intensive gun drill. We mixed well with the *Eggesford's* officers, and 658's crew were given the run of her facilities, especially the shower baths and the canteen.

On the last day of the blow, the ship's company of the *Eggesford* ran a party for the children of Mulat Island. The invitation was sent to the village through the Partisan authorities and there was a considerable delay before they heard whether the children would be coming. Eventually an officer arrived from Tito's Headquarters. Permission would be given for the children to be entertained provided an assurance was given by the Navy that no attempt would be made to influence their political thinking!

As we saw them climbing happily aboard, and later stuffing themselves with cakes, we wondered wryly whether they would be more influenced by the obvious gaiety and kindliness of *Eggesford's* sailors than by any amount of talking. It struck me that when I was five years old Stalin himself could not have influenced me if at the same time

[1] R.P.C.: Request the pleasure of the company.

someone had put me on a roundabout and given me enough sweets to keep me happy.

There were about twenty-five little Yugoslavs, and they were given a marvellous time. There was an Aunt Sally in the wardroom, side-shows all round the upper deck, the capstan was operated as a merry-go-round, and a huge tea was served on the messdeck. A genial petty officer acted as Father Christmas and distributed presents all round; and then came the biggest treat. The gunnery officer used all his old stock of signal rockets and flares to give a most impressive firework display, which was greeted with all the "Oooohs" and "Aaahs" we should have expected from British children. It was a fine illustration of the versatility of the British sailor, and it was obvious that the Active Service ratings knew all the tricks in staging an occasion of this sort.

When at last we singled up our lines and slipped from the *Eggesford*, we seemed to have been alongside her for much longer than five days. It had been a new experience—now we must get back on the job.

Straight away Morgan Giles planned a daring and rather hazardous patrol right inside the Planinski Channel. This channel—never much more than five miles wide and often as narrow as two—ran the whole length of the mainland almost as far south as Zara, protected by long islands on its seaward side. Along it ran the main enemy supply route, hugging the coast and bringing vital stores from Fiume southward to the German forces retreating slowly from the Zara area.

The guarding islands were almost continuous, and in many places were double or treble banked. Where there were gaps, minefields were marked on the charts and coastal batteries were believed to cover the entrances. The plan was that we should enter through one of these gaps where the minefield was believed to be laid rather deep, and where the guns were said not to be ready yet.

We looked at this Senjska Passage on the chart. It was just under half a mile wide, and was shaded in red. Red meant minefields, and it was all very well for someone to tell us the mines were laid deep. But once we were in, the possibilities were enormous. The sea had calmed quickly, there was no moon, and it was probable that the enemy might regard the "Plan-Chan" as impenetrable. They may be right, too—it looked it to us. Anyway, there was every chance that if we got inside we should achieve surprise.

So the patrol was on. First we all needed fuel, and we went into Mulat Cove, where we found 40-gallon barrels of 100-octane petrol stacked on the jetty with no one looking after them.

We found one important difference on this patrol, which made it one of the most arduous we had ever done. There was really no period of "being on the way"; even the passage was through enemy waters, with enemy-held islands on either side and the possibility of enemy shipping appearing at any moment. So concentration was necessary all the time, and nerves were tight; even before we reached the Senjska Passage we had been keyed up for nearly four hours. We could not use much speed, as we wanted to run on silenced engines for most of the time, and this demanded low revs. We slipped between Olib and Silba, past Trestenico Island, skirted the north-west coast of Rab, and began our run in to Senjska.

We were at action stations—had been for half an hour. Corny blinked "R"'s astern, and we reduced speed to crawling pace. It was a dark night, and with luck on silenced engines and with no bow wave, and wake reduced to a minimum, we might get through unseen. It wasn't only a question of getting *in* unscathed. If we were seen, shipping would be warned, and we might well have a nasty time getting out.

I looked round the bridge. Everyone was staring intently at one side or other of the gap. Nobody spoke. Corny had his glasses fixed on the lighthouse to starboard, Tony on the low shore to port. The guns were trained ready, evenly distributed between the two sides. If we were spotted, and firing started, the quicker our guns could knock out theirs the better for us. It would be quite like a ship-to-ship action at this range, with the important difference that we would not be able to sink a battery.

And then I thought of the mines. I had forgotten them for the moment. The visible hazards of the two jaws of the gap had pushed aside the thoughts of the invisible weapons which lurked beneath the waters. How far beneath? *That* was the important thing. It seemed an age before we were abreast of the lighthouse. The chart called it Strazica Point, and told me that in happier times the light would be flashing every six seconds and be visible for nine miles. I was glad it was not lit; we could do without light, thank you.

As soon as we were past, I turned to watch the others through. We were a real Commonwealth show tonight, I thought. Peter Hughes from South Africa, Dickie Bird from New Zealand, Ted Smyth from Ireland, Ken Golding from dear old England and Corny from Canada. I turned and reported to Corny.

"All through the gap now, sir."

We were past the preliminaries—now for the real thing. We swung northward and crept along the coast, the revolving aerials of our radar sweeping constantly across the width of the channel. For five hours we waited, searched and probed. Then it was time to go. After all that, our efforts were wasted.

Things had been so quiet that we lost interest in the Senjska Passage on the way out. It was still mined, it was still only half a mile wide, there was still supposed to be a battery there—but we couldn't believe that anything was going to happen now. We were right, but it was a dangerous frame of mind. I knew Corny would have loved to shoot up the lighthouse as we passed—just to leave his visiting card, as it were—but common sense prevailed: we might be coming back tomorrow, so there was no point in giving our presence away.

We got back to Mulat at 0600, and Corny ordered us in to fuel. There was an LCT there, with her bows to the beach, so I took 658 in on one side, and Ken Golding went in on the other and began fuelling straight away. We could not start for another two hours, so we turned in, with orders to the quartermaster to let us know when 633 finished.

The next I knew was being startled out of a deep sleep by shouts of "Fire!" Only people who have lived in a wooden boat containing five thousand gallons of petrol (or worse still, the vapour in half-empty tanks as we had that morning) know the urgency that that word brings.

The wings of fear took me up the hatch and on to the bridge. The sky was blotted out by thick black smoke which covered our bridge. I looked over to the LCT. Barrels of 100-octane were heaped all over her decks. Smoke and flames poured from her hold.

I rang the telegraphs violently to and fro, pressed the action-stations buzzer, and shouted: "Cast off everything!" The engine-room staff hated petrol more than most of us, and the engines burst into life even as I signalled for them. A quick glance round the deck told me everything was clear, and I moved the telegraphs to full astern. It was providential that we were not alongside the jetty, as we would not have been able to slip—but with the LCT at right angles to the beach we all had a clear run astern.

It was a fantastic sight. All five Dog-boats were speeding astern and the cloud of black smoke rose higher and higher into the sky. Every few seconds an ominous roar would tell of another barrel going, and a billow of flame would feed the inferno. The LCH was in Mulat Cove, beached further round and, as we watched from a safe distance we saw her moving closer to the LCT with fire hoses rigged and hard at work. Tiny, seemingly impotent figures still stood on the LCT's decks with foam extinguishers in their hands. Surely it had gone too far.

We did not see the end of the drama, as we were ordered to secure to buoys in the cove at Ist, but when we returned in the evening the fire was out, the LCT was in bad shape but still afloat, and there was no petrol left to fill us up.

Corny had a conference with Morgan Giles, and it was decided that we should have a go at the cove which was said to harbour the flotilla of explosive motor boats (EMBs) and small underwater craft, and then return in the morning to Ancona for fuel.

As we grouped ourselves to return to Ist to await the time of departure, a speck appeared on the horizon heading for the Maknare Channel. We were very intrigued, as no signal had been received, so no boat was expected. As it grew larger, my glasses made out the pendants fluttering from her mast.

"Victor Six Five Five," I read. "It's Derrick, by Jove!" We waved him alongside and greeted him with our congratulations and pleasure at seeing him again.

Immediately Corny briefed him so that he could join us in the assault on Cigale Cove. We spent six hours waiting, and then tried to flush out a few enemy craft by firing torpedoes into the cove. They resulted in magnificent explosions, but nothing emerged. We could only hope that the reason was inability, not absence.

We sailed over to Ancona, fuelled, and set off to return to Veli Rat. After two hours a Bora suddenly blew up and Corny was left with a difficult decision. He decided to turn back. As the dark horizon began to take the shape of the mountainous coast south of Ancona, Tony sighted two destroyers moving across our bows, and even as he reported them they began to challenge. To make things difficult, they challenged us with the wrong letter according to our list of signals.

However, we sent back the correct answer, only to be challenged once more with the wrong letter. Then the leading destroyer, getting impatient, flashed "AA" (What ship?). Since Corny had become S.O., we had carried a leading signalman aboard, and he now jumped to the lamp and rattled off the reply. There was a pause, and the lamp began to flash again. The signalman read off the message. "According—to—us—the—correct—answer—is—B—for—Baker!"

When we had stopped laughing, we tried to imagine the fate of the destroyers if we had been E-boats. As we had turned back they could not possibly have expected us in the area, and they would have been perfectly justified in blowing us out of the water. We were glad they hadn't, but felt they had been very slack. We were still puzzled by our wrong signals, but it turned out later that we had been given an incorrectly dated sheet. It might have been a costly error.

Next day we were able to make the passage, and had an uneventful voyage. Just before we got to Veli Rat we passed a very battered LCT with canvas stretched round the remains of her bridge and a charred, blackened hull. We could just recognize her as the victim of the Mulat fire. She was hobbling back to Ancona to see if she could be patched up. It showed an indomitable spirit.

We patrolled off Cigale Cove once more. It was so quiet that we tried every way we knew to provoke the Germans into movement. But they ignored us and we returned disconsolately to Mulat. It was only 0645, so I turned in for an hour, making sure first that no one was fuelling alongside. Once bitten, twice shy.

This time, it was not shouts of "Fire" which disturbed my sleep. It was the rough hand of the quartermaster, shaking my shoulder urgently.

"One of the Vospers is alongside, sir, and the skipper wants to see you."

It was Frank Dowrick (an ex-Dog-boat officer) and he was intensely agitated.

"Is Corny aboard?" he asked. "I think you'll have to do a rescue act—I left 371 and 287 three hours ago stuck on the putty way up north, on a small island near Cherso. It's nearly seventy miles. I couldn't get them off, and couldn't get any joy on the W/T, so I came down for help."

Corny was soon informed, and S.N.O.V.I.S. gave permission for us to sail north at speed with Ted Smyth (642) and Dickie Bird (643) on this errand of mercy. It was an interesting prospect, on reflection. We had seventy miles to travel, all off enemy coasts, and we might well be spotted and engaged by coast batteries, enemy ships or aircraft. It reminded me of Sicily. And when we got there, we could not be sure of our reception; if the two Vospers had been sighted, we might well be running into a well-prepared ambush.

We studied the chart. The island of Levrera was about two miles from Cherso, but there did not appear to be much settlement along the coast nearby. As far as we could see, Levrera was devoid of habitation; as it rose to two small hills, and the Vospers were on the north-west side, it was quite likely that they had not yet been seen, unless aircraft or patrol boats had had their eyes open.

We made about twenty-four knots northward, outside all the islands, and skirted Lussino by about six miles to give the shore batteries a wide berth. Suddenly one of the bridge lookouts exclaimed: "A bright light just flashed on the coast, sir!"

We soon knew what it was. A heavy shell exploded about two hundred yards away, and was followed immediately by three more, all much too close to be comfortable. Corny gravely ordered: "Port wheel," and we made a 90 degrees turn away to put a little more distance between us and the guns. We didn't shake off their attentions till the range was nine miles! Once past Lussino, we cut in towards Unie Island and then round the corner until the low outline of Levrera came into view.

Anxiously we swept our glasses along the beach.

"There they are," snapped Corny. "They seem to be undisturbed so far. Let's hope we all stay that way!"

As we approached, arms waved joyously from the Vospers' decks.

"I bet they've never been so pleased to see Dog-boats before!" grinned Tony. "We should be able to get a few good cracks in when the short-boat types start being superior again!"

Corny nosed up to the second one, and we rigged a towing hawser round her after gun turret. Carefully we took the strain and began to increase revs., until we were pulling at about 1,200 revs. 658 shook like an aspen leaf and the tow line quivered but the Vosper did not budge an inch.

Ted Smyth came up from astern and yelled through his megaphone: "Say, Corny, do you think it would help if I created a bit of a wash? It might lift her a few inches, and if you pull at the same time she might come off."

"O.K," said Corny, "Let's try it."

We stood by to heave, and Ted disappeared to gather speed for his run past. A minute or two later, he came thundering by only 50 yards off shore, doing full revs. As he passed, a great bow wave streamed out on either side. We were all ready. Corny increased to 1,400 revs. Fascinated, we watched the wave reach the Vosper. It lifted—and then wafted ten feet further up the beach and settled down with a groan.

"I think that's that, don't you?" said Corny. "Now I reckon they're on for good!"

After a brief discussion and many anxious glances at the skies (we expected the Luftwaffe to arrive at any moment), Corny and the two Vosper C.O.s decided to take off all the crews and all the secret or movable equipment, and destroy the boats. It took nearly an hour to do this, and our fo'c'sle was soon a mass of kit and equipment slung up from the quarterdeck of our Vosper. Ted did the same with the other, while 643 patrolled off the beach to give warning of any approach by enemy ships.

When all was complete, we lay off and pumped pom-pom starshell and incendiary Oerlikon shells into the two hulks from about 100 yards. They were soon burning brightly, and we judged that it was time we left the area as rapidly as possible.

We had an uneventful trip back to Ancona.


A week later 658 was still in the clutches of the Base staff at Ancona after some engine trouble, so Corny returned to the Islands in 649, and arrived at the right moment to lead two boats in a daylight operation against the German base in Cigale Cove, in company with the two Hunt-class destroyers *Brocklesby* and *Quantock*. *Brocklesby* was commanded by Lieutenant Tony Blomfield, D.S.C., R.N., who until recently had been the Senior Officer of the 7th Flotilla MTBs off the west coast of Italy, so Corny could be sure that the liaison between the two units would be closely maintained.

After waiting about most of the morning, the two destroyers, each with a Dog-boat astern ready to make smoke, moved in towards Cigale Cove and began their attack from close range.

The din was deafening. The roar of the 4-inch guns rolled round the bay, and came back off the shore. Shell after shell streamed into the cove, until it seemed that nothing could possibly be left alive.

When the destroyers seemed to have had enough, Corny requested permission to enter Cigale Cove to see what damage had been done. The greatest danger would be actually entering the cove, as there was a gun position on each side of the narrow entrance.

633 moved slowly towards the entrance, and the two destroyers obliged by bombarding each side of the entrance as they passed inside. Corny soon began to wish he hadn't asked for this support: there seemed to be more danger from stray 4-inch bricks than from a few small German guns.

But this was soon forgotten. The first thing they sighted inside the cove was a tiny enemy motor boat streaking towards them at high speed. It was about 20 feet long, seemed to taper to a point, and obviously meant business. Was it attacking or trying to leave in a hurry? Corny did not wait to find out. 633 opened fire with all guns, and the motor boat turned hard a-starboard and ran smack into the shore at about twenty-five knots. From it leapt a frantic figure of a man, stark naked, and he began to run over the rough ground at a phenomenal pace. For a moment or two he was pursued by shot and shell of every calibre, but he put up such a sporting show that the guns soon stopped firing and the gunners roared encouragement to him as he leapt from rock to rock and finally dropped out of sight behind a shoulder of the hill.

Soon two more motor boats were seen. The first was careering round in circles at the far end of the bay, obviously abandoned, and the other was hidden beneath camouflage netting in a little inlet. 633 made short work of them both.

All the time she had been in the cove, light machine-gun and rifle fire had been sporadically hitting 633 and such was the vulnerability of the Dogs to small-arms fire that two rifle bullets in the engine-room had put two engines out of action for the time being. That was not all, however. One able seaman had been killed and two injured by a burst of machine-gun fire which sprayed the pom-pom as 633 searched the northern shore of the cove.

Over in Ancona, we knew nothing of this operation, but it had an effect on us, just the same. Morgan Giles obviously decided that it would be a good idea to follow up the attack with a patrol off Lussino to see whether the Germans had been stirred into a reinforcement (or even evacuation) of the garrison. None of the boats in the Islands had the necessary fuel, so he sent a message to Ancona asking S.N.O.N.A. to send a patrol from there.

I was ashore, and sitting enjoying a very pleasant dinner in the Officer's Club when a messenger from the Base came in and handed me a signal. I put down my knife and fork, wiped my mouth with a napkin, and sighed. "They can even follow you this far," I thought.

"Return aboard immediately. Required for patrol. Slipping at 2100. Crew being recalled."

I looked at my watch. It was 2025. It would take me fifteen minutes to get back aboard. Quickly I finished the main course of the meal, and regretfully left without my sweet. When I climbed aboard, Tony reported that eight men were still ashore. Tim was alongside with

662, and he was going to lead for this patrol. He also had men ashore, but by 2100 only a few men from the two boats were missing, so we sailed.

It was quite a thrill to be out with Tim, and in any case my patrols in command had been sufficiently few and far between for me to regard every one as a special occasion. In my own mind I classed Tim and Corny together—their leadership was aggressive but not fool-hardy, and I knew that with either of them I could be sure of clear orders and a skilful, well-timed approach.

But this time there was nothing to find. Morgan Giles' hunch was wrong. I nearly sent him a bill for my unfinished dinner.

We were back in the Islands next day, and went off immediately for a repeat performance of our creep into the Planinski Channel. It was not quite as gruelling as our first attempt—nothing is really as disturbing as the unknown—but it was as long and tense and just as fruitless, and we all felt very tired on the way back to Veli Rat. To cap it all, the weather freshened and we had a wet trip.

It had become so traditional for me to be wakened abruptly for some emergency if I chose to snatch a quick sleep when we got in, that when I heard Corny shout "Rover!" I thought he was pulling my leg. I was wrong.

"Listen to this, young feller. A signal from C.C.F. 'The 56th Flotilla will proceed to Malta for rest and refitting as required.'"

I turned over in my bunk and stared at the deckhead. Malta again! It would be nice to be lazy for a while.

## Chapter XXIII

## BORA!

WE sailed at noon for Ancona. 658 led the flotilla westward: each boat rode with bows proudly high as it thundered exactly in the wake of the next ahead at twenty-two knots. All tiredness had gone; spirits were high. Tony and I talked over the refit and the repairs which would be necessary, and as we looked back down the line we could see little groups of seamen in animated conversation. We guessed that plans were being made and old adventures recounted. There was no doubting the popularity of Malta.

Suddenly, the peace of the afternoon was stripped away. Whereas till now we had ignored the sea and the sky, within a minute they began to demand full attention. In the north, the sky blackened and low ominous clouds spread rapidly over us. The wind, with no warning, whipped right up through the Beaufort Scale until we were in the fierce grip of a full gale.

This was the Bora—and we were just about in the middle of the Adriatic. There would be no escape to a sheltered anchorage this time. We would have to fight on through it.

The wind tore at my face and the first deluge of spray caught me completely unprepared. I ducked, turned my back, and swore. I was soaked. My open-necked shirt clung to my skin and I shivered.

I lifted the flap of the W/T voice-pipe and shouted:

"Send up my oilskins, Sparks—and tell the S.O. that we've got a Bora arriving."

But Corny was already climbing on to the bridge. He turned at once to the signalman.

"Make 'Act independently but try to keep in visual touch' to all boats," he ordered.

"I'll have to reduce, Corny," I said. "Would you like to take over?" He was still officially in command.

"No—carry on for now, Rover." He grimaced. "It may be a long job."

The sea already reflected the fury of the wind. Line after line of white curving waves hit us in rapid succession. The crests foamed and bubbled as the wind dragged the tops from them, and with every impact 658 tilted violently to port and spray lashed pitilessly over the side.

Within five minutes we were crawling at ten knots and still rolling in agonizing lurches. The Bora was sweeping down the Adriatic and we were trying to cross it. But we couldn't keep beam-on to this sea much longer—we should turn over. 658 was already doing her best to prove it.

Two choices lay before us. I knew we must get as far west as possible if we were ever to reach Ancona before our petrol ran out: the problem was whether we should steer south-west and run with the sea on our quarter, or turn north-west and put it on our bow. The south-westerly course would run us down the Adriatic, with little chance of a sheltered harbour for over a hundred miles; the north-westerly would certainly take us towards the coast of Italy, but to a part where the only welcome we could expect would be the barbed wire of a prisoner-of-war camp. Neither provided any basis for enthusiasm.

Eventually we turned south-west, and immediately the boat's motion eased slightly. I breathed a sigh of relief and looked round the upper deck. The whole crew was up top by now. A small boat in a rough sea makes too many frightening noises below decks to encourage anyone to stay there for long.

But the Bora had not reached its peak yet. Gradually the wind built up until its power was terrifying. The sea grew shorter and shorter, and the waves steeper and steeper. The quarter sea picked 658 up and sent her rushing forward in a mad corkscrew motion. The coxswain soon found the wheel almost impossible to control, and the ship's head slid about all over the place. As the bows rushed away to starboard, he would spin the wheel swiftly to port, and using all his strength struggle to hold it there. After an agonizing pause with the boat crabbing sideways at the edge of a trough, the head would begin to creep round, and then without warning slide frighteningly across, with the wheel now pushed hard the other way in a vain attempt to correct the swing.

It was hopeless. We would have to head into the sea and crawl even slower. It would be uncomfortable but safer. Corny agreed, and the coxswain, by now covered in perspiration, thankfully put the wheel over.

It was easy enough to order it, but we knew that the manoeuvre was liable to bring us into greater danger than anything the Germans had done yet. To get the bows round to face into the oncoming waves we had first to receive the full force of the beam sea, and the troughs were so horrifyingly deep and narrow that it was by no means certain that we would be able to escape from them. If 658 couldn't get round, she would stick in the trough and wallow there completely at the mercy of the sea. She might even turn over. But it had to be tried.

Gradually the ship's head moved round, and 658 shuddered as the first beam sea hit her squarely. Then came the frightful moment when she hung powerless in the trough. She heeled right over, a wave poised above her and the port gunwale dangerously near the water. The coxswain hauled wildly at the wheel, I clung to my voice-pipe, and the others slithered in a heap at the bottom of the bridge.

I tried to pray. We needed help now. We were closer to death than we had been in all our actions. Still we hung. And then she began to come round.

I gulped in air. I seemed to have been holding my breath for minutes. Corny picked himself up.

"For Pete's sake, Rover, haven't I taught you yet how to handle this barge?"

I grinned. After that we could face anything. Our bows climbed the next crest, hung, and plunged downhill in a mad tumble. At the bottom 658 buried her nose, shook, and started to rise again. A deluge of green water cascaded over us.

I had never seen anything like this before. The sea was short and steep, and far more dangerous to us than the gigantic swells of the Atlantic had been. The wheel was now such a handful that Corny, Tony, and the coxswain and I wrestled with it in turn, each taking a short spell. Beaver came up to report that several of the crew were looking very scared. I was not surprised. Had I been sitting around with nothing to do but wait and watch, I too would have been worried stiff by now. Every time we plunged over the crest, the stern went up at a fantastic angle.

Corny pulled at my arm.

"Just look at that deck strengthening," he yelled.

I looked over the side of the bridge, and watched the steel strip the Base had strapped us with after the Mljet Channel action. As we hung poised on a crest, the metal bent visibly. How long would it last?

By now every one of the guns was locked securely in place, and Tony had given the gunners orders to fall out. There was no chance of attack now—and every chance of losing someone overboard.

For two hours we bucked and plunged, hardly making any headway, and soon the shortage of fuel began to take first place in our minds. We had had the passage from Ancona to the Islands and a very long patrol up the Planinski Channel, since we last fuelled. Soon Burrows reported we had less than 1,000 gallons left.

"What's it like in the engine-room, Burrows?" I asked.

"'Orrible, sir. We just hang on like grim death and pray it'll be over soon."

"You're not the only ones doing that," I grinned. "Keep it up—it can't last for ever!"

Burrows looked sideways at me and said quietly: "The one we had alongside *Eggesford* lasted five days, sir."

There was no answer to that. It had. But gradually the wind eased a bit, and with it the height of the seas. I nudged 658's head slightly to westward. Half an hour later, I got her round another ten degrees. By six o'clock, with dusk approaching, we were able to increase speed to twelve knots, and the course was at least taking us towards Italy, even if rather further north than we wanted. Painfully and slowly we won our way westward, and eventually began to feel the benefit of the inshore ground swell.

With the gale still blowing hard, this lengthened the wave interval although it did not subdue the sea.

I was never so grateful to see the arms of Ancona's breakwaters stretched out to greet us. For the first time in our commission I had wondered if 658 would make it. She had, and I mentally took my hat off to her builders and designers.

The other boats, all battered, arrived within half an hour of each other, and we settled down alongside the jetty. Even if she fell to pieces on the way we would get 658 to Malta somehow, and there the engineers could enjoy themselves putting her together again.

We waited five days, and still had a rough passage to Malta. But we did not mind. We were in cheerful mood, and enjoyed ourselves.

It was exactly 0300 when we arrived off Malta, one lovely moonlight night exactly a week before Christmas. In spite of our E.T.A. signal,[1]

[1] E.T.A.: Estimated time of arrival.

we could not raise the slightest response from the signal station, and the boom was shut. It was rather like arriving home late without a key, and not being able to wake father.

We flashed and flashed, our Aldis lamp beam cutting the darkness like a miniature searchlight, but the duty signal staff were either making tea or were asleep, and it was twenty minutes before we got a reply.

Corny dictated a rude signal, and we all reflected how quickly Malta had forgotten the days when it was a front-line fortress. Obviously they were back to a peace-time routine. We were glad enough to find this true when it came to enjoying life ashore.

For me a great moment came only a couple of days after we arrived. Captain Stevens told me that he was appointing me in command of 658. I was to put up a second ring to keep everybody happy, and he would recommend me for accelerated promotion to lieutenant, as I could not receive it on age basis for another year. That night we celebrated aboard 658.

However, other celebrating had been going on. The first night in Malta, when leave was piped, the whole non-duty watch went ashore together, grimly determined to enjoy themselves. As Tony and I watched them go, he turned to me and said: "I wonder what headaches they'll have in the morning—and whether we'll have any on their account, too!"

He didn't know how prophetic his words were, for that night was to have far-reaching effects. Next morning, the coxswain reported: "All libertymen returned aboard, sir, except A/B Fletcher,[1] who is in hospital with suspected concussion. A/B Crowther[1] is aboard but I shall have to send him over to the sick bay, sir, because he's got a cut in his head which will need stitching."

We asked a few questions, but there was no case for making any charges, so we took the episode as a normal sort of brawl which could easily happen on the first night of a return to Malta. Fletcher returned a few days later, rather the worse for wear, but cheery as ever and very reticent about what had happened to him. We forgot about the affair for the time being.

We were mainly preoccupied with preparations for Christmas. Tony made frequent visits to NAAFI headquarters, and arranged that even at this short notice we should receive our ration of turkey, pork,

---

[1] Fletcher and Crowther were not the real names of these two ratings, nor of any ratings in the flotilla so far as I know. I have invented these names to avoid any embarrassment to those concerned.

sausage meat, crackers, beer, puddings, etc. Corny made it clear that he would be expecting every boat in the flotilla to keep Christmas in real Navy fashion. He would go his rounds at 1130 on Christmas morning.

In 658, the mess decks were gaily decorated, and we had the traditional switch round. Corny selected the youngest A/B aboard (Alf Tanner, from Thornton Heath) to become senior officer of the flotilla for the day, and the two changed uniforms. Corny made a magnificent matelot, and remained in his rig all day, both on board and in the Base, even to C.C.F.'s cocktail party. Tanner wore Corny's uniform—and responsibilities—very easily. I became coxswain, and Tony changed with the motor mechanic. At 1130 we set off for rounds, visiting 642 (where Ted Smyth made a huge and imposing stoker), 643, 649 and 655 in turn, and finally returning to 658.

In every boat—in fact on every messdeck—we were offered tots of rum; it was a very merry party which got back to the messdeck of 658 for the final fling. We escaped into the wardroom eventually, entertained the petty officers and leading hands, and then settled down to enjoy a vast dinner. The rest of the day was more restrained than it had been the previous year, and most of the crew were given leave.

After Christmas, we got down to the details of our refit. An army of engineers and mechanics came aboard and gave 658 a thorough inspection. Hull, fuel tanks, and engines, were all minutely checked, and finally it was decided that unless her hull was strengthened completely, 658 would be of little further use. And as we had been sailing around for nearly a year with three out of four wing petrol tanks filled with water, thus reducing our range considerably, the opportunity would be taken to repair them. This was in fact the longest and most complicated task in the refit, as in order to get at the tanks the engines had first to be removed, and then the tank-space bulkheads, which incidentally involved stripping all the electrical circuits.

So our plans were laid: dockyard for the hull repairs, which might take six weeks, and then back to C.F.B. for "putting together again". We were also to lose our pom-pom and goose gun, and be given in exchange semi-automatic 6-pounders in powered turrets both for'd and aft. It looked like being a long job.

While we were in the dockyard, we lost no opportunity to obtain improvements for both efficiency and comfort. Being quite experienced after two earlier stays, the first step we took was to throw a party in our wardroom to which we invited all those who would be involved in making decisions about repairs and stores during our stay. It was worth it in the long run. . . .

Our social life was soon well organized, too. We found no lack of partners from the Wrennery for picnics and dances, and thoroughly enjoyed ourselves. The civilizing effect of the Wrens was very noticeable. There were also excellent facilities for sport. The crew had a very good football team, in which I was sometimes allowed to play on the right wing—but I was left with no illusions on the captain's opinion of my play. He was an A/B, but no one would have thought it on the field. He had the authority of an admiral. To my great delight, we raised a Rugby XV from H.M.S. *Gregale*, and had several games before the decreasing rains and increasing temperatures made the ground too hard for play. The officers from the *Gregale* also ran hockey and soccer teams, and I turned out frequently for both. Captain Stevens played in goal for the Soccer XI.

In January, a list of awards was published which covered both our Mljet Channel action and Tim's big F-lighter battle in October. Tim was awarded the D.S.O., the first we had had in Dog-boats in the Med, and richly deserved. Next came a long list of "Bars to the Distinguished Service Cross", to Doug Maitland, Corny, Tom Ladner, Walter Blount and Bob Davidson. There was a long list of "mentions" for the first lieutenants, Gordon, Derrick, Freddie Mills, Johnnie Mudd —they were all there.

It was Corny who brought the list over to show us, and he was genuinely disturbed when he did so. "I'm afraid there's nothing there for you, Rover, but it's all a miserable mistake. We left you out because we were fully expecting something better to come through after the Elba scrap. But it didn't—and now I feel rotten about the whole thing."[1]

The crew's list of awards was imposing, too. Bert Burrows, now our chief motor mechanic in succession to Last, and A/B Duffill, the pom-pom gunner, both received the D.S.M., and Pountney of the starboard Oerlikon (one of our "originals") and Simpson the leading stoker were mentioned in despatches.

About six weeks after Christmas, the first lieutenant of *Gregale* sent over two summonses he had received for Fletcher and Crowther

---

[1] A year later, my name appeared in the New Year's Honours List. I had been awarded the Distinguished Service Cross " for distinguished service during the war in Europe ".

to appear at the police court. They were accused of assaulting the police and "inciting a concourse of more than four persons to commit a breach of the peace".

Both of the men had actually left 658 temporarily to go through a course for higher gunnery rating, but as they were old members of the crew, we were determined to do all we could for them. The amazing thing about the whole business was that no policemen had in fact been hurt, and yet both our sailors had suffered rough treatment from police truncheons; also, neither of these two was the sort to be vicious, even in his cups—they were above-average ratings, of pleasant disposition, and neither had been in trouble at all on board. Fletcher had always been willing and cheerful; he was very popular with everybody.

When the police court proceedings began, we found the sessions long-drawn-out and extremely tedious. The evidence could be given in Maltese or English, but had to be translated into English by the official court interpreter, and then written down in long-hand by the recorder. We heard several policemen give evidence and learned of a "very large gathering" in restive mood, which had congregated in the infamous "Gut" and which the police had had to move on. There had been bottle-throwing, and in the course of it a policeman had a button torn from his tunic. When the mob dispersed, Fletcher and Crowther were pounced upon. The police accused them of being the ringleaders, and gave them hefty blows with their truncheons. It looked to me like a case of "catch any two and make an example of them".

The case dragged on for three mornings and, as we expected, the two men were committed for trial at the next Quarter Sessions in March. The Navy briefed a Maltese counsel to appear for them, and they made their attendance once more. After two days, the case was adjourned pending further evidence. When we left Malta at the end of March that was the position, and unfortunately we were not able to take the two men with us. If we had known in the first place that summonses were to be issued, the men would have been drafted from Malta very quickly. Now it was too late.

All this time, 658 was an empty hull in the dockyard. There were no men living aboard, although we spent each day working ship in one way or another.

The greatest excitement among the Dogs was the arrival of a whole "new" flotilla from the U.K.—the 59th Flotilla, under Lt.-Cdr. J. A. Montgomerie R.N.V.R., who was known to everyone as "Monty". They had taken part in the invasion of Normandy, and after an extensive tropical refit had been sent to the Med to replace the Dogs which had been lost. Naturally, we could only regard them as new boys; their talk of D-Day cut no ice with us—we asked them "which one?" We had taken part in half a dozen D-Days.

Their boats were slightly different in design from the Dogs we knew; they were of more recent pattern and contained a good deal of equipment which we had never seen or even heard of in some cases. As they had not yet operated as fighting units with their present officers and crews they were a completely unknown quantity. They moved on to the Adriatic after a short stay in Malta.

Eventually, after many frustrating delays, we got somewhere near to completion as Easter approached. 658 was now put together in one piece, but we were having trouble with shaft bearings, and I was sure one of the shafts must be misaligned so that it was overheating badly. I found we were getting rather low priority from the Base, and as I was anxious to take my command to sea, and not spend the rest of the war alongside in Malta, I got impatient.

I went to see C.C.F. and appealed for his help to get us away by Easter. He smoothed the way, and the last week of the refit saw a miraculous change in tempo. From a heap of wires, pipes and disconnected parts, 658 suddenly re-emerged in fighting trim.

For some time I had known that Corny, Tommy and Doug would be leaving for Canada in the near future. They had completed their second two-year spell of operations, and were due to return to Canada for leave. I had been very anxious that 658's refit should be completed before they left; I felt that their last sight of the only surviving member of the "old firm" should be one worth carrying away in their minds.

In the end their date for departure was fixed for Good Friday. Two days later 658 was to sail for the Adriatic.

During the last week before Easter, some very disturbing news arrived to Tommy Ladner at his Operations Room. As soon as he could, he sent a signal over to me, and I arrived to hear from him that Derrick's boat (655) had been mined in the Northern Adriatic and that he and Johnnie Mudd were listed as "seriously wounded".

This was tragic news indeed. Everyone had been very impressed with Derrick's showing as C.O. of 655, as when he took her over she was in bad shape after being damaged in the Elba action. She had emerged as an efficient and happy ship, and her youthful officers had given her a good name on operations, too. That this fine ship—

so much in the mould of 663—should have suffered the same fate was a bitter blow to us, and must have been even greater for Derrick.

Tommy was undoubtedly very affected by the news. Apart from Derrick and Tony Marriott, many of 663's survivors had also gone to 655 and Petty Officer Nicholl (D.S.M. and Bar) had volunteered to join Derrick even though he had been badly injured when 663 was mined. Nichol had been with Tommy since 1941, first in MGB 75 in Hichens' flotilla, and then in 663. He had not been in a shore appointment since before the war. He had been torpedoed in destroyers at Narvik and Dunkirk. Finally (he later told Tommy) he decided that if he had to be in the water so often, he would rather be a bit closer to it. So he joined Coastal Forces. Now he was "missing, believed killed", and in a mining at night in enemy waters that could only mean one thing.

We heard two days later that Derrick had a broken thigh, and Johnnie a fractured knee cap; bad enough, but infinitely better than many things we had imagined.

Our last few days in Malta were unbelievably crowded. 658 needed finishing touches to make her completely habitable again; we had to prepare for a long voyage and operations after that. There were the last junketings and social round to perform, and then we had to say farewell to the "Three Musketeers" returning to Canada.

On Good Friday, Tony and I stood on the airfield and watched their aircraft dwindle into the distance. It seemed to mark the end of a chapter of life itself. I had spent all my commissioned service under their influence and leadership: their encouragement and advice had always been available. Now it was gone. Could we keep up the tradition? Could we ever recapture the spirit and atmosphere of those months at Bastia, or the team-work of the Battle of the Mljet Channel? It did not seem likely.

But we would do our best.

## Chapter XXIV

## THE LAST ROUND

IT was a sunny morning with a fresh breeze blowing when we sailed proudly out of Marxamaxett harbour, as we had so many times before. My heart was full; for the first time 658 was my very own. It was Easter Sunday, and the thousand bells of Malta rejoiced with us. Our tiny pendants fluttered from the whip aerial and the quartermaster's pipe shrilled the "still" as we saluted Fort Manoel.

Now that Corny had left for Canada, the 56th Flotilla had been disbanded, and 658 had been placed in the 59th Flotilla under Monty's leadership. We were to join him as soon as possible at either Ancona or Zara.

The weather worsened as we beat northward, and I decided to put into Augusta for the night rather than plunge into the long stretch across to the heel of Italy. The gale blew itself out during the night, and we sailed early next morning for Brindisi.

On the way, the motor mechanic reported that our shaft was still causing trouble, and when we got to Miraglia, Freddie Warner decided that we would have to stay two days to give his plumbers a chance of working on the bearings. It did not take me long then to discover that Derrick and Johnnie were at the 93rd General Hospital at Barletta, north of Bari, and I set out straightway to visit them.

After a long, dusty "hitch" I found the hospital and sought out the two casualties. They had hardly had a visitor in the week since they had been transferred, and were overjoyed to see a familiar face. We celebrated our miniature reunion with surreptitious swigs from the half bottle of gin I had brought for them. They were both in very good spirits and making fair progress, but it was too early to tell how their walking would be affected. I promised I would get to see them again if I could, and set off back to Brindisi.

Miraglia was buzzing with the news from Ancona. All through January, February and March, patrols had gone out in poor weather and worked really hard for very little result. The opposition was getting sterner all the time, and mines were taking an increasing toll. Apart from 655, two boats of Monty's new 59th Flotilla had been mined in the last few weeks. Tim and the 57th were still hard at it, and were still sinking ships, although they had been hard hit and had suffered casualties and damage in several recent actions.

But the news which caused a stir was the huge success of a new flotilla of Vosper MTBs under Charles Jerram, who had left 667 at Christmas to take them over. The 28th Flotilla had S.O. radar and torpedoes fitted with the non-contact pistols which had revolutionized attacks on shallow-draft targets. With these pistols the torpedoes did not have to hit to explode: they needed only to pass close to or below the target, and the ship's magnetism would do the rest.

They had combined these two scientific achievements and added the human factor by attaining perfection in plotting the movements of the enemy ships from the radar, and using the plot and radar to determine their firing angle. With this information carefully worked out at long range, they would then make an unobserved approach, fire their torpedoes, and wait for the bangs.

So far, this technique had achieved phenomenal results. Every time the flotilla operated, they seemed to sink something. The excitement on this particular night at Miraglia was the arrival of the news that they had fired six torpedoes at five F-lighters and they claimed to have hit with every one.

Our shafts were still not quite right, but we did not pause at either Manfredonia or Ancona for longer than was necessary to fuel. I was told that Monty was asking for every available boat to be sent over to Zara as soon as possible, and there seemed to be some urgency. It seemed strange to be sailing into Zara: when we had left for Malta three months before, Zara had still been in the enemy hands.

I was a little put out to find no Dog-boats at all alongside when I got there. I was directed to Captain Dickinson's office, and found him in the Operations Room. The boats were hiding up in a cove far to the north, and the invasion of Rab was under way. I was to fuel in the morning and then rendezvous with Monty and the others in their cove in the Planinski Channel.

The passage there was magnificent. To enter the Planinski Channel from Zara involved a zig-zag route up and down narrow channels between the parallel islands, penetrating further and further into the maze by means of narrow gaps like gates in a large field. And to sail up the Planinski Channel itself on a clear, calm day was breath-takingly beautiful: the bare grey-brown limestone mountains rose straight up to the east, and low ripples of islands sheltered the western side.

Vranjac Cove was an amazing sight when we arrived. It was so small, and so full of craft, that I wondered how I would get 658 in. Someone muttered: "You see how many boats are here already? Yes—twelve—that makes us the thirteenth! And blimey, it's Friday the thirteenth today." However, we had little time for superstitious speculation, as after a briefing session with Monty and a greeting from Eric Hewitt (670) and Joe Hill (643), we sailed almost immediately for a patrol in the northern end of the Planinski Channel where we had been twice with Corny before. Our role was to stop any reinforcement of the Rab garrison from Fiume now that the occupation was almost complete. Monty sailed with Eric, Dennis Booth (Monty's half-leader) was second in line with 697, and Joe Hill and I brought up the rear.

All was very quiet—as it had been on our previous visits—and at about 0130 we lay cut, close to the coast. I went down to the radar to inspect the plot and satisfied myself that nothing was about. At about 0215, though, an excited radar operator called the bridge and reported two large targets just entering the Channel from the north, about four miles away.

I immediately called Monty on R/T and passed him the news, and there was rapid reaction. All boats started up, and we got into line abreast. The echoes were larger than usual, and appeared to be destroyers, and this realization set us all tingling with anticipation. At last good torpedo targets with some MTBs in the unit! We continued to pass ranges and bearings to the S.O.

Every minute the radar operator passed up this information, and I relayed it to Monty. By this time, both Eric and Joe's sets were warmed up and they were confirming the echoes. At last, a little patch of denser blackness in my glasses told me that the leading ship was in sight, and at the same time we heard from Monty that he too had sighted the enemy.

"Preparative Flag Four," he ordered. "Range will be 1,500 yards."

I could imagine Eric and Dennis fiddling with the sight bar on their torpedo sights. . . . Still, they would have an accurate idea of the speed from the previous reports, and that was the most common error in firing torpedoes.

A few moments later, Monty ordered "Flag Four!" and we heard first Eric's, then Dennis's, fish leave the tubes. Immediately after, our loudspeaker yelled: "Come on, Rover, Flag Four!"

I was completely taken aback, and suddenly realized that Monty, who had probably never seen 658 before, let alone been aboard her, was under the horrible misapprehension that 658 was an MTB. I grabbed the microphone and replied: "Hallo, Monty, this is Rover. Sorry, I can't oblige—I wasn't made that way."

There was no time for Monty to reply, as the inky blackness was split by a most colossal explosion, and followed rapidly by two more. The fish had hit! The radar operator shouted up his voice-pipe : "Bridge, sir. The leading target has disappeared. The other is stopping."

Monty came over the R/T. "No need to hang about now—George 22, follow me." As we leapt forward in answer to this order, a starshell burst above us and provided a further incentive to get a move on. However, nothing but starshell was fired at us, and we moved in tight line ahead very swiftly southward.

Radar reported that the second craft had not waited about at all, but was already out of range on its way out at the northern end of the "Plan Chan". We made our way back to Vranjac Cove, and compared notes before pushing on to Zara. There a delighted Monty was told that the R.A.F. confirmed a great deal of wreckage and survivors on rafts at the point of attack, and also a Partenope-class torpedo boat (a small destroyer) limping towards Pola. Later an Intelligence report confirmed that one Partenope had been sunk with only thirty survivors whilst on its way to evacuate the Rab Garrison. The other ship had also suffered a hit and had not even waited to pick up survivors, but had turned and got out of the Planinski Channel as quickly as possible.

No sooner had we fuelled at Zara that afternoon, than I was instructed to proceed to Rab town where the occupation was just being completed, to bring back several local dignitaries. It was already early evening, and I set off on this lone mission with some misgivings. Our chart of Rab showed that the approach was down a very narrow channel which was also shown as completely mined. By sunset we were at Karlobag, some thirty miles short of our destination, and as it was another moonless night, I decided to stay the night and push on at first light in the morning. I sent a signal to S.N.O.N.A. expressing this intention, but it could not be got through as in this deep trough wireless signals were not easy to receive.

We arrived at Rab in time for breakfast, and seeing the entrance channel I was heartily glad of my discretion the previous night. It was less than a quarter of a mile wide, and five miles long! It turned out also that I was not expected till the morning, anyway, by the authorities at Rab. A different story awaited us at Zara when we got back there after an exhilarating run at twenty-two knots over glassy seas. Our signals had not been received, and three Spitfires had been sent out to look for us.

Two days later saw us at Rab again, this time in company with several other Dog-boats and MLs. The invasion of Krk, the last big island, was on, and our unit of three (Monty embarked with us, Dennis Booth in 697, and 633) was to move round the western side of Krk and patrol off Fiume to stop interference from that direction. In this task, our main bugbear, as ever, was mines. Captain Dickinson, in a briefing, warned us to go carefully. He had been assured that the Partisans had swept a channel around the coast, and aerial spotting had confirmed that if we kept within thirty yards of the shore, we should be all right.

"But you can't tell with these fellows, y'know," he said. "By sweeping they may mean stretching a wire between two rowing boats!"

Our charts showed the whole area as heavily mined, but orders were orders, so off we went. It was one of the most uncomfortable trips I ever made. None of the crew went below, and most of us spent the whole night in a state of highly-strung tension.

We had negotiated the gap between the islands and were sailing along the coast closer than I had ever conceived possible before, when there was a colossal explosion, which seemed to engulf us, and a lurid flash. We turned aghast and there, only thirty yards astern, was 697—split into two and the bows burning fiercely. 633, illuminated brightly in the glare, had just managed to stop in time. I began to turn short round—I had no desire to career about in such deadly waters—and we edged towards the wreckage and the men we could see in the water. Tony launched our dinghy, and Monty and he went rowing round searching for survivors. They found only one, a wounded seaman, but we had already picked up George Herd, 697's pilot, and three other injured survivors.

In the glare of the burning hull, about twenty yards from us, was the gleaming, polished and spiky surface of a very large mine, which had presumably been released from its mooring by the force of the explosion. As I watched from the bridge, it struck me that the scene was similar to an impressionist's painting of death and hell fire—a ravaged ship burning, a ghostly flickering light on the oily sea surface, the horns of that mine, and a dinghy moving silently across the scene like the boatman on the Styx.

Suddenly George Heard, dripping wet from his own immersion, and pale with tension and shock, pointed into the darkness and in a flash was diving into the sea and swimming strongly towards a man he had seen. He brought him back, and we helped him to bring the rescued man inboard. It was a very gallant act so soon after the horror of the explosion which had blown him into the water, and he was later awarded the RHS Bronze Medal in recognition of his courage.

A hail from 633 told us that they had Dennis Booth and quite a number of the crew aboard, and after we had got the dinghy inboard, there remained the task of getting out of this ill-fated channel and back to Zara. We in 658 had obviously set off the mine which sank 697, just as we had before in the case of 640. How many more mines had been "armed" by our passage over them on the way north?

The horror of the mining, its force and proximity, all seemed to Tony and me far greater than had that of 640 some twelve months before, and for Tony to admit that was something, as he had been aboard both 640 and 657 when they were mined. Moreover, mines had taken such a toll of our flotillas that they had become our most dreaded enemies, and the impersonal nature of the attack made it all the worse. So we turned and edged our way out of this unhealthy spot with heavy hearts and fear gripping us all.

Our prayers were answered, and we got back to Zara safely, to hand over our casualties to the same hospital craft which had received Derrick and Johnnie only a month before. One of the wounded had been in a very bad way, with an injury to his throat. We did our best for him, but his groans and heavy breathing were sounds which will long remain with me.

After this anti-climax, which was one of the last patrols in the islands, and which was to be 658's last really aggressive patrol of the war, we were sent back to Ancona and there had a new engine fitted.

The situation in the Adriatic was rapidly coming to a head (as in all theatres of the war) and each day we visited the "Ops Room" at the Base to read the latest Intelligence reports. The armies had at last broken out of their stalemate positions and were forging ahead, and the Partisans, as we had seen, had practically polished off all the Yugoslav islands and were pressing hard up the mainland. In Germany, too, the British and American armies were across the Rhine and moving fast to the east, and Russians were streaking across East Germany at a tremendous pace.

In our war, the major ports of Venice, Trieste, Pola and Fiume were still in German hands, and there were a large number of enemy ships using them; their destruction or surrender was our obvious aim. As the armies—and our patrols—had moved further and further north, these craft had been bottled into a smaller and smaller sea area. Intelligence reported about fifty ships ranging from small destroyers to E-boats in the four big ports. The big query in all our minds was: "Will they fight, scuttle, or surrender?"

Whatever the answer, it was obvious that very soon the whole Adriatic would be ours, and that the ports of Venice and Trieste would be vital to the supply of our troops, and so extensive plans were made to begin the sweeping of channels to these ports by MLs and fleet sweepers. This sweeping continued daily, and to save fuel and time, the sweepers anchored in a group at their operational area rather than return to Ancona each night.

The main danger was from E-boats, and we were given the job of anti-E-boat defensive patrols, in fact our old "zizz patrols" of Sicily days. We operated in sections of three, but to give wider protection we worked singly on each flank of the anchorage. On the first night I was detailed to the northern station, and there I stayed all night, eight miles north of the convoy, feeling rather lonely so much nearer to the enemy than everybody else! There was very little chance of being surprised by E-boats, however, as this was the bright moon period.

Through my glasses, I could see the sweepers eight miles away, and even managed to pick up the other Dog-boats, a much smaller "objective" at a similar distance. Unable to believe that such visibility was possible in moonlight, we switched on the radar and checked the distances, and found them to be correct. In the circumstances, there would appear to have been little worry on such a patrol; but the snag on our northerly beat lay in the fact that an E-boat lying eight miles down-moon from us would see us perfectly (as we could see the sweepers) but there was little chance of our spotting him until he was considerably closer.

I took the middle watch, and by the end of it, as my eyes tired with the strain, I had begun to imagine E-boat flotillas approaching from every direction. Down-moon, the sea horizon melted into the sky in an indeterminate line, quite different from the contrasting silver and pale blue of the up-moon horizon. We had done three of these quiet patrols when a bombshell arrived in the shape of a double signal from C.C.F.

*"Lieutenant Reynolds is required as witness in Trial by Grand Jury at Malta on 3rd May. Request he may be discharged by air accordingly. Suggest Lieutenant Robinson provides temporary relief—281134 (28th April)."*

*"A/B's Fennell and Tanner, and Tel. Anderson all of MGB 658 are to be discharged by air to Malta by first passage. Required as court witnesses in Trial by Grand Jury at Malta on 3rd May. Temporary reliefs are to be taken from non-operational craft if necessary—281135 (28th April)."*

At this stage of events this really was too bad. The war was obviously coming to an end, and it wasn't a time to be anywhere but on the bridge of 658.

I thought of signalling C.C.F., but knew that I couldn't get out of a direct order, so I began to make my arrangements. The first job was to get some Air Priority, and armed with a recommendation from the C.O. of the Base, I visited the necessary office and was promised seats aboard a Dakota next day via Bari and Catania. Terry Robinson was not available to relieve me, as he had become S.O.O. to S.N.O.N.A, but the job went to Chas Turner, the spare C.O. of the 59th, and not long out from U.K.

The next day I was driven out to the R.A.F. field outside Ancona, and I had my first experience of flying. I found the noise and vibration on the ground a little disturbing, but the flying itself was quite delightful, especially as there was the added interest of flying over the coast along which we had crawled so many times. Occasionally we passed over groups of small craft, and my excitement reached its peak when we spotted two Dog-boats sailing serenely northward, their glittering white wakes stretching behind them.

After a short stop at Bari, we followed the coast southward again for some miles, and then swung off to starboard to pass across the heel of the Italian boot and give me my first glimpse of Taranto, the Naval Base which had become famous by the great naval victory there earlier in the war. The flight continued westward across the Gulf of Taranto, and picked up the coast again for a majestic aerial view of the rugged mountains of Calabria. Quite suddenly we burst out over the Straits of Messina—that classic and familiar narrow neck of water which had been our concern for so many patrols in the late summer of 1943. Flying over it emphasized its narrowness. No wonder the shore batteries had been so unpleasant. We circled and landed at Catania, picked up more passengers, and took off almost immediately again for Malta.

Mount Etna loomed large but soon dropped away behind us as we flew south and I excitedly spotted the ports, points and bays of the coastline we had patrolled not only during "Husky" but before it as well. Augusta, Murro di Porco, Avola, Cap Passero, all sped by beneath us, and shortly after, there, like a dusty yellow jewel, lay Malta shimmering in the heat. We passed over Gozo, the northern island, picked out St. Paul's Bay, and finally circled slowly round to come down at Luqa airfield in the south-west of the Island.

I reported to C.C.F.'s office on arrival (he was in Italy himself) and heard that the case was due to begin in two days' time, and that, apart from the trial, I was a free agent.

I had a meeting with Fletcher and Crowther and found them, although very nervous, in quite good spirits. The whole thing appeared as incredible to them as it did to everyone; a wild night ashore had landed them into all this trouble when many similar nights had only resulted in bad headaches! I also visited the rooms of the barrister who who had been briefed on their behalf by the Navy. He impressed me as a very capable and confident young lawyer, and he confided that while he thought Crowther would get off owing to rather special identification circumstances, Fletcher would be lucky to get away with an acquittal, and would probably not succeed in doing so.

He questioned me carefully on the question of Crowther's beard, which had been growing at the time of the regrettable incident, and had been shaved off before the police court summons was issued. He also wanted me to testify as to character at the trial, and I was genuinely happy to do this, as neither of the men were in any way trouble-makers on board, and Fletcher in particular had a very good action record, besides being a pleasant and willing rating.

I could find little enthusiasm for social activity during the off-duty hours of this stay, as the trial and even more 658 up at Ancona, were in my mind the whole time. The news flooding over the radio showed more and more that the war would end in a day or two, and I didn't want to miss being aboard if the boats were to have a final fling.

The trial, which was less imposing than I had expected, took two days, and although an interesting experience, did not seem to conform to my vague ideas on justice and equity. In spite of all the trappings of the law, from the moment that the judge opened proceedings I felt that the nature of the charge had already decided the atmosphere of the court, and that hostility was general. Our counsel exploited the fact that no one could identify Crowther as the sailor specifically involved in one episode of the incident, and showed clearly that there was no hard and fast case against him; but Fletcher, who had been struck down by a policeman's truncheon and then remanded overnight and taken to hospital, had no hope in that direction. I had my say on their behalf, and pointed out that these men were enjoying their first shore leave after six months of strenuous operations in the islands of Yugoslavia.

When the judge summed up, he directed the jury rather strongly, I felt, on the principle of upholding the police in their difficult task of preserving law and order in the special conditions of the floating population of Malta. It was no surprise when the jury returned to indicate that they had found Fletcher guilty on two counts (fortunately *not* on that of "Inciting a concourse to commit a felony") and that against Crowther no case could be proved.

The judge then sentenced Fletcher to seven months' hard labour, and the whole thing was over—except for poor Fletcher.

I saw the C.O. of the Base to discover whether the Vice-Admiral, Malta could intervene to appeal for any mitigation of sentence on service grounds, but he was very unhopeful. However, there was a good chance that, with victory so close, there might be an amnesty proclaimed which would shorten the term or even release Fletcher after a few days. (I heard later that he actually served seven weeks before he was released, and that he had had quite enough by that time.)

I immediately set about arranging my transport back to Ancona, but found that my "Priority Three" was not sufficient to get me out next day, and I had to wait until May 5th before, after six hours hanging about at Luqa, I managed to get a plane. I had the seamen with me still, and they were in low spirits imagining the extra rum they would miss if they didn't get back aboard before victory was declared. We stopped at Catania as before, but in a chat to the pilot—a South African —I discovered to my delight that we would be taking a different route to Bari from that on the outward journey, and would be flying over the Straits of Messina and up the west coast of Italy, only turning east across the Apennines when the latitude of Bari was reached.

We had only just left Catania and were gazing down on the narrowing gap between Sicily and Italy when the navigator came out of the nose of the plane grinning all over his face. He lifted up a signal pad and shouted above the roar of the engines:

"The following signal has just been received. 'The Germans surrendered unconditionally at 6 a.m. today. 1400'."

A cheer went up all round the plane—but apart from a few hand-shakes, there was little emotion shown. Most of us withdrew into our own thoughts, and began to calculate the effect this would have on our immediate futures. I could only feel disappointment that I had not heard this news aboard my own boat, in which my war had been spent and should have ended. What was happening, I wondered, to the German Naval forces up there in the Northern Adriatic.

At Bari, it was at once evident that there would be even less chance of pressing on to Ancona now, for all aircraft were grounded as a precaution against over-enthusiastic celebration. I cheered up the three matelots considerably by getting them on a truck to Manfredonia, where I knew that they would be victualled in temporarily and would therefore be able to draw their tots next day!

There was a big party in the mess that night, but I was like a fish out of water. I knew no one there, and was glad to turn in after a miserable finish to what should have been a very memorable day.

However, after checking that it was hopeless to get a plane, next morning I set out once more to see Derrick and Johnny at the 93rd General Hospital. I took with me a bottle of gin again, and spent a hilarious couple of hours with them, which yanked me out of my depression. The hospital was celebrating and there was little adherence to rules that day, which added to the general gaiety of the atmosphere. Both Derrick and Johnny were getting along well, and expected to be sent home by hospital ship fairly soon. We listened to Mr. Churchill's speech together, and after an uproarious farewell, I thumbed my way back to Bari again.

There was good news waiting for me. I could fly to Ancona next morning.

It was a queer sensation to fly over Ancona harbour next day just before landing, and to see, lying alongside a berth at C.F.B., a trot of seven E-boats. Out in the bay were many other craft, some of familiar lines. F-lighters! It looked as though the boys had been busy.

I could hardly get to 658 quickly enough. Chas Turner, Tony and our new Pilot, Derek King, were having lunch when I arrived, and I joined them while, between mouthfuls, they recounted all the excitement of the last few days.

They all looked jaded (as I had expected), after celebrating hard for several days now. I gradually realized what I had missed. While I had been sitting in that court-room in Malta, 658 had (quite fortuitously) played a large part in accepting the surrender of a whole flotilla of E-boats.

Tony gave me the details. At 0600 on 3rd May, Tony had been shaken by the Base duty officer.

"There's a flotilla of E-boats just off the entrance, still fully armed and with torpedoes as far as we know," he gasped. "Get out there and make 'em surrender, for Pete's sake."

Tony sounded action stations, and in no time the engines burst into life, the crew were on deck, lines cast off and Chas heading for the entrance. In his hurry, he allowed the starboard quarter to crash against the jetty, and the wing propeller was flattened against a rocky projection.

658 was the first boat out of the entrance, closely followed by several Vospers of Jerram's 28th Flotilla. Chas picked out the foremost E-boat, which was flying a white flag, and closed her. As he got near, he hailed: "Are you surrendering?"

A voice in hard but competent English replied: "I wish to land troops as prisoners-of-war and then to proceed back to Pola for more. We do not wish to leave our prisoners to the hands of the Partisans."

Obviously Chas could not comment on this, although he knew well what the Germans meant. He suggested that the senior officer should accompany him into Ancona to parley with the N.O.I.C.

This was agreed, and 658 went alongside the E-boat. Captain Wupperman was a dignified, restrained officer, and created a favourable impression by his bearing. He appeared to be the German equivalent of Captain Coastal Forces, Mediterranean.

Of course, N.O.I.C. could not allow the E-boats to leave, and in the end they were escorted in to Coastal Force Base and their crews were mustered on the jetty and marched away.

So 658 had had the privilege that has fallen to few warships in naval history: she had received the surrender of her adversaries as a fitting finale to two years of battle.

And I had missed it.

Apart from this incident, there had been a grand climax at the northern end of the Adriatic, too. 658 had been returning from one of the minesweeper protection patrols when they had been passed by 634, 651 and 670 going north in a hurry. Aircraft had reported about thirty German ships sailing from Trieste towards Tagilamento, and Tim Bligh had been despatched to intercept them and to try to induce them to sail to Ancona.

I heard the story of this operation from Gordon, who as first lieutenant of 634 had the S.O. aboard.

When they first sighted the mass of shipping lying off the river mouth at Tagliamento, a British aircraft signalled the news that the ships were still firing at the Spitfires overhead, and that no white flags were visible. Nevertheless, Tim decided to close slowly to test reactions.

"We'll fly a large white flag, Gordon, and see if we can get anyone to parley."

Gordon brought up one of the wardroom sheets, and with this flapping in the breeze, the Dogs moved slowly in towards the convoy. Every gun had its crew closed up, but was left trained fore and aft to show peaceful intentions.

Tim flashed several enemy ships but could get nobody interested until a unit of R-boats appeared, and their S.O. was persuaded to go aboard 634 to parley. Eventually, a meeting of the R-boats' C.O.s was arranged and addressed by Tim, and they showed signs of weakening.

At about this time, three other ships signified their willingness to sail to Ancona, but at this stage, when the situation was beginning to look promising, the Army made an unwittingly badly-timed appearance along the shore and captured the port.

This only complicated matters for Tim, as his object was to get the enemy ships to Ancona, not to leave them scuttled in Tagliamento with the crews as prisoners of war. The Germans continued to hedge and tried (unsuccessfully) to persuade him that they could not possibly sail to Ancona.

More Dogs arrived, and as night came they formed a rough semi-circle and kept watch on the harbour. Next morning the Germans tried more delaying tactics, but the Dogs put small prize crews aboard and eventually took a total of fourteen vessels back to Ancona.

After the tension and difficulty of the parleying, Tim and his boats had now to contend with very bad weather, causing countless delays in towing, and reducing speeds even down to two knots, besides the hazards of the minefields.

For his extremely able handling of an unprecedented situation, Tim was later awarded the O.B.E.


All this had happened while I had been away. It would have been hard to believe without the solid evidence of that sleek, silent row of E-boats lying deserted, their teeth drawn, on the quayside ahead of us, and the queer, lumpy F-lighters lying at anchor in the bay.

I went up on the bridge and looked at them. At the masthead of each flew two flags—the White Ensign above the Black Swastika.

Our war was over.

# EPILOGUE

The end of the Mediterranean war was not the end of 658's life. For three more months she worked in the Adriatic at a variety of tasks. First she acted as a glorified lamp, directing convoys to Trieste along the swept channel; then she was reduced to the level of a mere liberty-boat for the cruisers lying off that great port.

After these indignities someone with imagination realized her value. Resplendent in light-grey paint, she joined the 59th Flotilla in "showing the flag" alongside the main piazza of Trieste, during the worst of the clashes with the Partisans. She finished, characteristically, with guns blazing—sinking mines as they were cut by a flotilla of fleet minesweepers.

And then it was Malta again, to pay off and to leave 658 to the caretakers. Behind all the parties and celebrations of that August, coinciding with the end of the war in Japan, was the sadness of parting with an old friend. Of the crew that commissioned 658 in March 1943, I alone was left in Malta on the day in August 1945 when we paid her off.

It was 1500 hours on August 27th. One of the care and maintenance party sounded the "still", and as the plaintive whine of the bosun's pipe hung in the clear afternoon air, Tony very slowly lowered the Ensign, and the Pilot the Union Flag for'd, whilst I saluted 658's dying moments from the bridge.


And even that was not her end, although it was the last I saw of her.

Later in 1945, several Dog-boats were towed to Alexandria by destroyers, to be sold to the Egyptians. 658 was in the first group of four, and on the way three foundered in a gale: only one survived. That one was not 658. I suspect she preferred to join 657 and 663 among the historic wreckage clothing the bed of the Mediterranean. Perhaps (and who can say she had no will?) she preferred to end her days with no dimming of the glory that had been hers.

# LIST OF OFFICERS APPOINTED TO H.M.M.G.B. 658

| | | |
|---|---|---|
| Lt.-Cdr. C. Burke R.C.N.V.R. | Commanding Officer. | March 1943 to Dec. 1944. |
| Lt. H. M. Pickard R.C.N.V.R. | First Lieutenant. | March 1943 to Oct. 1943. |
| Lt. L. C. Reynolds R.N.V.R. | Navigating Officer.<br>First Lieutenant.<br>Spare C.O. (in 658)<br>Commanding Officer. | March 1943 to Oct. 1943.<br>Oct. 1943 to Oct. 1944.<br>Oct. 1944 to Dec. 1944.<br>Dec. 1944 to Aug. 1945. |
| S/Lt. C. A. M. Brydon R.N.V.R. | Navigating Officer.<br>First Lieutenant. | Oct. 1943 to May 1944.<br>Oct. 1944 to Aug. 1945. |
| S/Lt. M. Walker-Munro R.N.V.R. | Navigating Officer. | May 1944 to Oct. 1944. |
| S/Lt. L. Battle R.N.V.R. | Navigating Officer. | Oct. 1944 to Feb. 1945. |
| S/Lt. D. King R.N.V.R. | Navigating Officer. | Feb. 1945 to June 1945. |
| S/Lt. G. Herd R.N.V.R. | Navigating Officer. | June 1945 to Aug. 1945. |

# LIST OF AWARDS MADE DURING SERVICE IN H.M.M.G.B. 658

| | |
|---|---|
| Lt.-Cdr. C. Burke R.C.N.V.R. | Distinguished Service Cross and 2 bars.<br>Mentioned in Despatches. |
| Lt. H. M. Pickard R.C.N.V.R. | Mentioned in Despatches. |
| Lt. L. C. Reynolds R.N.V.R. | Distinguished Service Cross. |
| S/Lt. C. A. M. Brydon R.N.V.R. | Distinguished Service Cross. |
| S/Lt. G. Herd R.N.V.R. | RHS Bronze Medal. |
| Ch.P.O./M.M. W. J. E. Last | Distinguished Service Medal.<br>Mentioned in Despatches. |
| P.O./M.M. A. E. Burrows. | Distinguished Service Medal. |
| A/B. G. Howe. | Distinguished Service Medal.<br>Mentioned in Despatches. |
| A/B. C. Preston. | Distinguished Service Medal.<br>Mentioned in Despatches. |
| A/B. K. Duffill. | Distinguished Service Medal. |
| L/Sto. G. Simpson. | Mentioned in Despatches. |
| A/B. C. Fennell. | Mentioned in Despatches. |
| A/B. H. Pountney. | Mentioned in Despatches. |

# SUMMARY OF RESULTS ACHIEVED IN ACTIONS BY UNITS WHICH INCLUDED H.M.M.G.B. 658

*Sunk or Destroyed*

1 Partenope Escort Vessel

3 E-boats

2 F-lighters
1 Pil boat
2 Trawlers
2 Schooners
1 Oil tanker
1 Harbour Defence Vessel
3 FW. 190s
2 Ju. 88s
1 Dornier 217

*Damaged (later destroyed)*

1 Trawler (Minelayer?)
  (driven ashore)
1 F-lighter
  (destroyed by R.A.F.)

*Damaged*

1 Partenope
  Escort Vessel
1 Corvette

1 K.T. ship
3 E-boats
2 F-lighters
3 small craft
1 Ju 88

# GLOSSARY

| | |
|---|---|
| BYMS | British Yacht Minesweeper |
| CCF | Captain Coastal Forces |
| CFB | Coastal Force Base |
| C in C | Commander-in-Chief |
| CO | Commanding Officer |
| Do | Dornier |
| DSC | Distinguished Service Cross |
| DSM | Distinguished Service Medal |
| DSO | Distinguished Service Order |
| EMB | Explosive Motor Boat |
| Flag A | 'Aircraft in sight' |
| Flag 4 | 'Fire torpedoes' |
| FW | Focke-Wulf |
| George (eg22) | Speed (22 knots) |
| HDML | Harbour Defence Motor Launch |
| Ju | Junkers |
| LCA | Landing Craft, Assault |
| LCF | Landing Craft, Flak |
| LCG | Landing Craft, Gun |
| LCI | Landing Craft, Infantry |
| LCT | Landing Craft, Tank |
| LST | Landing Ship, Tank |
| MGB | Motor Gun Boat |
| ML | Motor Launch |
| MM | Motor Mechanic |
| MTB | Motor Torpedo Boat |
| NOIC | Naval Officer in Charge |
| O/C | Officer Commanding |
| OD | Slang for Ordinary Seaman |
| PO | Petty Officer |
| RCNVR | Royal Canadian Naval Volunteer Reserve |
| RN | Royal Navy |
| RNVR | Royal Naval Volunteer Reserve |
| R/T | Radio Telephony |
| RTO | Railway Transport Officer |
| SGB | Steam Gun Boat |
| SNOL | Senior Naval Officer, Landing |
| SNONA | Senior Naval Officer North Adriatic |
| SNOVIS | Senior Naval Officer Vis |
| SO | Senior Officer |
| SOIS | Senior Officer Inshore Squadron |
| SOO | Staff Officer Operations |
| W/T | Wireless Telegraphy |
| USN | United States Navy |

# AUTHOR'S POSTSCRIPT to the 2002 EDITION

When I paid off MGB 658 in August 1945, I had in my possession a complete file of every 'Report of Proceedings' submitted after the numerous actions 658 had fought. At a time when it would have been difficult to obtain such reports from official sources, I had the key material to enable me to write as authentic an account of the boat's commission as was possible in 1955.

But that was not necessarily the whole picture, of course. As the years have passed, much more information has come to light: detail of the actual ships we fought, unknown conclusions to frenzied encounters, and facts which could only be secured from enemy sources.

The following notes are intended to add interest by revealing some facts which amplify the story of four episodes in 658's turbulent life.

## The encounter with U-boats in the Atlantic, 3 May 1943 *(pages 37-41)*

The convoy of MGBs, MTBs and MLs which sailed from Milford Haven to Gibraltar on 29 April 1943 entered the Atlantic at the very time when the U-boat menace reached its peak. By the end of May, the balance had turned in favour of the Allies as new attacking methods became more and more effective. In fact, the report from the Focke-Wulf Condor which had shadowed our convoy and which was passed to the nearest U-boat pack was the only such report to lead to an interception in the whole of that key month.

The U-boat pack of nine, code named 'Drossel', was ordered to get into position to attack both the MTB convoy and another further ahead consisting of twenty-eight landing craft. The U-boats split into two groups and moved off to intercept: U439 (von Tippelskirch) set out to attack the MTBs, and U659 (Stock) the landing craft. Each had to travel 300 miles on the surface throughout the whole of 3 May to reach their targets, and by 2300 U439 was in position close ahead of the MTBs. U659 failed to find the landing craft but saw star shell and tracer further north and set off at full speed towards it. The tracer indicated, in fact, the only attack pressed home, when U439 sighted MGB 657 and opened fire, securing hits immediately.

U439 was apparently disengaging from the MTBs at about 7 knots when suddenly U659 appeared immediately ahead of her. U439 ploughed into the control room of U659. Oil and water poured into U659's hull, a large wave swept over her and she plummeted to the bottom. U439 went astern, her diesel exhausts were blocked, and the boat filled with fumes. Von Tippelskirch tried to counter the flooding of the bow compartment by flooding the after end, but she began to sink. Once again, massive waves overwhelmed her, and she too was doomed. There were nine survivors from U439, and only three from U659, all picked up by the MTBs in the starboard column of the convoy.

*** *** ***

*The Battle of the Mljet Channel, 17/18 August 1944 (pages 177 - 187)*

The account I wrote in 1955 was derived from Lt Cdr Maitland's 'Report of Proceedings'. It was, of course, prepared after consultation with Corny Burke and Tom Ladner, but not surprisingly it differs in some detail from the enemy's report of the action, which was discovered many years later.

Most Motor Gun Boat actions were conducted in darkness, at close range, and often with sudden changes of course; approaches from different angles therefore led to the consequent possibility of confusion. It was also often extremely difficult to recognise accurately the make up of a convoy, or to be certain whether a target was sunk or just severely damaged. There were dozens of examples - on both sides - where seemingly doomed boats later made a painful return to harbour, defying all odds.

The Mljet Channel action was no exception. We now know that the two schooners (adapted as 'gun coasters') were the *Jota* and the *Dora*; there were two barge-tankers, not three, named *Helga* and *Peter*; and there was no F-lighter but two I-lighters (a small version of the 'F') numbered 168 and 148. Four were definitely sunk, but *Helga* and 168, although both heavily damaged, hid close inshore and eventually got back to Korcula.

The only real surprise was that Maitland had been sure that an E-boat had been sunk in the second run, and yet no E-boat was apparently involved in close defence. Indeed, the activities of the four E-boats previously detected on radar is shrouded in mystery, because although their role was intended to be that of defensive screen, they were three miles away when the battle began, and never intervened, stating in their report that they stood off for virtually the whole of the engagement 'because they were unable to distinguish friend from foe'. Perhaps one of the E-boats *did* get involved.

Although 658 was so badly damaged that she was not available on the following night, Tom Ladner took 663 out again with two other boats, and this time the unit found the same E-boats, engaged them, and 663 sank S57 (Lt Buschmann).

★★★

*The Battle of the Planinski Channel, 12/13 April 1945 (pages 232-233)*

It is now possible to give far more accurate detail about the success of the attack by Lt Cdr Montgomerie with 670, 697, 643 and 658 on two large enemy vessels at the northern end of the Planinski (now Velebit) Channel - the last action of the Mediterranean Coastal Forces' war.

The detail came very indirectly and strangely from a Yugoslav diving enthusiast who wrote to the author several years ago. Following up local reports from 'the old fishermen who remembered a naval battle in 1945' he dived in the indicated area, and found the wreck of a destroyer 60 metres down. He was astonished to discover that the ship was in two pieces, with the stern section ahead of the forward half, which had a great hole at the bow. Clearly, two torpedoes had struck, one midships which broke the ship in half, and the other at the bow.

He researched the battle in German records, and obtained the report by the Commander of the First Escort Group (Adriatic) in Trieste. The ship sunk was identified as TA45, and was named *Spiza*. 'T' signified 'Torpedo Boat' (regarded as a destroyer) and 'A' the fact that it was not German built. She was one of six

Italian destroyers being built in Trieste and Fiume when the Germans occupied those ports in 1943. They were classified as the Ariete class and completed by the Germans. Astonishingly, 12 April 1945 was her first – and of course last – patrol against the enemy. Leading the two ships was TA40 (Kpt Fridrich Birnbaum) and his descriptive report concludes:

'We in TA40 managed to avoid two torpedoes which passed on each side of us, but immediately after, we heard two explosions. The stern of TA45 stood straight up in the air, and we could see the stern passing forward. She sank quickly and we in TA40 turned away at full speed, firing at the MTBs, and returned to Fiume.'

His unit had had a very short war.

*658's end: sunk when she foundered while on tow to Alexandria, January 1946 (page 244)*

Research by the author reveals that the scale of the losses was far greater than realised in 1955.

In all, eleven boats were dispatched to Alexandria for sale to the Egyptian Government in this disastrous convoy. They were 633, 634, 637, 638, 642, 643, 658, 659, 698, 700 and almost certainly 674. They were towed by four destroyers – *Jervis*, *Chevron*, *Chequers* and *Chaplet* – each with two or three in tow.

The group was sailed despite a very bad forecast of gales, on the orders of Vice Admiral Malta, and the boats were soon wallowing, waterlogged, in mountainous beam seas. Tows parted and the destroyers were ordered to sink each in turn by gunfire as hazards to shipping.

All these boats had fine records, and many of them feature in this book. For the officers and men who had served in them, it seemed a cruel end for boats which had earned their deep respect and affection.

*** 

*What happened to some of the main participants in the story of MGB 658? A look back over the years from 1945 to 2002.*

In the preface to the original 1955 edition, I suggested that the spirit of comradeship found in 658 and indeed throughout Coastal Forces was exceptional.

I could not possibly have known then of the extent to which that spirit would remain and develop throughout the lives of many affected by their wartime experiences. Now, 58 years since it began for me, it has proved to have had an astonishing personal influence on my life, and surely for many others too.

In the early years after the war, when we were all starting or restarting our careers, the main incentive for contact was the annual reunion dinner of Mediterranean officers. And in those years, the six 'Junior Dogs' (see page 138) attended each other's weddings whenever possible, so that the wives too became friends, and occasional meetings were arranged and greatly enjoyed. Now, only three of the six survive, but the widows are closely bound in fellowship. Similarly, contact with the 'Senior Dogs' in Canada grew, as they made visits to London and stayed in our homes, and these visits were reciprocated by our visits to Canada.

As retirement neared, during the 1980s this blossomed into gatherings which became larger and larger. They began when the Canadian COs wrote to challenge us to track down the crews of the six boats of the 56th Flotilla for a reunion weekend in London. Eventually over 100 (including 40 wives) sat down to dinner aboard HMS *Belfast* and met again next day for lunch at the Naval Club. It was both hilarious and moving.

This was followed by the chartering of a schooner to take twenty of us cruising the Dalmatian Coast northward from Dubrovnik via Vis and past Zara (now Zadar) to Rab in the north, greeted daily by Partisan veterans at formal (and informal) receptions wherever we stopped. Reunions followed in British Columbia, Tuscany (with a visit to Bastia), Brittany, and many in London. The culmination in 1993 was a 50th anniversary of our time together - quite incidentally marking the 70th birthdays of the surviving Junior Dogs.

The fellowship has endured for a lifetime.

★★★

An individual account of post-war lives must start with Corny Burke, to whom this book is still dedicated.

### Lt Cdr Cornelius Burke DSC and two bars, RCNVR

Returning to Vancouver after the war he was soon involved as a senior partner for 10 years in the operation of a tug-boat company off the coast of British Columbia. He then founded Western Canada's largest travel agency – 'Burke's Worldwide' - becoming well known for his daily radio broadcasts, in which he recounted his travel experiences.

He was an avid fly-fisherman, and a keen long range cyclist. He cycled the routes of the rivers of Europe - the Rhine, the Danube, and the Moselle, and pedalled around Ireland, across France and from Lands End to John O'Groats. He wrote vivid accounts of all these adventures. A lively raconteur, a ready wit and a celebrated eccentric, the years brought him a worldwide host of friends, who bade him farewell in 1999 at the age of 82, having lived a rich and colourful life.

### Lt Thomas Ellis Ladner DSC and bar RCNVR

CO of MGB 663, Tom Ladner had already seen much action in home waters and in all was mentioned in despatches four times. He was Corny's life-long friend, and it was fitting that they should spend nearly four years serving in Coastal Forces out of their five in the Royal Navy together.

On returning to Vancouver, Tom rejoined his father's legal firm, which became one of the largest in British Columbia. He was appointed Queen's Counsel early in his professional career.

His links with his First Lieutenant, Derrick Holden Brown, became even stronger over the passing years.

### Lt Cdr J. Douglas Maitland DSC and bar, Cde G, RCNVR

The leader of the 'Three Musketeers', the Vancouver friends who by design came together in the Mediterranean, he commanded MGB 657. The first SO of the all-Canadian led 56th Flotilla, he was the senior of the trio and commanded great respect. He too returned to take a major part in Vancouver life, and ran a highly successful insurance business. He was Commodore of the Royal Vancouver Yacht Club, retired to Powell River and died in 1997.

### Lt Herbert M. Pickard RCNVR

Known as 'Pick', he was the original First Lieutenant of 658 and a great friend and support to me throughout my first few months as a Midshipman. When I took over from him, he became CO of MTB 655 and was wounded in action and returned to Canada. He joined the law firm in Winnipeg where he had been an articled student before the war and in 1953 he qualified and joined the Canadian Pacific Railway. He moved up within that major corporation until in due course he was Executive Vice-President of Canadian Pacific Investments and headed the Realty Division and the Hotels Company. He retired in 1977 to Calgary, and maintains contact with his wartime friends.

★★★

Next must come the 'Junior Dogs', the Navigators and First Lieutenants in the Flotilla who became great friends and are mentioned frequently. First, my closest friend and best man at my wedding in 1946, now *Sir Derrick Holden-Brown*.

Derrick had been blown off the bridge of his command, MTB 655, in March 1945 – his second mining – and after a spell in hospital in Italy, returned home for convalescence. He had a short spell in an Admiralty office before studying and qualifying as a chartered accountant. There followed rapid advancement in the food and drink industry: from Hiram Walker to managing a brewery in Ireland, to responsible posts at Grants of St James's and Victoria Wine. From there he was Finance Director of Allied Breweries and eventually Deputy Chairman and then Chairman and Chief Executive of Allied Lyons. He was knighted in 1979 for his services to the industry, and was sought as a director of other companies – Midland Bank and Sun Alliance. He worked tirelessly for naval charities and was Chairman of the White Ensign Association. Later he chaired the Portsmouth Naval Heritage Trust and is now very active in the Coastal Forces Heritage Trust.

*Tony Brydon*, whose DSC in 658 was one of very few such awards made to a junior navigating officer, and thoroughly well deserved, survived two minings, and was a stalwart friend and excellent First Lieutenant when I became CO. After the war, he carried on the family's whisky broking firm in the City, and after several other business ventures ran his own gardening enterprise. He was highly valued in his community for his excellence and kindness. He died of cancer, bravely borne, in 1991.

*Tony Marriott*, who succeeded Derrick Brown as navigator of 663 and whose Anglo-French parentage proved an asset in Corsica, became a young executive in Courtaulds, spending much time in New York and Paris. He gave this up to run a poultry farm in Hampshire, and later returned to Paris to establish an office for a London property firm. However, he was based in the U.K. and devoted much time to the British Legion. He died in 2000.

*John Mudd* first served in MGB 659 as pilot, and later joined Derrick as his First Lieutenant in MTB 655. He was alongside him when she was mined in the Adriatic in March 1945, was wounded and returned home. He spent the next 35 years with Lucas in Birmingham, becoming Personnel Director of the company. He also served as a Captain in the Warwickshire Yeomanry TA, wearing the Atlantic Star ribbon on his uniform to the confusion of inspecting Generals. After retirement he withstood serious illness, lives now in Worcestershire but keeps closely in touch.

*Gordon Surtees*, Tim Bligh's navigating officer in 662, was later First Lieutenant of MTB 634 with Walter Blount and saw much action in the 57th Flotilla. After reading History at Oriel College, Oxford, he taught and was later a Housemaster at Malvern College for fifteen years. He was then Headmaster of Rishworth School in Yorkshire and of The John Lyon School at Harrow, part of the Harrow Foundation. He, like me, served as a headmaster on the Admiralty Interview Board. A great sportsman, he died of a heart attack whilst playing in a very competitive golf match in 1990.

\*\*\*

*This record would be incomplete without some detail of the illustrious careers of four senior officers who were all significant in the story of MGB 658 and Mediterranean Coastal Forces.*

### Commander Robert A. (Bobby) Allan

later Baron Allan of Kilmahew, commanded several MTBs from 1940 before becoming the Commanding Officer of each Advanced Base from which we operated: Bone, Augusta, Maddalena and Bastia. He achieved miracles of diplomacy and was totally respected and admired by all who came under his command. His DSO for the special operations he led using LCGs to sink F-lighters was acclaimed by all, and he was honoured by the French and USA for his work at Bastia.

He left the Mediterranean in May 1945 to contest - unsuccessfully - a seat in the General Election, but entered Parliament in 1951. Almost at once, he began to assume responsible posts as a Whip, a PPS to the Prime Minister, and as a Minister at the Admiralty and the Foreign Office. A change of direction saw him overseeing the finances of the Conservative Party until 1966.

Retiring from politics, he was a Governor of the BBC and of Harrow School, Chairman of Ladybird Books, and a Director of Pearson Longmans Penguin. He was created a Life Peer in 1973, and died in 1979.

### Lt Cdr Timothy J. Bligh OBE DSO DSC and bar RNVR

After two years commanding a Vosper MTB of the 7th Flotilla, he was CO of MGB 662 - at first in the 20th MGBs, and then as SO of the 57th. After the war, he entered the Civil Service as an Assistant Principal in the Treasury and in a meteoric rise was rapidly a Principal, and Secretary to the Head of the Civil Service. By 1959 he was PPS to two Prime Ministers - first to Harold Macmillan and then Sir Alec Douglas Home. He was knighted in 1963 and left the Civil Service to join the Thomson Organisation as Assistant Managing Director. He was an Alderman of the GLC by 1967. He died, aged 50, in 1969.

### Lt Cdr M.C.Morgan-Giles DSO OBE GM RN

as we knew him when we came under his wing in 1944-5, was then Senior Naval Officer Vis - operating all naval craft 'in the Islands' and liaising with Tito's Partisans, the Commandos and the RAF on the island of Vis.

He was rapidly promoted after the war, and as a Captain was in succession Chief of Naval Intelligence in the Far East, Captain (D) of the Dartmouth Training Squadron, and in command of HMS *Belfast*. On reaching Flag rank, he was President of the Royal Naval College at Greenwich before retiring at his own request in 1964, as a Rear Admiral. He entered Parliament in the same year as MP for Winchester and held the seat till 1979. He played a major part in the preservation of HMS *Belfast*, was a Deputy Lieutenant for Hampshire and knighted in 1985. He is a great supporter of Coastal Forces.

### Captain John Felgate Stevens RN

became Captain Coastal Forces (Mediterranean) in July 1943 and had a huge influence on the development of Coastal Forces – and our fortunes – until almost the end of the war, receiving a CBE in recognition of his outstanding services. Post-war, he commanded the aircraft carrier *HMS Implacable*, flagship of the Home Fleet, was Director of Naval Training and then Chief of Staff to the Head of the Joint Services Mission in Washington. Appointed Vice Admiral in 1952, he was made a Companion of the Bath, was Flag Officer, Home Fleet Training Squadron, and finally C in C America and West Indies Station and Deputy Supreme Allied Commander, Atlantic. He was made KBE shortly before retiring in 1955.

He demonstrated his affection for his young Coastal Forces officers – and perhaps especially the Canadians – when he visited them from his fleet off British Columbia at their holiday home on Pasley Island off Vancouver. Later, Corny and I with our wives visited him several times at his home in Surrey before he died in his ninetieth year in 1989 – as Vice Admiral Sir John Stevens KBE CB.

★★★

And, if it is of any interest – what happened to me?

I decided that my career was destined to be in teaching. Thankfully that was to give me thirty-two years of fulfilment and happiness, and ultimately a secure and purposeful retirement. After two periods of higher education at London University, I emerged with a First in geography, taught in two fine grammar schools before gaining my first Headship at Kendal Grammar School in 1960 and then moved to Maidenhead, retiring in 1981.

I remained enthusiastically in the Scout Movement, which had led to my nickname 'Rover' in war-time, active at Group, District, County and Headquarters levels, which led – totally unexpectedly – to an OBE in 1981. I served as a JP on both the Kendal and Maidenhead Benches for a total of thirty years, seven of them in the Chair. I was invited in 1962 to join the Admiralty Interview Board, selecting prospective officers for Dartmouth and the Royal Marines. I served for thirty years, and greatly enjoyed my contacts with the Service. I was made a Deputy Lieutenant of Berkshire in 1977. In retirement, I was encouraged by the Imperial War Museum to research and write a trilogy of books covering the operations of all the Royal Navy's MTBs and MGBs in the Second World War, which kept me (and Win, my wife for 55 years, who typed every word) busy for a total of sixteen years.

It has been a good life.

L. C. Reynolds 2002

# INDEX